The Collected Works of

Langston Hughes

Volume 11

Works for Children and Young Adults:
Poetry, Fiction, and Other Writing

Projected Volumes in the Collected Works

The Poems: 1921–1940

The Poems: 1941–1950

The Poems: 1951–1967

The Novels: *Not without Laughter*
  and *Tambourines to Glory*

The Plays to 1942: *Mulatto* to *The Sun Do Move*

Gospel Plays, Operas, and Later Dramatic Works

The Early Simple Stories

The Later Simple Stories

Essays on Art, Race, Politics, and World Affairs

Fight for Freedom and Other Writings on Civil Rights

Works for Children and Young Adults: Poetry,
  Fiction, and Other Writing

Works for Children and Young Adults: Biographies

Autobiography: *The Big Sea*

Autobiography: *I Wonder As I Wander*

The Short Stories

The Translations: Federico García Lorca, Nicolás Guillén,
  and Jacques Roumain

An Annotated Bibliography of the
  Works of Langston Hughes

Publication of

The Collected Works of Langston Hughes

has been generously assisted by

Landon and Sarah Rowland

and

Morton and Estelle Sosland

The Collected Works of

Langston Hughes

Volume 11

Works for Children and Young Adults:
Poetry, Fiction, and Other Writing

Edited with an Introduction
by Dianne Johnson

University of Missouri Press
Columbia and London

Library of Congress Cataloging-in-Publication Data

Hughes, Langston, 1902–1967
    [Works. 2001]
The collected works of Langston Hughes / edited with an introduction by
    Dianne Johnson
    p. cm.
    Includes bibliographical references.
    ISBN 0-8262-1498-3 (v. 11 : alk. paper)
    1. African Americans—Literary collections. I. Johnson, Dianne, II. Title.
PS3515 .U274 2001
818/.5209—dc21   00066601

♾™This paper meets the requirements of the
American National Standard for Permanence of Paper
for Printed Library Materials, Z39.48, 1984.

Designer: Kristie Lee
Typesetter: BOOKCOMP, Inc.
Printer and binder: Thomson-Shore, Inc.
Typefaces: Galliard, Optima

Contents

"First" Books

Acknowledgments

The University of Missouri Press is grateful for assistance from the following individuals and institutions in locating and making available copies of the original editions used in the preparation of this edition: Anne Barker and June Deweese, Ellis Library, University of Missouri–Columbia; Teresa Gipson, Miller Nichols Library, University of Missouri–Kansas City; Ruth Carruth and Patricia C. Willis, Beinecke Rare Book and Manuscript Library, Yale University; Ann Pathega, Washington University.

The *Collected Works* would not have been possible without the support and assistance of Patricia Powell, Chris Byrne, and Wendy Schmalz, Laura Bucko, and Phyllis Westberg of Harold Ober Associates, representing the estate of Langston Hughes, and of Arnold Rampersad and Ramona Bass, co-executors of the estate of Langston Hughes.

The editor would like to extend a special thanks to Carol Johnson, sixth-grade teacher extraordinaire.

Chronology
By Arnold Rampersad

1902 James Langston Hughes is born February 1 in Joplin, Missouri, to James Nathaniel Hughes, a stenographer for a mining company, and Carrie Mercer Langston Hughes, a former government clerk.

1903 After his father immigrates to Mexico, Langston's mother takes him to Lawrence, Kansas, the home of Mary Langston, her twice-widowed mother. Mary Langston's first husband, Lewis Sheridan Leary, died fighting alongside John Brown at Harpers Ferry. Her second, Hughes's grandfather, was Charles Langston, a former abolitionist, Republican politician, and businessman.

1907 After a failed attempt at a reconciliation in Mexico, Langston and his mother return to Lawrence.

1909 Langston starts school in Topeka, Kansas, where he lives for a while with his mother before returning to his grandmother's home in Lawrence.

1915 Following Mary Langston's death, Hughes leaves Lawrence for Lincoln, Illinois, where his mother lives with her second husband, Homer Clark, and Homer Clark's young son by another union, Gwyn "Kit" Clark.

1916 Langston, elected class poet, graduates from the eighth grade. Moves to Cleveland, Ohio, and starts at Central High School there.

1918 Publishes early poems and short stories in his school's monthly magazine.

1919 Spends the summer in Toluca, Mexico, with his father.

1920 Graduates from Central High as class poet and editor of the school annual. Returns to Mexico to live with his father.

1921 In June, Hughes publishes "The Negro Speaks of Rivers" in *Crisis* magazine. In September, sponsored by his father, he enrolls at Columbia University in New York. Meets W. E. B. Du Bois, Jessie Fauset, and Countee Cullen.

1922   Unhappy at Columbia, Hughes withdraws from school and breaks with his father.

1923   Sailing in June to western Africa on the crew of a freighter, he visits Senegal, the Gold Coast, Nigeria, the Congo, and other countries.

1924   Spends several months in Paris working in the kitchen of a nightclub.

1925   Lives in Washington for a year with his mother. His poem "The Weary Blues" wins first prize in a contest sponsored by *Opportunity* magazine, which leads to a book contract with Knopf through Carl Van Vechten. Becomes friends with several other young artists of the Harlem Renaissance, including Zora Neale Hurston, Wallace Thurman, and Arna Bontemps.

1926   In January his first book, *The Weary Blues,* appears. He enrolls at historically black Lincoln University, Pennsylvania. In June, the *Nation* weekly magazine publishes his landmark essay "The Negro Artist and the Racial Mountain."

1927   Knopf publishes his second book of verse, *Fine Clothes to the Jew,* which is condemned in the black press. Hughes meets his powerful patron Mrs. Charlotte Osgood Mason. Travels in the South with Hurston, who is also taken up by Mrs. Mason.

1929   Hughes graduates from Lincoln University.

1930   Publishes his first novel, *Not Without Laughter* (Knopf). Visits Cuba and meets fellow poet Nicolás Guillén. Hughes is dismissed by Mrs. Mason in a painful break made worse by false charges of dishonesty leveled by Hurston over their play *Mule Bone.*

1931   Demoralized, he travels to Haiti. Publishes work in the communist magazine *New Masses.* Supported by the Rosenwald Foundation, he tours the South taking his poetry to the people. In Alabama, he visits some of the Scottsboro Boys in prison. His brief collection of poems *Dear Lovely Death* is privately printed in Amenia, New York. Hughes and the illustrator Prentiss Taylor publish a verse pamphlet, *The Negro Mother.*

1932   With Taylor, he publishes *Scottsboro Limited,* a short play and four poems. From Knopf comes *The Dream Keeper,* a book of previously published poems selected for young people. Later, Macmillan brings out *Popo and Fifina,* a children's story about Haiti written with Arna Bontemps, his closest friend. In June, Hughes sails to Russia in a band of twenty-two young African

Americans to make a film about race relations in the United States. After the project collapses, he lives for a year in the Soviet Union. Publishes his most radical verse, including "Good Morning Revolution" and "Goodbye Christ."

1933 Returns home at midyear via China and Japan. Supported by a patron, Noël Sullivan of San Francisco, Hughes spends a year in Carmel writing short stories.

1934 Knopf publishes his first short story collection, *The Ways of White Folks*. After labor unrest in California threatens his safety, he leaves for Mexico following news of his father's death.

1935 Spends several months in Mexico, mainly translating short stories by local leftist writers. Lives for some time with the photographer Henri Cartier-Bresson. Returning almost destitute to the United States, he joins his mother in Oberlin, Ohio. Visits New York for the Broadway production of his play *Mulatto* and clashes with its producer over changes in the script. Unhappy, he writes the poem "Let America Be America Again."

1936 Wins a Guggenheim Foundation fellowship for work on a novel but soon turns mainly to writing plays in association with the Karamu Theater in Cleveland. Karamu stages his farce *Little Ham* and his historical drama about Haiti, *Troubled Island*.

1937 Karamu stages *Joy to My Soul,* another comedy. In July, he visits Paris for the League of American Writers. He then travels to Spain, where he spends the rest of the year reporting on the civil war for the *Baltimore Afro-American*.

1938 In New York, Hughes founds the radical Harlem Suitcase Theater, which stages his agitprop play *Don't You Want to Be Free?* The leftist International Workers Order publishes *A New Song,* a pamphlet of radical verse. Karamu stages his play *Front Porch*. His mother dies.

1939 In Hollywood he writes the script for the movie *Way Down South,* which is criticized for stereotyping black life. Hughes goes for an extended stay in Carmel, California, again as the guest of Noël Sullivan.

1940 His autobiography *The Big Sea* appears (Knopf). He is picketed by a religious group for his poem "Goodbye Christ," which he publicly renounces.

1941 With a Rosenwald Fund fellowship for playwriting, he leaves California for Chicago, where he founds the Skyloft Players. Moves on to New York in December.

1942   Knopf publishes his book of verse *Shakespeare in Harlem*. The Skyloft Players stage his play *The Sun Do Move*. In the summer he resides at the Yaddo writers' and artists' colony, New York. Hughes also works as a writer in support of the war effort. In November he starts "Here to Yonder," a weekly column in the Chicago *Defender* newspaper.

1943   "Here to Yonder" introduces Jesse B. Semple, or Simple, a comic Harlem character who quickly becomes its most popular feature. Hughes publishes *Jim Crow's Last Stand* (Negro Publication Society of America), a pamphlet of verse about the struggle for civil rights.

1944   Comes under surveillance by the FBI because of his former radicalism.

1945   With Mercer Cook, translates and later publishes *Masters of the Dew* (Reynal and Hitchcock), a novel by Jacques Roumain of Haiti.

1947   His work as librettist with Kurt Weill and Elmer Rice on the Broadway musical play *Street Scene* brings Hughes a financial windfall. He vacations in Jamaica. Knopf publishes *Fields of Wonder*, his only book composed mainly of lyric poems on nonracial topics.

1948   Hughes is denounced (erroneously) as a communist in the U.S. Senate. He buys a townhouse in Harlem and moves in with his longtime friends Toy and Emerson Harper.

1949   Doubleday publishes *Poetry of the Negro, 1746–1949*, an anthology edited with Arna Bontemps. Also published are *One-Way Ticket* (Knopf), a book of poems, and *Cuba Libre: Poems of Nicolás Guillén* (Anderson and Ritchie), translated by Hughes and Ben Frederic Carruthers. Hughes teaches for three months at the University of Chicago Lab School for children. His opera about Haiti with William Grant Still, *Troubled Island*, is presented in New York.

1950   Another opera, *The Barrier*, with music by Jan Meyerowitz, is hailed in New York but later fails on Broadway. Simon and Schuster publishes *Simple Speaks His Mind*, the first of five books based on his newspaper columns.

1951   Hughes's book of poems about life in Harlem, *Montage of a Dream Deferred*, appears (Henry Holt).

1952   His second collection of short stories, *Laughing to Keep from Crying*, is published by Henry Holt. In its "First Book" series for children, Franklin Watts publishes Hughes's *The First Book of Negroes*.

1953   In March, forced to testify before Senator Joseph McCarthy's subcommittee on subversive activities, Hughes is exonerated after repudiating his past radicalism. *Simple Takes a Wife* appears.

1954   Mainly for young readers, he publishes *Famous Negro Americans* (Dodd, Mead) and *The First Book of Rhythms*.

1955   Publishes *The First Book of Jazz* and finishes *Famous Negro Music Makers* (Dodd, Mead). In November, Simon and Schuster publishes *The Sweet Flypaper of Life*, a narrative of Harlem with photographs by Roy DeCarava.

1956   Hughes's second volume of autobiography, *I Wonder As I Wander* (Rinehart), appears, as well as *A Pictorial History of the Negro* (Crown), coedited with Milton Meltzer, and *The First Book of the West Indies*.

1957   *Esther,* an opera with composer Jan Meyerowitz, has its premiere in Illinois. Rinehart publishes *Simple Stakes a Claim* as a novel. Hughes's musical play *Simply Heavenly,* based on his Simple character, runs for several weeks off and then on Broadway.

1958   Hughes translates and publishes *Selected Poems of Gabriela Mistral* (Indiana University Press). *The Langston Hughes Reader* (George Braziller) also appears, as well as *The Book of Negro Folklore* (Dodd, Mead), coedited with Arna Bontemps, and another juvenile, *Famous Negro Heroes of America* (Dodd, Mead). John Day publishes a short novel, *Tambourines to Glory,* based on a Hughes gospel musical play.

1959   Hughes's *Selected Poems* published (Knopf).

1960   *The First Book of Africa* appears, along with *An African Treasury: Articles, Essays, Stories, Poems by Black Africans,* edited by Hughes (Crown).

1961   Inducted into the National Institute of Arts and Letters. Knopf publishes his book-length poem *Ask Your Mama: 12 Moods for Jazz. The Best of Simple,* drawn from the columns, appears (Hill and Wang). Hughes writes his gospel musical plays *Black Nativity* and *The Prodigal Son.* He visits Africa again.

1962   Begins a weekly column for the *New York Post.* Attends a writers' conference in Uganda. Publishes *Fight for Freedom: The Story of the NAACP,* commissioned by the organization.

1963   His third collection of short stories, *Something in Common,* appears from Hill and Wang. Indiana University Press publishes

Five Plays by Langston Hughes, edited by Webster Smalley, as well as Hughes's anthology *Poems from Black Africa, Ethiopia, and Other Countries.*

1964   His musical play *Jericho–Jim Crow,* a tribute to the civil rights movement, is staged in Greenwich Village. Indiana University Press brings out his anthology *New Negro Poets: U.S.A.,* with a foreword by Gwendolyn Brooks.

1965   With novelists Paule Marshall and William Melvin Kelley, Hughes visits Europe for the U.S. State Department. His gospel play *The Prodigal Son* and his cantata with music by David Amram, *Let Us Remember,* are staged.

1966   After twenty-three years, Hughes ends his depiction of Simple in his Chicago *Defender* column. Publishes *The Book of Negro Humor* (Dodd, Mead). In a visit sponsored by the U.S. government, he is honored in Dakar, Senegal, at the First World Festival of Negro Arts.

1967   His *The Best Short Stories by Negro Writers: An Anthology from 1899 to the Present* (Little, Brown) includes the first published story by Alice Walker. On May 22, Hughes dies at New York Polyclinic Hospital in Manhattan from complications following prostate surgery. Later that year, two books appear: *The Panther and the Lash: Poems of Our Times* (Knopf) and, with Milton Meltzer, *Black Magic: A Pictorial History of the Negro in American Entertainment* (Prentice Hall).

The Collected Works of
Langston Hughes

Volume 11

Works for Children and Young Adults:
Poetry, Fiction, and Other Writing

Introduction

The final sentence of Langston Hughes and Arna Bontemps's *Popo and Fifina: Children of Haiti* (1932) reads: "We had a grand trip." In this scene, Popo and Fifina and the other members of their family have just returned from a visit to the beach and a lighthouse. The larger story is about Popo and Fifina's everyday lives as Haitian peasants. Through the details of the lives of common people, Hughes and Bontemps show how anyone's life can, indeed, be a grand trip, figuratively and in fact. Hughes's writings for children take his readers on many trips, all over the world and through the emotional and imaginative landscapes he creates. It is a body of work that should be celebrated along with his better-known writing for adults.

The same might be said of the works for children by other writers. Gwendolyn Brooks, James Baldwin, Lucille Clifton, Nikki Giovanni, and Ernest Gaines are just a few of the African American writers who have devoted some of their energies to the creation of literature for the young. Arguably, this has happened more in the world of African American literature than in mainstream literature. This says something about the worldviews and life experiences of African American writers and their communities. African American writers have long understood that children's literature is a useful and powerful vehicle through which to revise skewed histories, to inspire black children to live up to their potential, and to cultivate a love of and appreciation for literature in future generations.

In Hughes's case, part of his project was to open up the world to children. He acted on this as early as 1921, the year after he was graduated from high school. In that year he met W. E. B. Du Bois and published "The Negro Speaks of Rivers" in the NAACP's *Crisis* magazine. He also became a contributor to *The Brownies' Book*, a black children's magazine edited by Du Bois and the accomplished writer Jessie Fauset.[1] Hughes's biographer Arnold Rampersad suggests, "It was fitting, almost inevitable, that when he sought to enter the world as a poet . . . Hughes

---

1. For further information, see Dianne Johnson-Feelings, ed., *The Best of the Brownies' Book* (New York: Oxford University Press, 1966).

offered material written from a child's point of view, or with deliberately childlike technique, to a magazine for black children."[2] Although the magazine was a private venture, it functioned as the children's counterpart to the NAACP's *Crisis* magazine. Pan-African and international in its orientation, *The Brownies' Book* was an ideal starting point for Langston Hughes's "grand trip" in the world of children's literature. He sent in not only poetry, essays, and stories, but even a few Mexican games. His concluding note to the latter said: "Dear Little Friends: These are three games which the children play in your beautiful neighbor country, Mexico. I hope you will enjoy them." Clearly, he thought it was important to introduce young readers to children from other parts of the world. The reference to America's neighbors demonstrates the extent to which Hughes was interested in relationships between individuals and between peoples, relationships of kin and of communities.

Some of the poems Hughes contributed to the magazine are simple verses with titles such as "An April Rain Song" or "Thanksgiving Time." However, others that seem benign actually express important ideas. "Winter Sweetness," for example, is a four-line poem about a house made of sugar, with a "maple-sugar child" peeping out the window. During an era when *The Story of Little Black Sambo* (1899) was one of the most popular children's books in the United States, a maple-sugar child constituted a quiet but powerful alternative vision. Hughes's description forces readers to look at black children in new ways and with a new vocabulary. Likewise, his simple poems celebrating the seasons of nature nudge readers toward an appreciation of the natural environment, as do his pieces from *The Brownies' Book* that might be described as ethnographic writing, "In a Mexican City" and "Up to the Crater of an Old Volcano," both published in 1921.

In the first piece, Hughes notes that in Toluca "the climate is cool and often cold, but the poor folks never have shoes to wear." Discussing homes and furnishings, he mentions later in the essay, "Only a few of the well-to-do people have a great deal, so most of the homes use chairs as their principal space fillers." In the second piece, recounting an afternoon adventure to visit a volcano, in addition to describing the natural environment, he notes: "These dark faced, friendly school boys were about like other dark skinned boys of my own race whom I

2. George P. Cunningham, afterword to *The Sweet and Sour Animal Book* (New York: Oxford University Press, 1994), n.p.

had known in the United States. They made me remember a hike that the colored Y.M.C.A. fellows, in Chicago, took out to the sand dunes one summer." In these essays that go into great detail about landscape, climate, architecture, food, cultural traditions, and everyday life, Hughes is interested in issues of class and color as well. And his writing suggests that he thinks children should be interested in those things too. More than a decade later, writing more and more for children, he would continue to demonstrate the same preoccupations.

In the first few pages of *Popo and Fifina,* for example, readers learn that the family is a peasant family. Papa Jean is described as "a big powerful black man" who "walked proudly." Most of the story revolves around the various goings-on of the family and community—going to the market, making and playing with a kite, participating in communal celebrations such as dancing the congo. Just as important, however, are the implicit statements Hughes and Bontemps make about society at large and the role the common person has played (and can play) in social transformation. What's more, *Popo and Fifina* celebrates the role of the storyteller both in recounting history and in inspiring future activism. Specifically, a character named Uncle Jacques tells the story of the building of Haiti's Citadel during the Haitian Revolution. As Uncle Jacques talks, "Popo began to understand. The Haitians had once been slaves to the French. They had freed themselves, fighting. Then they had built that fort, the Citadel, as a protection, so that the French might not come and make them slaves again." Not surprisingly, Hughes was exploring the same subject matter in his writing for adults. As Arnold Rampersad's chronology reminds us, in 1936 the Karamu Theater in Cleveland, Ohio, staged *Troubled Island,* Hughes's historical drama about Haiti. His writing for children was part and parcel of his entire project as a writer for and of the people.

The title character in Hughes and Bontemps's *The Pasteboard Bandit* (written in 1935 but not published until 1997), which is set in Mexico, also invokes a kind of revolutionary spirit. The pasteboard bandit is only a toy hoping to be selected from the many at a stall in the market, thinking to himself, "Somebody, he was sure, would admire the way he clinched his tiny fists and held one hand in the air, making a strong gesture." In commenting on Hughes's 1934 trip to Mexico to settle his father's affairs, Cheryl A. Wall mentions his association with writers and artists there and notes, "He also shared their allegiance to leftist politics." Wall contends, "As always, the poet of the blues responded intensely to the masses, and it is their influence that informs *The Paste-board Bandit*."[3]

Wall points out, too, that *The Pasteboard Bandit* is, to a large degree, a story about cultural relativism. This might be one of the reasons Hughes and Bontemps were unsuccessful in getting it published during their lifetimes.[4] As in *Popo and Fifina*, the central family, with whom readers are led to identify, is poor. The American family living temporarily in Mexico has the surname of Strange. They are other. But the bandit, Tito, is entirely comfortable with both the Mexicans and the Americans. Because "Tito could understand both languages, it made no difference at all to him" what language was being spoken. Certainly, Tito mirrors Hughes himself in some ways. He was well traveled, well spoken, and comfortable among all people. Whether or not they have the means to travel themselves, young people see in Hughes's life a model of world citizenship.

In the world Hughes created in his writing, children can recognize similarities in experiences and identities that are not connected to nationality. Perhaps this is why the major piece of fiction he published in *The Brownies' Book*, "The Gold Piece: A Play That Might Be True," is set in no particular time or place. The play concerns a young, impoverished married couple who give all of their money to an elderly woman who needs to hire doctors to cure her son's blindness. Essentially, it is a fairy tale with a moral about generosity and the immensity of the human spirit.

To a large extent, the human spirit is what Hughes's 1932 collection, *The Dream Keeper*, is about. Although the poems in the book were published in various venues prior to this compilation, they were assembled explicitly for an audience of young people. This is clear in the introduction written by Effie Power, at that time the director of Work with Children at the Cleveland Public Library, in which she expressed Hughes's popularity with young people of that day. Hughes's writing represents the same things to young readers now that it did in 1932—that one is not alive if one does not dream. The dream keeper of the title poem

3. Cheryl A. Wall, afterword to *The Pasteboard Bandit* (New York: Oxford University Press, 1997), 89.

4. For more on the Hughes/Bontemps legacy, see Dianne Johnson, *Telling Tales: The Pedagogy and Promise of African American Literature for Youth* (Westport, Conn.: Greenwood Press, 1990).

(and the opening poem in the volume) protects dreams "from the too-rough fingers / Of the world." Simultaneously, this protection insures the survival of those dreams *in* the world.

The themes and tones of the poems in *The Dream Keeper* are wide ranging—the poems are religious, fanciful, gentle and contemplative, sad, romantic, exuberant, and humorous. The collection includes many of Hughes's most famous poems: "The Weary Blues," "When Sue Wears Red," "Dream Variation," "My People," "The Negro Speaks of Rivers," and "Mother to Son." Underscoring the intended audience, the collection ends with "Youth":

> We have tomorrow
> Bright before us
> Like a flame.
>
> Yesterday
> A night-gone thing,
> A sun-down name.
>
> And dawn-today
> Broad arch above the road we came.
>
> We march!

The grand trip, the journey, is ongoing.

But again, it is important to acknowledge the full range of the poems gathered between "The Dream Keeper" and "Youth." Although both of those poems are positive and forward-looking, on the whole the collection represents a balancing act between exploration of harsh realities and celebration of the little joys of living. In the larger world of American children's literature, the happy ending has been the norm until the last twenty or thirty years. But African American writers for young audiences have not had the luxury of indulging in the happy-ever-after fantasy. In many cases, the closest they come is writing that might be described as bittersweet. Thus, *The Dream Keeper* includes an author's note on the blues and numerous poems in that genre.

It is out of the same dynamics that Hughes's *The Sweet and Sour Animal Book* developed. First written during the thirties and revised in the fifties, the volume suffered countless rejections and wasn't published until 1994, with illustrations by students of the Harlem School of the Arts. It is an alphabet book with each letter representing a different animal. In the book's afterword, George Cunningham says, "Although this little collection of light rhymed verse does not betray a racial focus, the denizens of Hughes's fanciful menagerie all seem to find their way into a blues paradox; each poem is a little existential vignette about the rewards of living." Consider the "L" poem:

> A lion in a zoo,
> Shut up in a cage,
> Lives a life
> Of smothered rage.
>
> A lion in the plain,
> Roaming free,
> Is happy as ever
> A lion can be.

Alex Bontemps, the son of Arna Bontemps, suggests, "For my father— and I would think also for Langston—the promise he saw in writing for children was that 'they readily identify with all other children (as they do also with animals).'"[5] So, even though these poems are about lions and zebras and apes on the surface, not far from the surface in most of the poems is their application to human experience and existential concerns as profound as freedom and rage, happiness, right and wrong.

Right and wrong is what Hughes is concerned with in *Black Misery* (1969). The book is made up of black-and-white drawings by Arouni with a caption accompanying each image; Hughes finished writing these captions just before his death in 1967. The only animals in this book are black cats, keeping company with the phrases "black arts" and "black-ball," and a dog: "Misery is when somebody meaning no harm called your little black dog 'Nigger' and he just wagged his tail and wiggled." No happy endings. No sugarcoated children. Just page after page of situations and interactions and realizations about the negativity associated with blackness in the United States. A child is at the center of each scenario, but if this is a children's book, it is the cruelest children's book. Whether or not adults would share it with young people is questionable. But it would have been impossible for *Black Misery* to have the same balance as some of the other books without losing its integrity. Admittedly, the scenarios are quite nuanced. They express the pain of those who have been targets of racism, the confusion of the young people who must make sense out of nonsensical racial dynamics, the power of

5. Alex Bontemps, introduction to *The Sweet and Sour Animal Book*, 8.

the images and stereotypes rampant in popular culture. There is no way to sugarcoat the misery of a black child who feels shame upon seeing a drunk black man "talking out of his mind." Does the child understand why the man is talking out of his mind or why he has lost his sanity?

Finally, there is the consuming misery of institutionalized racism. The last caption of the book reads: "Misery is when you see that it takes the whole National Guard to get you into the new integrated school." No matter how many silly poems he wrote, for Langston Hughes education was all-important. The speaker in one of his uncollected poems, "The Kids in School with Me," rattles off a catalog of classmates from various ethnic backgrounds who consider themselves "Just American kids together" and whose motto is "One for All and All for One." The speaker concludes,

> When I studied my A-B-C's
> And learned arithmetic,
> I also learned in public school
> What makes America tick.

So perhaps a valuable kind of understanding comes with integration. Perhaps embedded in the misery of that last page are also the potentially fruitful changes promised by the actions of the National Guard.

Between 1952 and 1960—the *Brown v. Board of Education* decision was handed down in 1954—Langston Hughes wrote five books, all published by Franklin Watts, that were neither poetry nor fiction, but instead nonfictional, educational works: *The First Book of Negroes* (1952), *The First Book of Rhythms* (1954), *The First Book of Jazz* (1955), *The First Book of the West Indies* (1956), and *The First Book of Africa* (1960). Reading them does constitute a journey—a grand trip, if you will—for Hughes's audience. *The First Book of Negroes* is, in fact, constructed as the journey of a fictional character named Terry through the history of black people in America, beginning with the Moroccan explorer Estevanico in the early 1500s and ending with contemporary life in New York City.

The only shortcoming of this book is that Terry does not appear until several chapters into the narrative, after which he is present throughout the remainder of the book. But on the whole, Terry's presence makes the book more engaging for young readers. Interestingly, he is the child of southerners who have relocated to Harlem to escape the Jim Crow South. In Harlem, Terry is being educated in integrated schools, has friends from various ethnic backgrounds, and, the narrator points out, is himself the descendant of people from many racial backgrounds, like most African Americans. Terry is comfortable ice skating at Rockefeller Center or visiting the United Nations Plaza. In short, he is preparing to live the American dream.

One of the more powerful messages of the book is that one must know the history of one's people in order to move toward a productive future. To that end, Hughes's book covers an enormous time span and a substantial amount of material. He makes note of black kings and queens, the black presence in the Bible, ancient African empires, colonialism, black people in South America, slavery, famous Negroes, Negro History Week, the United Nations' Universal Declaration of Human Rights, and more. Despite the title of the book, Hughes is ahead of his time in referring to African Americans as "black men and women." But in other ways, to a large extent, the book is a document that reveals much about the time in which it was written, especially in terms of issues of class. For example, a passage about language reads this way: "Terry's grandmother graduated from Fisk University, so she does not say 'ain't,' or use bad grammar, except when she is reciting folk poems or telling stories." Of course, this is an ironic comment. However, it is somewhat unfortunate that Hughes, a man who understood and appreciated both standard English and African American vernacular English in ways that few do, did not offer a comment on language that would be more accessible to young readers.

Perhaps intentionally, what will stay with some readers is the thought that one must master standard English to be successful in American society. For as wide-ranging as the subject matter of the book may be, its final passage is all about the virtues of democracy and Terry's stance that he would prefer living in America to any other place in the world. *The First Book of Negroes* was published in 1952. In 1953 Hughes testified before Joseph McCarthy's infamous subcommittee on un-American activities and repudiated his former radicalism. Terry's father could have testified as well:

> "I agree, it is good to live in America, Terry. Our country has many problems still to solve, but America is young, big, strong, and beautiful. And we are trying very hard to be, as the flag says, 'one nation, indivisible, with liberty and justice for all.' Here people are free to vote and work out their problems. In some countries people are governed by rulers, and ordinary folks can't do a thing about it. But here all of us are a part of democracy. By taking an interest in our government, and by treating our neighbors as we would like to be treated, *each one of us* can help make our country the most wonderful country in the world."

The most direct connection between *The First Book of Negroes* and *The First Book of Africa* is Hughes's discussion of Liberia, which he characterizes as the "Godchild of the U.S.A." and a "child of American freedom." As he does in the earlier book, in the later one Hughes includes generous discussion of ancient African civilizations, making a point that they had firmly established governments and standing armies. In addition, he addresses the topics of missionaries and explorers. It would be interesting to see how Hughes would write about some of these topics today. Would he still use the term *discover* when speaking about explorers making contact with places and civilizations that were foreign to them previously? He does, interestingly enough, examine the term *Dark Continent* and make a distinction between the primitive and the savage.

Two points in particular stand out in his final contribution to the First Book series. First, he is interested in the processes of modernization and the future of Africa. Speaking directly to his young audience, the caption beneath the final photograph in the book reads: "Students are preparing to take their place in the new Africa." Second, the importance of the choice to use photographs instead of illustrations in *The First Book of Africa* cannot be overstated. This decision might have been Hughes's or it might have been made by the publisher. It could have been made for financial reasons rather than artistic or content concerns. In any case, the end result is that the photographs constitute a kind of evidence that Africans are in fact a part of the modern world. Too often in children's literature up through the early years of the twenty-first century, when African peoples were depicted at all they were represented as caricatures. The photographs leave no doubt that the people Hughes wrote of are real. Unfortunately, this is an idea that needed (and needs) to be shared with all audiences, including American black people, who often have no appreciation of the relationship between themselves and continental Africans.

This relationship is part of what Hughes might have been trying to communicate not only in this book but also in *The First Book of Jazz*. Although he talks about the fact that jazz is a uniquely American music, he repeatedly establishes the larger context of the creation of jazz, making it clear that there would not be jazz without the rhythm of the African drums. He informs his readers, "Now jazz concerts are often held in Carnegie Hall where formerly only symphonies were heard. So from the Congo to Carnegie went the rhythms of African drums, from New Orleans to New York, and from New York to the whole world."

In *The First Book of Rhythms,* he points out, "The music on your radio now is Cuban, its drums are the bongos of Africa, but the orchestra playing it is American. Rhythms go around the world, adopted and molded by other countries, mixing with other rhythms, and creating new rhythms as they travel." It is clear that, for Hughes, Africans and African cultures contribute to a world culture and a world community. Further, he respects both traditional and contemporary forms of art and arts training. In *The First Book of the West Indies,* for example, he mentions prominently DeWitt Peters, founder in 1944 of the Haitian Art Center at Port-au-Prince, which served both trained and untrained artists. And, while he shows a certain respect for Carnegie Hall, most moving is the respect he shows for traditional African arts, asserting in *The First Book of Africa* that "African art is not 'art for art's sake.' Rather, it is art applied to useful objects."

He might have added that art skills can be applied not only to objects but to useful purposes as well—purposes such as writing books to educate, entertain, and inspire children. And this Langston Hughes did ingeniously. *The First Book of Rhythms* is a model of how he addressed all of those aims simultaneously. It is a fascinating book about the very concept of rhythm, whether demonstrated in music, dance, seashells, architecture, handwriting, poetry, sermons, athletics, or machinery. He explores, too, the idea of the broken rhythm and its lack of beauty. Part of the brilliance of this book is that Hughes hits just the right tone, being neither condescending nor simplistic. Consider this passage: "If a friend is drawing with you, see how different your friend's circles are from your circles. It is fun to make something yourself with your *own* rhythm because it will always be different from what anyone else will make. Your circles and rhythms are yours alone." Hughes is engaging, speaking to each reader individually, showing an absolute interest in self-identity, but also making a powerful statement about collectivity: "*All* the rhythms of life in some way are related, one to another. You, your baseball, and the universe are brothers through rhythms."

Langston Hughes's literature for children and young adults is a gift. Whether fiction, poetry, or nonfiction, it is true literature into which he put much research, thought, creative energy, and love. Alex Bontemps is a witness to the rapport young readers experience with Hughes and his work. In his introduction to *The Pasteboard Bandit* he remembers:

> Hughes was one of the modern poets who, my father thought, had not abandoned children, either in his affections or in his writing. My own

recollections of Hughes confirm that impression. From the moment I met Langston, I saw that he was one of those adults who have the ability to relate to children. We were in a crowded room, but he seemed to be making contact with me as an equal. Hughes had the child in him, and children really zeroed in on him. It was unmistakable, something in his eye, something I knew even before he talked to me.[6]

There could be no more convincing testimony.

Langston Hughes's young readers sense that they are just as important as his adult audience, that the two audiences are related. They know that Hughes trusts them to shape a future worth living, while recognizing his own responsibility in preparing them to do that. He hopes that each reader's reading, each reader's life, is a grand trip. This is work both to be enjoyed and to be taken seriously. It remains entertaining, moving, and beautiful, and relevant.

6. Ibid., 6–7.

A Note on the Texts

For this volume, we have used the first edition of each work, as indicated below, for our text. Capitalization, punctuation, and word compounding have been retained as they originally appeared, although obvious typographical errors and misspellings have been corrected.

Works from *The Brownies' Book:* "Mexican Games," January 1921, p. 18; "In a Mexican City," April 1921, pp. 102–5; "The Gold Piece: A Play That Might Be True," July 1921; "Up to the Crater of an Old Volcano," December 1921, pp. 334–38. Reprinted in *The Best of the Brownies' Book*, ed. Dianne Johnson-Feelings. New York: Oxford University Press, 1996.

The Dream Keeper and Other Poems. Illustrations by Helen Sewell. Introduction by Effie L. Power. New York: Knopf, 1932. Reprinted 1960, 1986. Reprinted with illustrations by Brian Pinkney, 1994.

The Sweet and Sour Animal Book. Introduction by Ben Vereen. Afterword by George P. Cunningham. Illustrations by students from the Harlem School of the Arts. New York: Oxford University Press, 1994.

Popo and Fifina: Children of Haiti, with Arna Bontemps. Illustrations by E. Simms Campbell. New York: MacMillan Co., 1932. Reprinted, New York: Oxford University Press, 1993.

Black Misery. Illustrations by Arouni. New York: Paul S. Eriksson, 1969. Reprinted, New York: Oxford University Press, 1994.

The Pasteboard Bandit, with Arna Bontemps. Illustrations by Peggy Turley. Introduction by Alex Bontemps. Afterword by Cheryl Wall. New York: Oxford University Press, 1997.

The First Book of Negroes. Pictures by Ursula Koering. New York: Franklin Watts, 1952.

The First Book of Rhythms. Pictures by Robin King. New York: Franklin Watts, 1954. Reprinted with illustrations by Matt Wawiorka. New York: Oxford University Press, 1995.

The First Book of Jazz. Pictures by Cliff Roberts. New York: Franklin Watts, 1955. Reprinted, Hopewell, N.J.: Ecco Press, 1995.

The First Book of the West Indies. Pictures by Robert Bruce. New York: Franklin Watts, 1956.

The First Book of Africa. Illustrated with photographs. New York: Franklin Watts, 1960.

A Note on the Illustrations

The illustrations for *The Dream Keeper* are quiet but poignant, while those for *Popo and Fifina* are graphic and bolder, though few in number. The illustrations in the "First Book" series are less successful artistically than those in the aforementioned books, but important nonetheless. The images in *Black Misery* are integral to that project, with an illustration accompanying each page of text. But the text is powerful even without all of the images.

Relatively few illustrations are included in the present volume largely due to permissions considerations. But those readers who are interested may consult directly some of the early volumes as well as recent editions, some with new art, as noted above in the listing of texts.

In *The First Book of Rhythms*, a few sentences referring to the original illustrations are included for accuracy's sake but will require readers to use their imaginations when those illustrations do not appear.

The editor's hope is that the illustrations that are included here are sufficient to convey the tone and texture of those of Hughes's projects that are, to some extent, incomplete without the original images. But ultimately, what endures are the images created in the minds of Hughes's audience by the gift of his words.

Contributions to
The Brownies' Book

(1921)

Mexican Games

Lady White

One child is chosen as Lady White and another as Don Philip, her suitor. All the other players join hands to form a large circle, thus making a house for Lady White, who stands in the center. Don Philip comes to call and begins to walks around the circle, but finds every hand tightly joined and so he can not get in. The children forming the ring then sing the following verse three times:

> *Sweet Lady White is sheltered*
> *In walls of silver and gold;*
> *Her lover must break a window,*
> *The Lady to behold.*

Then Lady White asks:

Who is walking around my house?

And the lover answers:

Don Philip Philipon.

And the Lady says:

Why, who can this fat person be?

And the suitor replies:

Don Philip Philipon.

Then the players in the circle all sing:

> *You can't get into this house,*
> *Don Philip Philipon;*
> *Unless you break a window out,*
> *Don Philip Philipon.*

Then Don Philip attempts to break through the circle in order to reach the inside. As soon as he succeeds in getting in, however, Lady White must run out and Don Philip has to catch her. Then the game may be played over again with two different children taking the parts of Don Philip and Lady White.

The Lost Donkey

Here is a game to be played when there is an odd number of children present so that when pairs are formed there will always be one left over. All the players walk about in different directions and pretend to be gathering flowers while they sing this little song:

> *Benny goes a walking,*
> *Picking pretty flowers.*
> *Benny goes a walking*
> *Under shady bowers.*
> *But he shall lose his way,*
> *Little donkey,*
> *And be alone all day,*
> *Little donkey,*
> *And be alone all day,*
> *Little donkey.*

At the third *Little Donkey* all the players must run to join hands with another player so as to have a partner and the one who is left without a partner is the *Little Lost Donkey* until the next game gives him a chance to get one.

The Priest and the Teacher

In this game one child is a priest, another is a teacher and the third a storekeeper. The priest and the teacher are buyers. All the other children are articles of merchandise and should sit down in a long line. To each one in line the storekeeper gives a secret name such as *Butter, Sugar, Cinnamon,* and so on, which the buyers must not know. Then the priest and the teacher take turns at buying and can only ask for one article at a time. For example, if the priest calls for *cheese*, the player who has that name must rise and follow him, but if there is no *cheese* the storekeeper says so and the priest must wait until his next turn to ask for something else. When the storekeeper has sold all his merchandise the priest and the teacher count their articles and the one who has the most can be storekeeper for the next time, and he also has the privilege of choosing the new priest and the new teacher.

Dear Little Friends:

These are three games which the children play in your beautiful neighbor country, Mexico. I hope you will enjoy them.

In a Mexican City

Toluca sits in the highest plateau of Mexico at the foot of the old and long extinct volcano "Xinantecatl," which is said to be named after one of the ancient Indian kings. All around us there are mountains and our valley is broad and fertile. Here the climate is cool and often cold, but the poor folks never have shoes to wear nor do the rich use stoves in their houses. In summer it is the rainy season and every day brings long showers and misty clouds that hide the mountains. In winter the sky is clear and the sun shines warm at mid-day, but in the shade it is always cool.

The house where I live faces a little plaza or park and from my window I can see many interesting things. Every morning a bare-footed old woman in a wide straw hat and long skirts drives a little flock of white sheep down the street, and sometimes she has a tiny baby lamb in her arms. They go to the country to graze all day and in the evening they come back again. Often I see a funeral procession passing through the plaza on the way to the Panteon and as they do not have hearses here, the men carry the casket on their shoulders while the mourners walk behind them. On Sundays the park is full of black-shawled women and men wrapped in *serapes* or blankets who come in the early morning to say mass in the quaint old church in front with its pretty tower and its most unmusical bells.

There are many churches here and all of them are very old. Some were built before the Independence, when Mexico was still under Spanish rule, and have beautiful domes and tall, graceful towers. Practically every one is Catholic and they keep many feast days. On the day of the Innocent Saints there is a custom that reminds one of our April Fool. On this date things should never be loaned and if you forget, the article is sure to be sent back by the joking friend who borrowed it, accompanied by a tiny box full of tiny toys and a note calling you a "poor little innocent saint." On the second of November, which is a day in honor of the dead, they sell many little cardboard coffins and paper dolls dressed as mourners, and if a person meets you in the street and says "I'm dying," you must give him a gift unless you have said "I'm dying" first; then, of course, he has to treat you to the present. On a certain day in January the people take their animals to be blessed and in the church-yard one sees everything from oxen to rabbits. Each is wearing a bit of gay-colored ribbon and they wait patiently for the priest to come.

The houses here from the outside all look very much alike and are but a succession of arched doors and windows with small balconies facing the sidewalk. They often have lovely court-yards and verandas but these are hidden from the passers-by behind high walls, and the fronts of the houses never tell anything about the beauty that may be within them. When one enters a house the door usually leads directly into the court-yard or sometimes into the long open corridor from which every room has its entrance. In the *patio* or court-yard there are flowers the year round and if it is a large one, there may be a garden or trees. On the railing of the long veranda, too, there are many pots of red and pink geraniums and fragrant heliotrope. Inside the house there will probably be little furniture. Only a few of the well-to-do people have a great deal, so most of the homes use chairs as their principal space fillers. In a friend's parlor I counted twenty-seven one day and the only other articles of furniture were two small tables. Most of the parlors of the middle-class folk show the same emptiness but perhaps it is a good idea, for on holidays there is plenty of room to dance without moving anything out.

The kitchens here are very different from American ones, for they do not use stoves or gas ranges. The fuel is charcoal and the stoves are made of stone or brick, built into the wall like a long seat, except that they have three square grates on top for the fire and three square holes in front for removing the ashes. Some are prettily built and covered with gaily colored tiles. To make the fire several splinters of pine are lighted in the grate and then the black pieces of charcoal piled on top. Then one must fan and fan at the square holes in front until the charcoal on top begins to blaze, and in a little while you have a nice glowing fire ready to cook with.

The shops here in the portals, which is Toluca's "uptown," are much like the American stores, but in the little *expendios* in the side streets one can buy a penny's worth of wood or a tablespoonful of lard or a lamp full of oil. The poor here do not have much money. These little shops paint themselves all sorts of colors and have the funniest names. One I know is called "The Wedding Bouquet." Others are "The Light of America," "The Big Fight," "The Fox," and so on, and one tinner's shop is even called "Heart of Jesus." The last store on the edge of town, where the road leads off to San Juan, has the very appropriate name of "Farewell." One who did not know Spanish could acquire a whole vocabulary just by reading the store names which are painted in large colored letters across the front and are often accompanied by pictures or decorations to illustrate their meanings. For instance, the meat market called "The Bull of Atenco" has the animal's picture on one side of the door and a bull-fighter's on the other, painted over a background of bright blue.

Friday is market-day in Toluca and the square outside the market-house is one sea of wide Mexican hats, as buyer and trader jostle and bargain. The surrounding streets are lined with Indians from the country who squat behind their little piles of vegetables, or fruit, or herbs, which they have to sell and which they spread out on the ground before them. One old woman will have neat little piles of green peppers for a cent a pile. Another will have beans and another wild herbs for seasoning soup or making medicine. The fruit sellers, of course, always have a most gorgeous and luscious display. Under a canopy created from four sticks and some sort of covering to make a spot of shade, are piled all sorts of strange, delicious fruits. There one finds creamy alligator pears and queer-tasting mangoes; red pomegranates and black zapotes; small, round melons and fat little bananas and the delicately flavored granada, which feels like a paper ball and has a soft seedy pulp inside. Then there are oranges that come up to us from the hot country, along with limes and juicy lemons that are not sour like the ones we know up North.

Here people never buy without bargaining. If the price asked for a thing is two cents, they are sure to get it for one. These price arguments are always good-natured and the merchant, knowing that he will have to come down, usually asks more than he should in the first place. Everyone going to market must carry his own baskets and sacks and even the paper for his meat, as everything is sold without wrapping.

A market-day crowd is composed of all sorts of people. A rich señorita with her black scarf draped gracefully about her shoulders is doing the family buying, while the servants carrying baskets follow behind. Indian women with sacks of vegetables on their backs; others with turkeys or chickens in their arms; little ragged brown boys seeking a chance to earn a few cents by carrying a customer's basket; and beggars, numberless beggars, blind, lame and sick beggars, all asking patiently for pennies or half-rotted fruits; these are the folks one sees on market-day pushing and elbowing their way through the crowd which is so thick that nobody can hurry.

On one side of the plaza are the sellers of hats and the large yellow mats that the Indians spread down on the floor at night for sleeping purposes. The Mexican straw hats have wide round brims and high peaked crowns and, though cheap, most of them are prettily shaped. The Indian, upon buying a new hat, will not take the trouble to remove his old one, but puts the new one on top and marches off home with his double decked head gear. Sometimes a hat merchant, desiring to change his location, will put one hat on his head, and as each peaked crown fits snugly over the other, he then piles his whole stock on top of himself and goes walking down the street like a Chinese pagoda out for a stroll.

Here everything that people do not carry on their backs they carry on their heads. The ice-cream man crying *nieve,* balances his freezer, and the baker-boys carry a shallow basket as big around as a wagon wheel. This basket has a crown in the center and when filled with bread it fits over the head like a very wide Mexican hat, while its wearer underneath is as insignificant as the stem of a mushroom. Sometimes we see fruit sellers, too, with great colorful mounds of fruit piled upon their wooden trays and balanced gracefully on their black-haired heads. When a thing is too heavy or too unwieldy to put on the head, then it is carried on the back, and the Indians bear immense burdens in this way. Men, women and even small children are often seen with great loads of wood or charcoal, or sacks of grain, on their backs, and the only carriage that the little Indian baby ever knows is its mother's back, where it rides contented all day long, tied in her *rebosa* or shawl.

The Gold Piece
A Play That Might Be True

Characters

A Peasant Boy
A Peasant Girl, his wife
An Old Woman

Scene: The interior of a hut by the roadside. It is twilight. A boy and a girl are lying before the fireplace, a gold piece on the floor between them. There is a door at the right of the fireplace and a window at the left. During the play the twilight deepens into darkness.

THE GIRL *(Looking at the coin)*—Just to think that this bright gold piece is ours! All ours! Fifty whole loren!

THE BOY *(Smiling happily)*—The ten old pigs were fat ones, Rosa, and brought us a fine price in the market.

THE GIRL—Now we can buy and buy and buy.

THE BOY—Sure we can. Now we can buy all the things we've wanted ever since we've been married but haven't had the money to get.

THE GIRL—Oh! How good, Pablo! It seems we've been waiting an awfully long time.

THE BOY—We have, but now we shan't wait any longer. Now we can get the wooden clock, Rosa. You know—the one that we've wanted since we first saw it in the old watch-maker's window. The one so nicely carved, that strikes the hours every day and runs for a whole week with a single winding. And I think there is a cuckoo in it, too. It will make our little house look quite elegant.

THE GIRL—And now you can buy the thick brown boots with hob nails in them to work in the fields.

THE BOY—And you may have the woolen shawl with red and purple flowers on it and the fringe about the edges.

THE GIRL—O-o-o! Can I really, Pablo? I've dreamed of it for months.

THE BOY—You surely can, Rosa. I've wanted to give it to you ever since I knew you. It will make you look so pretty. And we'll get two long white candles, too, to burn on Sundays and feast days.

26

THE GIRL—And we'll get a little granite kettle for stewing vegetables in.

THE BOY—And we'll get a big spoon to stir with.

THE GIRL—And two little blue plates to eat from.

THE BOY—And we'll have dried fish and a little cake for supper every night.

THE GIRL—And—but Oh! Pablo—It's wonderful!

THE BOY—Oh! Rosa! It's fine!

THE GIRL AND THE BOY *(Rising and dancing joyously around and around the little gold piece which glistens and glitters gaily on the floor before the open fire as if it knew it were the cause of their joy)*—Oh! How happy we are! Oh! How happy we are! Because we can buy! Because we can buy! Because we can buy and buy and buy!

> *(Just then an old woman's figure passes the window and there is a timid knock at the door. The dancing stops. THE BOY picks up his shining gold piece and clutches it tightly in his hand.)*

THE GIRL *(With a little frown of annoyance)*—Who's there?

> *(The door opens slowly and a bent old woman leaning on a heavy stick enters.)*

THE BOY *(Rudely)*—Well, Grandmother, what do you want?

THE OLD WOMAN *(Panting and weak)*—I've come such a long way today and am very tired. I just wanted to rest a moment before going on.

> *(THE GIRL brings her a stool and she sits down near the fireplace.)*

THE GIRL *(Sympathetically)*—But surely, Old Woman, you aren't going any further on foot tonight?

THE OLD WOMAN—Yes, I am, child, because I must.

THE GIRL—And why must you, Old Lady?

THE OLD WOMAN—Because my boy is in the house alone and he is blind.

THE GIRL—Your boy is blind?

THE OLD WOMAN—Yes, for eighteen years. He has not seen since he was a tiny baby.

THE BOY—And where have you been that you are so late upon the road?

THE OLD WOMAN—I've been into the city and from sunrise I have not rested. People told me famous doctors were there who could make my blind boy see again and so I went to find them.

THE GIRL—And did you find them?

THE OLD WOMAN—Yes, I found them, but *(her voice becomes sad)* they would not come with me.

THE GIRL—Why would they not come?

THE OLD WOMAN—Because they were great and proud. They said, "When you get fifty loren, send for us and then perhaps we'll come. Now we have no time." One who was kinder than the rest told me that a simple operation might bring my boy's sight back. But I am poor. I have no money and from where in all the world could a worn out old woman like me get fifty loren?

THE BOY AND THE GIRL *(Quickly)*—We don't know!

THE BOY *(Keeping his fist tightly closed over the gold piece)*—Why, we never even saw fifty loren!

THE GIRL—So much money we never will have.

THE BOY—No, we never will have.

THE OLD WOMAN—If I were young I would not say that, but I am old and I know I shall never see fifty loren. Ah! I would sell all that I have if my boy could only see again! I would sell my keepsakes, my silken dress that I've had for many years, my memories, anything to bring my boy's sight back to him!

THE GIRL—But, Old Lady, would you sell your dream of a wooden clock, a clock that strikes the hour every day and need not be wound for a whole week?

THE OLD WOMAN—Yes, Child, I would.

THE BOY—And would you sell your wish for white candles to burn on feast days and Sundays?

THE OLD WOMAN—Oh! Boy, I would even sell my labor on feast days and Sundays were I not too weak to work.

THE GIRL—And would you give up your dream of a woolen shawl with red and purple flowers on it and fringe all around the four edges of it?

THE OLD WOMAN—I would give up all my dreams if my son were to see again.

> *(There is a pause. THE GIRL, forgetting for a moment her own desires, begins to speak slowly as if to herself.)*

THE GIRL—It must be awful not to know the sunshine and the flowers and the beauty of the hills in springtime.

THE BOY—It must be awful never to see the jolly crowds in the square on market days and never to play with the fellows at May games.

THE GIRL—And the doctor says that maybe this boy could be made well.

THE BOY—And the Old Woman says that it would cost but fifty loren.

THE GIRL—*(Suddenly)*—I have no need of a gay shawl, Pablo.

THE BOY—We have no shelf for a wooden clock, Rosa.

THE GIRL—Nor vegetables to cook in a granite kettle.

THE BOY—And a big spoon would be such a useless thing.

THE OLD WOMAN *(Rising)*—Before the night becomes too dark I must go on. *(She moves toward the door.)*

THE BOY—Wait a moment, Mother. Let us slip something into your pouch.

THE GIRL—Something bright and golden, Mother.

THE BOY—Something that shines in the sunlight.

THE GIRL—Something from us to your boy.

> *(They open THE OLD WOMAN's bag and THE BOY slips the gold piece into it. THE OLD WOMAN does not see what they have given her.)*

THE OLD WOMAN—Thank you, good children. I know my boy will be pleased with your toy. It will give him something to hold in his hands and make him forget his blindness for a moment. God bless you both for your gift and—Good-Bye.

THE BOY and THE GIRL—Good-Bye, Old Woman.

> *(The door closes. It is dark and the room is lighted only by the fire in the grate.)*

THE GIRL—Are you happy, Pablo?

THE BOY—I'm very happy. And you, Rosa?

THE GIRL—I'm happy, too. I'm happier than any wooden clock could make me.

THE BOY—Or hob-nailed shoes, me.

THE GIRL—Or me, a flowered shawl with crimson fringe.

> *(They sit down before the fireplace and watch the big logs glow. The wood crackles and flames and lights the whole room with its warm red light. Outside through the window a night star shines. THE BOY and THE GIRL are quiet while the curtain falls.)*

Up to the Crater of an Old Volcano

Near Toluca, Mexico, is an old volcano, Xinantecatl. The fires which once burned within its bosom have long ago gone out and now, in the deep crater that in past centuries held boiling lava and red hot ashes, two calm blue lakes sparkle like dainty jewels in a rough setting. No one knows when the last eruption of this volcano took place but some say that it was long before the time of Christ, and when the Aztec Indians came down from the North to found their powerful empire, Xinantecatl, for so they called it, had long been sleeping. Now, like a dead giant at rest, it is still great and majestic. Rising above the puny cities and little low hills that cluster about its base, it is as some nature king rising above a subject people. The ancient Indians thought it a god and climbed its steep sides carrying gold and jewels and precious gifts on their backs as an offering to the mountain deity. Even today the rural Indians say that when shots are fired in the crater or stones thrown into the blue lakes, the mountain becomes angry and calls the clouds to hide its peaks and send rain down upon its disturbers. We in Toluca, however, are not afraid of Xinantecatl. It is like a well-known friend to us and one whom we see every day. On clear mornings its peaks are sharp and distinct in the blue sky; at evening the whole mountain makes a great black silhouette against the twilight colors.

When the boys of the Instituto, Toluca's high school, began to plan a two-day walking trip to the crater, and invited me to go with them, I accepted eagerly. They, with the customary Mexican politeness, put my name first on the list of those who were to go and several of the students went with me to aid in choosing the proper kind of "trumpeate," a sort of bag for carrying food. It is woven from marsh grass and is light of weight. They also saw that I bought a wide Mexican hat, as protection from the sun, and told me all the things that I would need to carry. First, plenty of lunch; then, two warm blankets because we were to sleep in the open mountains; my camera for pictures; a bottle for water; a small amount of cognac or some other liquor in case of mountain sickness in the high altitude; and a pistol. "But above all," they said, "take onions!" Those who had been up to the volcano before claimed that they were the very best things to smell if one began to feel ill in the thin air near the summit. I thought to myself that if I should get sick, the scent of onions would only make me worse. Nevertheless I took them and when the time arrived for their use I found my mind completely changed about their smell.

It was a beautiful sunny morning when we left Toluca. From the platform of the small station, where we were to board the seven o'clock train for Calimaya, we could see the white, sparkling snow peaks of the volcano and they seemed very high and far away. There were forty of us going on the trip and, before leaving time, the first coach of the tiny train was completely filled with Instituto boys. The aisle of the car was one jumble of blanket rolls and fat "trumpeates" of food, and the windows were crowded with faces—mostly brown faces of laughing young fellows, all talking at once and watching the late comers hurrying down the platform. These dark faced, friendly school boys were about like other dark skinned boys of my own race whom I had known in the United States. They made me remember a hike that the colored Y.M.C.A. fellows, in Chicago, took out to the sand dunes one summer. There the car windows were crowded with dark faces, too, and everybody talked at once. The only difference was that in Chicago they were speaking English and when a late member of the party reached the platform, every one cried out, "Hurry up!" while here, when Rudolfo, the tardy, came running through the gates, every one in the window shouted, "Apurese!" which means the same in Spanish.

The little train went click, click, click, down the pretty valley. We passed several small villages: Metepec, with its great church large enough to hold its whole population; San Francisco, a collection of small huts, and a white temple; Mexicaltzingo, where the country bullfights are held; and then Calimaya, where the road to the volcano begins.

We found Calimaya a small, clean town with cobblestone streets and a stream of water running down the center of each one, where the cows and long horned oxen stopped to drink.

We piled our blankets and bags in one corner of its arched "Portales" to wait while two of the boys went for the guide and the burros—patient little beasts of burden—who were to carry our things. After a long while the burros came. There had been some disagreement in regard to the money to be paid, so we learned, the guide having set a price and then suddenly changing his mind, saying that he could not risk his animals in the cold mountain air for such a small sum. But finally an agreement was reached and we had three burros, a boy and two men to drive them, and a guide—all for a price that would amount to but five American dollars, and this for a two-day trip!

When the word "Vamanos" was given, the three small animals were almost hidden under their loads of blankets and lunch-bags, but being strong, sturdy little beasts, they did not seem to mind. They started off down the road with a trot, the two drivers and the boy running behind shouting, "Burro! Burro!" to make them go faster. The members of the hiking party, freed of their luggage, had nothing to pack now except the canteens or water bottles and their guns. Very few having pistols, there was an unusual variety of fire-arms in sight, from a modern rifle to ancient carbines. The reason for so many shooting machines was that we might meet bandits on the road, and, though it was only a *might*, every one should be prepared. During the revolutions and until a year or so ago the hills were full of robbers, who, not content with taking travelers' money, would ofttimes take their clothes, even to their shoes, leaving the robbed ones to get home as best they could. Now, though such robberies are infrequent, no one goes far into the country unarmed. The boys of the Instituto, going through the quaint streets of Calimaya, looked like a small militia.

The road leading to the foothills was quite bare of trees. High in a cloudless sky, the sun beat down upon our heads without pity, while the dust rose in clouds from under our feet. On either side the road was lined with maguey and cactus plants which served as a sort of fence around the fields, where lazy, slow moving oxen were pulling wooden plows yoked to their horns, and wide-hatted peons pricked them languidly with sharp-pointed sticks. After about an hour's walking we passed Zaragoza, a small village which, like all Mexican villages, had its tall old church towering sad and beautiful above the miserable little huts. By this time all our water bottles were empty and our throats were dry. The guide promised us that we should come to a river soon and when we finally reached its friendly banks, after what seemed like an eternity of tramping in dust and sun, we lay on our stomachs like dogs and drank the cool clear water that came rippling down from the hills.

Soon the road began to ascend and we found ourselves climbing a slope covered with little pine trees. Before us, when we reached the summit, we saw only pine clad hills and then more hills, hiding the volcano from us. Looking back, we saw the wide valley of Toluca below, dotted with red roofed villages and the white towers and domes of old, old churches. At its opposite side we saw the mountains rising like a wall about the valley, shutting it in from the rest of the world and protecting it with their grey and purple strength.

The road now led upward, and it was not easy climbing through the forest of stunted trees with the sun like a hot ball overhead. About one o'clock, when everybody was aching and tired, the guide showed us a little cañon at one side of the road and said that here was the last water to be found before reaching the crater, the next morning; so he advised us to stop for lunch and to fill our water bottles. The burros were unloaded and everyone searched in the pile of "trumpeates" for his lunch-bag. As each woven sack looked just about like another, there was much opening and exchanging and inspecting before each one had his own. Then we scattered about the slope and prepared to eat. One of the boys from each group went down to the spring for water, and it was deliciously sweet and cool. After lunch we decided to rest a while. The guide said we had made good time and in three hours we could reach the timber line, where we were to make camp on the edge of the woods.

At three o'clock we climbed up to the road, loaded the burros and were off again—up, up, up. We had left the foot-hills behind us now and were on the very slope of the volcano itself. Here the trees, taller and thicker, made what we call a real forest. Perhaps we had eaten too much lunch, or perhaps we were tired, but anyway the trail seemed difficult. Then, too, we had begun to notice the lightness of the air and at every hundred yards or so we had to stop for breath. Some of the boys began to feel ill and at this juncture the onions put in their appearance. I felt none too well, so I began to search in my pockets for my onions, too,—and when, with a dull ache in my head and a breathless feeling in the lungs, I pressed them to my nose, all the former aversion to their scent disappeared. I kept them under my nose all the way to camp. And whether due to the onions or not, I didn't feel any worse while some of the fellows had to walk so slowly that they were left behind the rest of the party.

In the late afternoon we passed through a part of the forest where it seemed as if more than half the trees had been torn up by the roots. Great tree trunks, so large that we could hardly climb over them, lay across the path. Looking down, I could see whole hillsides strewn with these fallen members of the forest. Some of the boys explained to me how, two years before, a hurricane had swept across the mountains and tried to carry the whole forest off with it. The fallen trees were a bad impediment to our progress because, in an atmosphere where one cannot walk without getting out of breath, to climb over a gigantic trunk is an exercise that is not taken with pleasure.

It was almost six o'clock when we arrived at the spot chosen for camp, just below the timber line, where the trees of the mountain end. We were close to the peaks now and one of them, that looked very near, loomed between us and the sinking sun so that all the mountain-side was in shadow. Down below we saw the valley—far, far beneath—bathed in a twilight mist of rose and purple; the little river, that had been a winding, silver thread all day, had now turned golden in the sunset.

We began to make camp. Some unloaded the burros and tied them fast to trees. Others searched for the dry limbs and branches of the pine in order to make the fires. And still others, too tired and out of breath to do anything, sank down upon the ground to rest, for the last hour of the ascent had been the hardest of all.

The shadows on the mountain-side deepened and the sunset colors faded from the sky. For me, the evening passed quickly. There was supper around the blazing camp-fires, of which each group of fellows had its own; then songs and stories and more songs, to which the two burro drivers contributed a love ballad which they said they had learned down in the "hot country." At nine, the first guards were posted and the camp became still. The only noise to be heard was the occasional sob-like "hee-hooing" of the burros and the strong "Alerta" of the watchers, crying to each other from the four corners of the camp.

At two o'clock, when my turn came to stand guard, the moon had gone down behind the mountain and the forest was in inky blackness. The low burning camp-fires gave a little light. A long way off and deep down in the night-covered valley, we saw the white lights of Toluca, shining like a cluster of sunken stars in the darkness.

The next morning, at sunrise, we were off for the crater. A half hour's walk took us past the timber line, out of the forest, and to the open mountain-side. In a little while we found ourselves at the foot of one of the volcanic peaks, which, if we chose to climb it, would give us a view down into the crater. About half the party chose to go up; the others took the burro path which led around the side of the peak, entering the crater at the lowest opening. The peak, which near the top was covered with large patches of snow, did not appear to be very high. But we soon found that the steepness of its slope and the lightness of the air made the ascent more laborious than we thought it would be, and at every eight or ten steps we had to stop for breath. It seemed as if we would never reach the summit. The rocks and sand and gravel, of which the mountain was made, slipped beneath our feet and made us slide half-way back at every forward movement. We had to cross the snow covered spaces on our hands and knees—they were so slippery. When we finally gained the summit, it seemed as if our last breath had gone. We were very high and, between us and the hills below, the white clouds drifted by.

As we turned to look down into the crater, we saw it as a sort of double one, divided into two parts by a long hump-backed hill. On each side of the hill there was a blue lake with a rocky shore. The sides of the crater were steep and many colored, and the three highest of the tall, jagged peaks that formed its ragged edge had snow upon them. We, on top of our laboriously climbed summit, had an excellent view down into that part of the volcano where La Laguna Chica (The Little Lake) sparkled in the morning sun. Those who had taken the burro path were already resting on its shore and the height from which we saw them made them appear very tiny. Feeling the pangs of hunger, as we had not yet eaten breakfast, and knowing that the burros carrying the lunch-bags were waiting for us below, we began to descend. Half running, half sliding in the loose sand and gravel of the inner slope, we reached the bottom much more quickly than we had ascended. On the sandy shore, scattered with big boulders taller than a man, we ate our breakfast and drank the cold, refreshing water of the clear blue lake.

After breakfast we decided to see La Laguna Grande (The Big Lake), and so, circling around the side of The Little Lake, we began to climb one of the low ends of the hump-backed hill. In a short while, from the top of its rocky ridge, we saw below us the deep blue waters of La Laguna Grande, so beautiful and lovely and calm that it gave one a thrill of surprise at finding it buried in this old volcano's burnt, scarred walls. Some people say that this pretty lake has no bottom and that swimmers who venture far into its cold waters may be drawn down into unknown depths. Its smooth, innocent surface, however, gives no indications of such treachery, and the charm of its beauty makes one think it is a good fairy lake and not the wicked old witch with the pretty face, which reputation has given it.

We walked all around the rocky shore, stopping now and then to pick up small queer-colored stones or the sulphur coated rocks found on the beach. To reach the other end of the lake's long oval required more time than we had expected, for distances are deceiving in the high clear air. We stopped often to rest, sitting down on the large boulders and admiring the beautiful colors in the sides of the crater whose walls were sometimes deep crimson capped with jagged peaks, sometimes bright red or soft orange streaked with purple, and sometimes just gray rock covered with snow patches near the rim. And the blue lake was always like a jewel in a rough setting. At the other end of the oval we found erected on the sandy shore, a large wooden cross which a band of religious people had carried up the steep trail some years before. They held a mass in the crater. Behind the cross rose "El Pice de Fraile," the highest of the Xinantecatl peaks, glittering snow white in morning sun. From its tooth-like summit on a clear day, one who has a pair of strong binoculars can see, off the coast of Guerrero, more than a hundred miles away, the silver waters of the Pacific.

When we climbed back over the hump-backed hill and down to the wider shore of the Little Lake, the burros were already packed with our blankets and much diminished lunch bags. Before we reached the spot where we had eaten, the first ones started off. We filled our water bottles and canteens from the lake and started after them. When we came to the highest point in the narrow road we turned for a last look at the little blue lake below, the hump-backed hill and the opposite red and purple walls of the volcano. Then we turned and followed the path which curved, at a dizzying height, onto the steeply sloping outer sides of the crater, where a false step too near the edge would have sent one tumbling down a mile or so into a green tree-covered valley. We took care not to make the false step.

When, at sunset, we unloaded the burros in the clean little "Portales" of Calimaya, although stiff and footsore and weary, everybody was happy and agreed that it had been a fine trip. A few minutes later, sitting on the platform of the country station, awaiting the last train for Toluca, we could see, high and far away, the sharp, jagged peaks of the old volcano faintly outlined against the sunset sky. They seemed so very high and so very far from us we could scarcely believe that just ten hours before we had visited them and drunk the cool snow water of their clear blue lakes.

Poetry

The Dream Keeper and Other Poems

Illustrations by Helen Sewell

(1932)

To My Brother

The author wishes to thank the editors of the various magazines, including *The New Republic, Survey Graphic, Vanity Fair, The Crisis, Opportunity,* and *The World Tomorrow* for their permission in reprinting certain of these poems.

Contents

The Dream Keeper

The Dream Keeper

Bring me all of your dreams,
You dreamers,
Bring me all of your
Heart melodies
That I may wrap them
In a blue cloud-cloth
Away from the too-rough fingers
Of the world.

Winter Moon

How thin and sharp is the moon tonight!
How thin and sharp and ghostly white
Is the slim curved crook of the moon tonight!

Fairies

Out of the dust of dreams
Fairies weave their garments.
Out of the purple and rose of old memories
They make rainbow wings.
No wonder we find them such marvellous things!

Autumn Thought

Flowers are happy in summer.
In autumn they die and are blown away.
　Dry and withered,
Their petals dance on the wind
Like little brown butterflies.

Dreams

Hold fast to dreams
For if dreams die
Life is a broken-winged bird
That cannot fly.

Hold fast to dreams
For when dreams go
Life is a barren field
Frozen with snow.

April Rain Song

Let the rain kiss you.
Let the rain beat upon your head with silver liquid drops.
Let the rain sing you a lullaby.

The rain makes still pools on the sidewalk.
The rain makes running pools in the gutter.
The rain plays a little sleep-song on our roof at night—

And I love the rain.

After Many Springs

Now,
In June,
When the night is a vast softness
Filled with blue stars,
And broken shafts of moon-glimmer
Fall upon the earth,
Am I too old to see the fairies dance?
I cannot find them any more.

Winter Sweetness

This little house is sugar.
    Its roof with snow is piled,
And from its tiny window
    Peeps a maple-sugar child.

Quiet Girl

I would liken you
To a night without stars
Were it not for your eyes.
I would liken you
To a sleep without dreams
Were it not for your songs.

Poem

I loved my friend.
He went away from me.
There's nothing more to say.
The poem ends,
Soft as it began—
I loved my friend.

Joy

I went to look for Joy,
Slim, dancing Joy,
Gay, laughing Joy,
Bright-eyed Joy—
And I found her
Driving the butcher's cart
In the arms of the butcher boy!
Such company, such company,
As keeps this young nymph, Joy!

Sea Charm

Water-Front Streets

The spring is not so beautiful there—
But dream ships sail away
To where the spring is wondrous rare
And life is gay.

The spring is not so beautiful there—
But lads put out to sea
Who carry beauties in their hearts
And dreams, like me.

Long Trip

The sea is a wilderness of waves,
A desert of water.
We dip and dive,
Rise and roll,
Hide and are hidden
On the sea.
    Day, night,
    Night, day,
The sea is a desert of waves,
A wilderness of water.

Sea Calm

How still,
How strangely still
The water is today.
It is not good
For water
To be so still that way.

Sailor

He sat upon the rolling deck
Half a world away from home,
And smoked a Capstan cigarette
And watched the blue waves tipped with foam.

He had a mermaid on his arm,
An anchor on his breast,
And tattooed on his back he had
A blue bird in a nest.

Seascape

Off the coast of Ireland
As our ship passed by
We saw a line of fishing ships
Etched against the sky.

Off the coast of England
As we rode the foam
We saw an Indian merchantman
Coming home.

Mexican Market Woman

This ancient hag
Who sits upon the ground
Selling her scanty wares
Day in, day round,
Has known high wind-swept mountains,
And the sun has made
Her skin so brown.

Beggar Boy

What is there within this beggar lad
That I can neither hear nor feel nor see,
That I can neither know nor understand
And still it calls to me?

Is not he but a shadow in the sun
A bit of clay, brown, ugly, given life?
And yet he plays upon his flute a wild free tune
As if Fate had not bled him with her knife!

Parisian Beggar Woman

Once you were young.
Now, hunched in the cold,
Nobody cares
That you are old.

Once you were beautiful.
Now, in the street,
No one remembers
Your lips were sweet.

Oh, withered old woman
Of rue Fontaine,
Nobody but death
Will kiss you again.

Irish Wake

In the dark they fell a-crying
For the dead who'd gone away,
And you could hear the drowsy wailing
Of those compelled to stay—
But when the sun rose making
All the dooryard bright and clear
The mourners got up smiling,
Happy they were here.

Death of an Old Seaman

We buried him high on the windy hill,
But his soul went out to sea.
I know, for I heard, when all was still,
His sea-soul say to me:

Put no tombstone at my head,
For here I do not make my bed.
Strew no flowers on my grave,
I've gone back to the wind and wave.
Do not, do not weep for me,
For I am happy with my sea.

Sea Charm

Sea charm
The sea's own children
Do not understand.
They know
But that the sea is strong
Like God's hand.
They know
But that sea wind is sweet
Like God's breath,
And that the sea holds
A wide, deep death.

Dressed Up

A Note on Blues

The five poems in this section on pages 62, 63, 64, 67, and 69 are written in the manner of the Negro folk songs known as Blues. The Blues, unlike the Spirituals, have a strict poetic pattern: one long line, repeated, and a third line to rhyme with the first two. Sometimes the second line in repetition is slightly changed and sometimes, but very seldom, it is omitted. Unlike the Spirituals, the Blues are not group songs. When sung under natural circumstances, they are usually sung by one man or one woman alone. Whereas the Spirituals are often songs about escaping from trouble, going to heaven and living happily ever after, the Blues are songs about being in the midst of trouble, friendless, hungry, disappointed in love, right here on earth. The mood of the Blues is almost always despondency, but when they are sung people laugh.

Dressed Up

I had ma clothes cleaned
Just like new.
I put 'em on but
I still feels blue.

I bought a new hat,
Sho is fine,
But I wish I had back that
Old gal o' mine.

I got new shoes—
They don't hurt ma feet,
But I ain't got nobody
For to call me sweet.

Reasons Why

Just because I loves you—
That's de reason why
Ma soul is full of color
Like de wings of a butterfly.

Just because I loves you
That's de reason why
Ma heart's a fluttering aspen leaf
When you pass by.

Negro Dancers

"Me an' ma baby's
Got two mo' ways,
Two mo' ways to do de Charleston!
  Da, da,
   Da, da, da!
Two mo' ways to do de Charleston!"

Soft light on the tables,
Music gay,
Brown-skin steppers
In a cabaret.

White folks, laugh!
White folks, pray!

"Me an' ma baby's
    Got two mo' ways,
Two mo' ways to do de Charleston!"

The Weary Blues

Droning a drowsy syncopated tune,
Rocking back and forth to a mellow croon,
    I heard a Negro play.
Down on Lenox Avenue the other night
By the pale dull pallor of an old gas light
    He did a lazy sway. . . .
    He did a lazy sway. . . .
To the tune o' those Weary Blues.
With his ebony hands on each ivory key
He made that poor piano moan with melody.
    O Blues!
Swaying to and fro on his rickety stool
He played that sad raggy tune like a musical fool.
    Sweet Blues!
Coming from a black man's soul.
    O Blues!
In a deep song voice with a melancholy tone
I heard that Negro sing, that old piano moan—
    "Ain't got nobody in all this world,
    Ain't got nobody but ma self.
    I's gwine to quit ma frownin'
    And put ma troubles on de shelf."
Thump, thump, thump, went his foot on the floor.
He played a few chords then he sang some more—
    "I got de Weary Blues
    And I can't be satisfied.

Got de Weary Blues
And can't be satisfied—
I ain't happy no mo'
And I wish that I had died."
And far into the night he crooned that tune.
The stars went out and so did the moon.
The singer stopped playing and went to bed.
While the Weary Blues echoed through his head
He slept like a rock or a man that's dead.

Homesick Blues

De railroad bridge's
A sad song in de air.
De railroad bridge's
A sad song in de air.
Ever time de trains pass
I wants to go somewhere.

I went down to de station.
Ma heart was in ma mouth.
Went down to de station.
Heart was in ma mouth.
Lookin' for a box car
To roll me to de South.

Homesick blues, Lawd,
'S a terrible thing to have.
Homesick blues is
A terrible thing to have.
To keep from cryin'
I opens ma mouth an' laughs.

Wide River

Ma baby lives across de river
An' I ain't got no boat.
She lives across de river.
I ain't got no boat.
I ain't a good swimmer
An' I don't know how to float.

Wide, wide river
'Twixt ma love an' me.
Wide, wide river
'Twixt ma love an' me.
I never knowed how
Wide a river can be.

Got to cross that river
An' git to ma baby somehow.
Cross that river,
Git to ma baby somehow—
Cause if I don't see ma baby
I'll lay down an' die right now.

Minstrel Man

Because my mouth
Is wide with laughter
And my throat
Is deep with song,
You do not think
I suffer after
I have held my pain
So long?

Because my mouth
Is wide with laughter,

You do not hear
My inner cry?
Because my feet
Are gay with dancing,
You do not know
I die?

A Black Pierrot

I am a black Pierrot:
   She did not love me,
   So I crept away into the night
   And the night was black, too.

I am a black Pierrot:
   She did not love me,
   So I wept until the red dawn
   Dripped blood over the eastern hills
   And my heart was bleeding, too.

I am a black Pierrot:
   She did not love me,
   So with my once gay-colored soul
   Shrunken like a balloon without air,
   I went forth in the morning
   To seek a new brown love.

Bound No'th Blues

Goin' down de road, Lawd,
Goin' down de road.
Down de road, Lawd,
Way, way down de road.
Got to find somebody
To help me carry dis load.

Road's in front o' me,
Nothin' to do but walk.
Road's in front o' me,
Walk . . . and walk . . . and walk.
I'd like to meet a good friend
To come along an' talk.

Hates to be lonely,
Lawd, I hates to be sad.
Says I hates to be lonely,
Hates to be lonely an' sad,
But ever friend you finds seems
Like they try to do you bad.

Road, road, road, O!
Road, road . . . road . . . road, road!
Road, road, road, O!
On de No'thern road.
These Mississippi towns ain't
Fit fer a hoppin' toad.

Song

Lovely, dark, and lonely one,
Bare your bosom to the sun.
Do not be afraid of light,
You who are a child of night.

Open wide your arms to life,
Whirl in the wind of pain and strife,
Face the wall with the dark closed gate,
Beat with bare, brown fists—
And wait.

Passing Love

Because you are to me a song
I must not sing you over-long.

Because you are to me a prayer
I cannot say you everywhere.

Because you are to me a rose—
You will not stay when summer goes.

When Sue Wears Red

When Susanna Jones wears red
Her face is like an ancient cameo
Turned brown by the ages.

Come with a blast of trumpets,
    Jesus!

When Susanna Jones wears red
A queen from some time-dead Egyptian night
Walks once again.

Blow trumpets, Jesus!

And the beauty of Susanna Jones in red
Burns in my heart a love-fire sharp like pain.

Sweet silver trumpets,
    Jesus!

Po' Boy Blues

When I was home de
Sunshine seemed like gold.
When I was home de
Sunshine seemed like gold.
Since I come up North de
Whole wide world's turned cold.

I was a good boy,
Never done no wrong.
Yes, I was a good boy,
Never done no wrong,
But this world is weary
An' de road is hard an' long.

I fell in love with
A gal I thought was kind.
Fell in love with
A gal I thought was kind.
She made me lose ma money
An' almost lose ma mind.

Weary, weary,
Weary early in de morn.
Weary, weary,
Early, early in de morn.
I's so weary
I wish I'd never been born.

Song for a Banjo Dance

Shake your brown feet, honey,
Shake your brown feet, chile,
Shake your brown feet, honey,
Shake 'em swift and wil'—
   Get way back, honey,
   Do that rockin' step.
   Slide on over, darling,
     Now! Come out
     With your left.
Shake your brown feet, honey,
Shake 'em, honey chile.

Sun's going down this evening—
Might never rise no mo'.
The sun's going down this very night—
Might never rise no mo'—
So dance with swift feet, honey,
  (The banjo's sobbing low)
Dance with swift feet, honey—
  Might never dance no mo'.

Shake your brown feet, Liza,
Shake 'em, Liza, chile,
Shake your brown feet, Liza,
  (The music's soft and wil')
Shake your brown feet, Liza,
  (The banjo's sobbing low)
The sun's going down this very night—
Might never rise no mo'.

Night and Morn

Sun's a settin',
This is what I'm gonna sing.
Sun's a settin',
This is what I'm gonna sing:
I feels de blues a comin',
Wonder what de blues'll bring?

Sun's a risin',
This is gonna be ma song.
Sun's a risin',
This is gonna be ma song:
I could be blue but
I been blue all night long.

Feet o' Jesus

Feet o' Jesus

At de feet o' Jesus,
Sorrow like a sea.
Lordy, let yo' mercy
Come driftin' down on me.

At de feet o' Jesus,
At yo' feet I stand.
O, ma precious Jesus,
Please reach out yo' hand.

Sinner

Have mercy, Lord!

Po' an' bowed
An' humble an' lonesome
An' a sinner in yo' sight.

Have mercy, Lord!

Prayer

I ask you this:
Which way to go?
I ask you this:
Which sin to bear?
Which crown to put
Upon my hair?
I do not know,
Lord God,
I do not know.

Judgment Day

They put ma body in de ground,
My soul went flyin' o' de town.

Lord Jesus!

Went flyin' to de stars an' moon
A shoutin' God, I's comin' soon.

O Jesus!

Lord in heaben,
Crown on His head,
Says don't be 'fraid
Cause you ain't dead.

Kind Jesus!

An' now I'm settin' clean an' bright
In de sweet o' ma Lord's sight,—
   Clean an' bright,
      Clean an' bright.

Ma Lord

Ma Lord ain't no stuck-up man.
Ma Lord, he ain't proud.
When he goes a walkin'
He gives me his hand.
"You ma friend," he 'lowed.

Ma Lord knowed what it was to work.
He knowed how to pray.
Ma Lord's life was trouble, too,
Trouble ever day.

Ma Lord ain't no stuck-up man.
He's a friend o' mine.
When He went to heaben,
His soul on fire,
He tole me I was gwine.
He said, "Sho you'll come wid Me
An' be ma friend through eternity."

Baby

Albert!
Hey, Albert!
Don't you play in dat road.
   You see dem trucks
   A goin' by.
   One run ovah you
   An' you die.
Albert, don't you play in dat road.

Lullaby

(For a Black Mother)

My little dark baby,
My little earth-thing,
My little love-one,
What shall I sing
For your lullaby?

   Stars,
   Stars,
   A necklace of stars
   Winding the night.

My little black baby,
My dark body's baby,
What shall I sing
For your lullaby?

   Moon,
   Moon,
   Great diamond moon,
   Kissing the night.

Oh, little dark baby,
Night black baby,

   Stars, stars,
   Moon,
   Night stars,
   Moon,

For your sleep-song lullaby!

Prayer Meeting

Glory! Halleluiah!
De dawn's a-comin'!
Glory! Halleluiah!
De dawn's a-comin'!
A black old woman croons
In the amen-corner of the
Ebecanezer Baptist Church.
A black old woman croons—
De dawn's a-comin'!

Walkers with the Dawn

Walkers with the Dawn

Being walkers with the dawn and morning,
Walkers with the sun and morning,
We are not afraid of night,
Nor days of gloom,
Nor darkness—
Being walkers with the sun and morning.

African Dance

The low beating of the tom-toms,
The slow beating of the tom-toms,
　　Low . . . slow
　　Slow . . . low—
Stirs your blood.

　　Dance!
A night-veiled girl
　　Whirls softly into a
　　Circle of light.
　　Whirls softly . . . slowly,
Like a wisp of smoke around the fire—
　　And the tom-toms beat,
　　And the tom-toms beat,
And the low beating of the tom-toms
　　Stirs your blood.

Aunt Sue's Stories

Aunt Sue has a head full of stories.
Aunt Sue has a whole heart full of stories.
Summer nights on the front porch
Aunt Sue cuddles a brown-faced child to her bosom
And tells him stories.

Black slaves
Working in the hot sun,
And black slaves
Walking in the dewy night,
And black slaves
Singing sorrow songs on the banks of a mighty river
Mingle themselves softly
In the flow of old Aunt Sue's voice,
Mingle themselves softly
In the dark shadows that cross and recross
Aunt Sue's stories.

And the dark-faced child, listening,
Knows that Aunt Sue's stories are real stories.
He knows that Aunt Sue
Never got her stories out of any book at all,
But that they came
Right out of her own life.

And the dark-faced child is quiet
Of a summer night
Listening to Aunt Sue's stories.

Alabama Earth

(At Booker Washington's grave)

Deep in Alabama earth
His buried body lies—
But higher than the singing pines
And taller than the skies
And out of Alabama earth
To all the world there goes
The truth a simple heart has held
And the strength a strong hand knows,
While over Alabama earth
These words are gently spoken:
Serve—and hate will die unborn.
Love—and chains are broken.

My People

The night is beautiful,
So the faces of my people.

The stars are beautiful,
So the eyes of my people.

Beautiful, also, is the sun.
Beautiful, also, are the souls of my people.

Lincoln Monument: Washington

Let's go see old Abe
Sitting in the marble and the moonlight,
Sitting lonely in the marble and the moonlight,
Quiet for ten thousand centuries, old Abe.
Quiet for a million, million years.

Quiet—

And yet a voice forever
Against the
Timeless walls
Of time—
Old Abe.

Dream Variation

To fling my arms wide
In some place of the sun,
To whirl and to dance
Till the white day is done.
Then rest at cool evening
Beneath a tall tree
While night comes on gently,
    Dark like me—
That is my dream!

To fling my arms wide
In the face of the sun,
Dance! Whirl! Whirl!
Till the quick day is done.
Rest at pale evening. . . .
A tall, slim tree. . . .
Night coming tenderly
    Black like me.

Sun Song

Sun and softness,
Sun and the beaten hardness of the earth,
Sun and the song of all the sun-stars
Gathered together—
Dark ones of Africa,
I bring you my songs
To sing on the Georgia roads.

The Negro Speaks of Rivers

I've known rivers:
I've known rivers ancient as the world and older than the flow of human
blood in human veins.

My soul has grown deep like the rivers.

I bathed in the Euphrates when dawns were young.

I built my hut near the Congo and it lulled me to sleep.
I looked upon the Nile and raised the pyramids above it.
I heard the singing of the Mississippi when Abe Lincoln went down to
    New Orleans, and I've seen its muddy bosom turn all golden in the
    sunset.

I've known rivers:
Ancient, dusky rivers.

My soul has grown deep like the rivers.

The Negro

I am a Negro:
    Black as the night is black,
    Black like the depths of my Africa.

I've been a slave:
    Caesar told me to keep his door-steps clean.
    I brushed the boots of Washington.

I've been a worker:
    Under my hand the pyramids arose.
    I made mortar for the Woolworth Building.

I've been a singer:
    All the way from Africa to Georgia
    I carried my sorrow songs.
    I made ragtime.

I've been a victim:
    The Belgians cut off my hands in the Congo.
    They lynch me now in Texas.

I am a Negro:
    Black as the night is black.
    Black like the depths of my Africa.

Mother to Son

Well, son, I'll tell you:
Life for me ain't been no crystal stair.
It's had tacks in it,
And splinters,
And boards torn up,
And places with no carpet on the floor—
Bare.
But all the time
I'se been a-climbin' on,
And reachin' landin's,
And turnin' corners,
And sometimes goin' in the dark
Where there ain't been no light.
So, boy, don't you turn back.
Don't you set down on the steps
'Cause you finds it kinder hard.
Don't you fall now—
For I'se still goin', honey,
I'se still climbin',
And life for me ain't been no crystal stair.

As I Grew Older

It was a long time ago.
I have almost forgotten my dream.
But it was there then,
In front of me,
Bright like a sun—
My dream.

And then the wall rose,
Rose slowly,
Slowly,
Between me and my dream.
Rose slowly, slowly,
Dimming,

Hiding,
The light of my dream.
Rose until it touched the sky—
The wall.

Shadow.
I am black.

I lie down in the shadow.
No longer the light of my dream before me,
Above me.
Only the thick wall.
Only the shadow.

My hands!
My dark hands!
Break through the wall!
Find my dream!
Help me to shatter this darkness,
To smash this night,
To break this shadow
Into a thousand lights of sun,
Into a thousand whirling dreams
Of sun!

I, Too

I, too, sing America.

I am the darker brother.
They send me to eat in the kitchen
When company comes,
But I laugh,
And eat well,
And grow strong.

Tomorrow,
I'll sit at the table
When company comes.
Nobody'll dare

Say to me,
"Eat in the kitchen,"
Then.

Besides,
They'll see how beautiful I am
And be ashamed—

I, too, am America.

Youth

We have tomorrow
Bright before us
Like a flame.

Yesterday
A night-gone thing,
A sun-down name.

And dawn-today
Broad arch above the road we came.

We march!

The Sweet and Sour Animal Book

(1994)

A

There was an ape
Who bought a cape
To wear when he went
Downtown.

The other apes
Who had no capes,
Said, "Look at that
Stuck-up clown!"

B

A bumble bee flew
Right in the house
And lit on a bouquet
Of flowers.

It turned out the flowers
Were papier-mâché—
So that bee looked for honey
For hours.

C

There was a camel
Who had two humps.
He thought in his youth
They were wisdom bumps.

Then he learned
They were nothing but humps—
And ever since he's
Been in the dumps.

D

Rover Dog
Is quite brave when
He's chasing Tom Cat
Around the bend.

But when Tom Cat
Scratches him on the nose,
Rover Dog turns tail
And goes.

E

Elephant,
Elephant,
Big as a
House!

They tell me
That you
Are afraid of a
Mouse.

F

There was a fish
With a greedy eye
Who darted toward
A big green fly.

Alas! That fly
Was bait on a hook!
So the fisherman took
The fish home to cook.

G

What use
Is a goose
Except to quackle?

If a goose
Can't quackle
She's out of whackle.

H

Dobbin used to be
A fire horse
Pulling a truck
With pride.

Now the village has
A motor truck—
Old Dobbin's
Cast aside.

I

Ibis,
In case you have not heard,
Is a long-legged
Wading-bird.

Happiest
Where fish are found,
He hates to set foot
On dry ground.

J

Jaybird,
Jaybird,
Do you know
What I would do?
"Naw!"

I wouldn't try
To sing at all
If I were you!

"Caw!"

K

A little white kitten
Got caught in the rain.
The mud and the wetting
Caused him great pain.

When he got in the house
And lay down to dry,
He started to purring,
"How happy am I!"

L

A lion in a zoo,
Shut up in a cage,
Lives a life
Of smothered rage.

A lion in the plain,
Roaming free,
Is happy as ever
A lion can be.

M

Jocko is
A peanut fiend.
He can eat peanuts
Like an eating machine.

When the peanuts are gone
And his fun is done,
Jocko can chatter
Like a son-of-a-gun!

N

Newt,
Newt, newt,
What can you be?

*Just
A salamander, child,
That's me!*

O

At night the owl
In a hollow tree,
With one eye shut,
Still can see.

But daylight changes
All of that—
By day an owl
Is blind as a bat.

P

There was a pigeon,
A mighty flier,
His friends all called him
Pigeon McGuire.

But he perched upon
An electric wire—
And that was the end of
Pigeon McGuire!

Q

Quail
Are happy,
And fleet on their feet—

Till the hunter
Comes gunning
For something to eat!

B-O-O-M!

R

Peter Rabbit
Had a habit
Of eating garden plants—

Until Mrs. Rabbit
Caught Peter Rabbit
And warmed his little pants.

S

Mrs. Squirrel
Can look so sweet
When she finds
Her nest is neat.

When baby squirrels
Mess up her bower,
Mrs. Squirrel
Indeed looks sour.

T

Turtle, turtle,
I wonder why
Other animals
Pass you by?

Turtles travel
Very slow,
Still I get
Where I want to go.

U

The unicorn
Has a single horn—
Except that there is
No unicorn!

In fairy tales alone
They're born.
Happy unreal
Unicorn!

V

The vixen is
A female fox,
Pleased the woods
To roam.

If a trapper
Puts her in a box
She never feels
At home.

W

A pretty white mouse
Smooth as silk
Made a misstep
And fell in the milk.

When she got out
She was soaked to the skin
And mad as a hatter
Because she fell in!

X

X,
Of course,
Is a letter, too.

But I know *no* animal
Starts with an
X.

Do you?

Y

Yaks are shaggy
And yaks are strong,
Happiest where
The winters are long.

But when summer sun
Is bright and bold,
A yak had rather be
Where it's cold.

Z

Zebra.
Zebra.
Which is right—

White on black—
Or black on white?

No More

So with a riddle,
My young friend,
From A to Z,
We come to the end.

Uncollected Poems for Children

Signs of Spring

Bright, jolly sunshine and clear blue skies,
Green trees and gardens and gay butterflies,
Soft little winds that balmy blow,
A golden moon with love light glow,
And the music of bird songs, blithe and clear,
Are the things which tell us that Spring is here.

The Lament of a Vanquished Beau

Willy is a silly boy,
   Willy is a cad.
Willy is a foolish kid,
   Sense he never had.
Yet all the girls like Willy—
   Why I cannot see,—
   He even took my best girl
Right away from me.

I asked him did he want to fight,
   But all he did was grin
And answer, "Don't be guilty
   Of such a brutal sin."

Oh, Willy's sure a silly boy,
   He really is a cad,
Because he took the only girl
   That I 'most ever had.

Her hair's so long and pretty
   And her eyes are very gay;
I guess that she likes Willy
   'Cause he's handsome, too, they say.
But for me, he's not good looking;
   And he sure has made me mad,
'Cause he went and took the only girl
   That I 'most ever had.

Mister Sandman

The Sandman walks abroad tonight,
  With his canvas sack o' dreams filled tight.

Over the roofs of the little town,
  The golden face of the moon looks down.

Each Mary and Willy and Cora and Ned
  Is sound asleep in some cozy bed,

When the Sandman opens his magic sack
  To select the dreams from his wonder pack.

"Ah," says the Sandman, "To this little girl
  I'll send a dream like a precious pearl."

So to Mary Jane, who's been good all day,
  A fairy comes in her sleep to play;

But for Corinne Ann, who teased the cat,
  There's a horrid dream of a horrid rat,

And the greedy boy, with his stomach too full,
  Has a bad, bad dream of a raging bull;

While for tiny babes, a few days old,
  Come misty dreams, all rose and gold.

And for every girl and every boy
  The Sandman has dreams that can please or annoy.

When at pink-white dawn, with his night's work done,
  He takes the road toward the rising sun,

He goes straight on without a pause
  To his house in the land of Santa Claus.

But at purple night-fall he's back again
  To distribute his dreams, be it moon light or rain;

And good little children get lovely sleep toys,
  But woe to the bad little girls and boys!

For those who'd have dreams that are charming and sweet,
  Must be good in the day and not stuff when they eat,

'Cause old Mister Sandman, abroad each night,
  Has a dream in his sack to fit each child just right.

Thanksgiving Time

When the night winds whistle through the trees and blow the crisp
    brown leaves a-crackling down,
When the autumn moon is big and yellow-orange and round,
When old Jack Frost is sparkling on the ground,
  It's Thanksgiving time!

When the pantry jars are full of mince-meat and the shelves are laden
    with sweet spices for a cake,
When the butcher man sends up a turkey nice and fat to bake,
When the stores are crammed with everything ingenious cooks can
    make,
  It's Thanksgiving time!

When the gales of coming winter outside your window howl,
When the air is sharp and cheery so it drives away your scowl,
When one's appetite craves turkey and will have no other fowl,
  It's Thanksgiving time!

Trip: San Francisco

I went to San Francisco.
I saw the bridges high
Spun across the water
Like cobwebs in the sky.

Garment

The clouds weave a shawl
Of downy plaid
For the sky to put on
When the weather's bad.

The Kids in School with Me

When I studied my A-B-C's
And learned arithmetic,
I also learned in public school
What makes America tick:

The kid in front
And the kid behind
And the kid across the aisle,
The Italian kid
And the Polish kid
And the girl with the Irish smile,
The colored kid
And the Spanish kid
And the Russian kid my size,
The Jewish kid
And the Grecian kid
And the girl with the Chinese eyes—
We were a regular Noah's ark,
Every race beneath the sun,
But our motto for graduation was:
One for All and All for One!
The kid in front
And the kid behind
And the kid across from me—
Just American kids together—
The kids in school with me.

We're All in the Telephone Book

We're all in the telephone book,
Folks from everywhere on earth—
Anderson to Zabowski,
It's a record of America's worth.

We're all in the telephone book.
There's no priority—
A millionaire like Rockefeller
Is likely to be behind me.

For generations men have dreamed
Of nations united as one.
Just look in your telephone book
To see where that dream's begun.

When Washington crossed the Delaware
And the pillars of tyranny shook,
He started the list of democracy
That's America's telephone book.

City

In the morning the city
Spreads its wings
Making a song
In stone that sings.

In the evening the city
Goes to bed
Hanging lights
About its head.

To Make Words Sing

To make words sing
Is a wonderful thing—
Because in a song
Words last so long.

Gypsies

Gypsies are picture-book people
Hanging picture-book clothes on a line.
The gypsies fill the vacant lots
With colors gay as wine.

The gypsies' skins are olive-dark,
The gypsies' eyes are black fire.

The gypsies wear bright headcloths dyed
By some elfin dyer.

The gypsies wear gay glassy beads
Strung on silver threads
And walk as though forever
They've had suns about their heads.

There's Always Weather

There's always weather, weather,
Whether we like it or not.
Some days are nice and sunny,
Sunny and bright and hot.

There's always weather, weather,
Whether we like it or don't.
Sometimes so cold and cloudy!
Will it soon snow, or won't?

If days were always just the same,
Out-of-doors would be so tame—
Never a wild and windy day,
Never a stormy sky of gray.

I'm glad there's weather, weather,
Dark days, then days full of sun.
Summer and fall and winter—
Weather is so much fun!

New Flowers

So many little flowers
Drop their tiny heads—
But newer buds come to bloom
In their place instead.

I miss the little flowers
That have gone away,
But the newly budding blossoms
Are equally gay.

Year Round

Summertime
Is warm and bright,
With light-bugs
At night.

Autumn time
Is not so sunny,
But Halloween
Is funny.

Winter
Changes most of all,
Bright, then gray,
Then snowflakes fall.

But Spring
I like the very best
When birds come back
To nest.

Also in the
Springtime rain
Flowers start
To bloom again.

Country

My mother said,
A house we'll buy
In the country where the sky
Is not hidden by tall buildings.

I said,
We'll have a hill
For coasting in the wintertime
Or climbing in the summertime—
   I love to coast!
   I love to climb!

Grandpa's Stories

The pictures on the television
Do not make me dream as well
As the stories without pictures
Grandpa knows how to tell.

Even if he does not know
What makes a Spaceman go,
Grandpa says back in his time
Hamburgers only cost a dime,
Ice cream cones a nickel,
And a penny for a pickle.

Piggy-Back

My daddy rides me piggy-back.
My mama rides me, too.
But grandma says her poor old back
Has had enough to do.

Shearing Time

It must be nice to be a sheep
With nothing to do but graze and sleep.
But when it's time the wool to shear,
That poor old sheep bleats, "Oh, dear!"

Brand New Clothes

My mama told me,
Kindly, please,
Do not get down
On your knees
With your brand new
Clothes on.

I said, Mom,
I'm already down.
Can't I stay
On the ground
With my brand new
Clothes on?

My mother said,
No, I say!
So my mother had her way—
That's why I'm so clean today
With my brand new
Clothes on.

Problems

2 and 2 are 4.
4 and 4 are 8.

But what would happen
If the last 4 was late?

And how would it be
If one 2 was me?

Or if the first 4 was you
Divided by 2?

Not Often

I seldom see
A kangaroo
Except in a zoo.

At a whale
I've never had a look
Except in a book.

Another thing
I never saw
Is my great-
Great-great-grandpa—
Who must've been
A family fixture,
But there's no
Picture.

Grocery Store

Jimmy, go
To the store, please,
And bring me back
A can of peas.

Also, get
A sack of flour,
And kindly do not
Stay an hour.

Poor Rover

Rover was in clover
With a bone
On the front lawn—
But Rover's fun was over
When his bone
Was gone.
Poor Rover!

The Blues

When the shoe strings break
On *both* your shoes
And you're in a hurry—
That's the blues.

When you go to buy a candy bar
And you've lost the dime you had—
Slipped through a hole in your pocket somewhere—
That's the blues, too, *and bad!*

Silly Animals

The dog ran down the street
The cat ran up the drain
The mouse looked out and said,
  There they go again!

Old Dog Queenie

Old Dog Queenie
Was such a meanie,
She spent her life
Barking at the scenery.

Little Song

Carmencita loves Patrick.
Patrick loves Si Lan Chen.
Xenophon loves Mary Jane.
Hildegarde loves Ben.

Lucienne loves Eric.
Giovanni loves Emma Lee.
Natasha loves Miguelito—
And Miguelito loves me.

Ring around the Maypole!
Ring around we go—
Weaving our bright ribbons
Into a rainbow!

Friendly in a Friendly Way

I nodded at the sun
And the sun said, *Howdy do!*
I nodded at the tree
And the tree said, *Howdy, too!*

I shook hands with the bush.
The bush shook hands with me.
I said to the flower,
Flower, how do you be?

I spoke to the man.
The strange man touched his hat.
I smiled at the woman—
The world is smiling yet.

Oh, it's a holiday
When everybody feels that way!
What way?—*Friendly
In a friendly way.*

Shepherd's Song at Christmas

Look there at the star!
I, among the least,
Will arise and take
A journey to the East.
But what shall I bring
As a present for the King?
What shall I bring to the Manger?

    I will bring a song,
    A song that I will sing,
    A song for the King
    In the Manger.

Watch out for my flocks,
Do not let them stray.
I am going on a journey
Far, far away.
But what shall I bring
As a present for the Child?
What shall I bring to the Manger?

    I will bring a lamb,
    Gentle, meek, and mild,
    A lamb for the Child
    In the Manger.

I'm just a shepherd boy,
Very poor I am—
But I know there is
A King in Bethlehem.
What shall I bring
As a present just for Him?
What shall I bring to the manger?

    I will bring my heart
    And give my heart to Him.
    I will bring my heart
    To the Manger.

Fiction

Popo and Fifina: Children of Haiti

By Arna Bontemps and Langston Hughes
Illustrations by E. Simms Campbell

(1932)

Contents

Popo and Fifina

Going to Town

Popo and Fifina were walking barefooted behind two long-eared burros down the highroad to the little seacoast town of Cape Haiti. Bags,
woven of grass, were hung across the backs of the pack animals, and in
these were all the belongings of their family. Popo and Fifina were moving. They were moving from their grandmother's home in the country
to a new home in town.

Their parents, Papa Jean and Mamma Anna, were peasant farmers. But
they had grown tired of the life on their lonely hillside, and they were
going to Cape Haiti, where Papa Jean planned to become a fisherman.

The sunshine was like gold. The little dusty white road curved ribbon-
like among the many hills. It was overhung with the leaves of tropical
trees. On the warm countryside there was no sound but the droning of
insects and the sudden crying of bright birds. There was no hurry or
excitement. And the burros' lazy steps set the speed for the little band
of travelers.

From the rear of their tiny caravan, Popo could see the members of his
family stretched along the road, one after another, like a line of ducks.
First was Papa Jean himself, a big powerful black man with the back
torn out of his shirt. He wore a broad turned-up straw hat and a pair of
soiled white trousers; but, like all peasants of Haiti, he was barefooted.
He walked proudly, and there was a happy bounce in his step as he led
his little family toward the town of his dreams.

Next came Mamma Anna with the baby, Pensia, swinging from her
side as Haitian babies do. Mamma Anna was also barefooted, and she
wore a simple peasant dress and a bright peasant headcloth of red and
green. She was a strong woman with high glossy cheek bones. She
followed her husband step for step in the dusty road. The two loaded
burros came next. They were shaggy animals, and their heads were
lowered as they trudged along. Great bright-winged flies rode on their
flanks and buzzed around their heads.

Fifina, Popo's ten-year-old sister, walked so close behind the second
burro that she could reach out her hand and smack him on the flanks if
he stopped to nibble grass on the roadside. She wore a little blue dress
that reached her knees.

But Popo, who walked behind her, was only eight, and all he wore was a shirt that didn't even reach his waist. At home he wouldn't have been wearing this; but when a person is making a long journey to an important town like Cape Haiti, he has to dress up a little. So Popo had worn his Sunday clothes. And Sunday clothes for black peasant boys in Haiti usually consist of nothing more than the single shirt Popo was wearing to town.

Like all dressed-up people, Popo was proud of himself this afternoon. He was proud also to be going to town to live by the ocean and to see new wonders. So while the little procession swung slowly along, he frisked about like a young colt, stamping the dust and kicking up his heels. Late in the day, near their journey's end, the road led up a hill and they passed between thickets of dense foliage. Beautiful flowering trees were plentiful, their blossoms red like fire, or white as milk.

Looking back, Popo could see forests of palms, mangoes, banana trees, and coffee bushes bordering the road; but he spent very little time in looking back. His mind was set on reaching the top of the hill. He wanted to get a glimpse of the town that was to be their home, and the great ocean from which Papa Jean would fish food and make a living for his family.

Papa Jean was perspiring as he led the way up the mountain. His naked back flashed like metal in the sun.

"Do you think we're almost to the top?" Popo asked Fifina.

"It isn't far," she said. "But you won't help us to get there any sooner by frisking around as you do."

"I can hardly wait, Fifina! If Papa Jean would let me, I could run ahead and be at the top in a minute. Why do you suppose he makes me stay back here, Fifina?"

"Why, it's plain as anything. It's because he knows you'd run so far ahead we could never catch you."

Popo became silent. He couldn't understand the ways of old people. And his thoughts made him sad. "Oh, my!" he said to himself. Then he settled back into the slow gait of the others and made up his mind to be patient till they reached the hilltop.

Presently Papa Jean reached the high point and stood with his hands on his hips. A few moments later Mamma Anna reached his side. Popo could see their backs against the sky—Papa Jean and Mamma Anna standing on the top of the world at the place where the mountain touches the sky. They were in the middle of the road, and soon the faithful burros were there also. One stopped beside Popo's mother and the other beside his father. Then Fifina reached the top and stood beside one of the burros; but before she got there Popo forgot his place, ran ahead of her, and took his stand beside the other animal.

"Well, here we are," Papa Jean said.

"H'm," Mamma Anna hummed without parting her lips. "H'm." She was pleased.

"How fine!" Fifina exclaimed. "Oh, how fine the ocean is! And what a big town!"

Really the town was small, but, compared with the villages Fifina had seen, it was quite impressive.

Popo said nothing. He was too excited to speak, but his eyes swept the whole bright scene below.

This is what he saw: rows of small white houses and buildings that stretched along the curved water front almost as far as his eyes could reach, old ruins and battlements overlooking the water at several places, trees growing right down to the water's edge, sailboats in the harbor moving under a slow steady wind, others being sculled by half-naked men, and a number of tiny rocking boats anchored along the beach.

"We've got to keep moving," Papa Jean said, after a long pause. "We've got to find a house in town and get unpacked before night. Then, too, we'll need a bed."

"H'm," Mamma Anna agreed.

Fifina clapped her hands in excitement, and Popo danced with glee as the party of travelers took their former positions in the road and started down the hillside to their new home.

Work to Do

"Children," said Papa Jean, when they had found their house, "I want you to make yourselves useful this afternoon. It is getting late, and Mamma will have many things to do before night. She will need your help. Can I depend on you?"

"Oh, yes, Papa Jean," Popo and Fifina assured him.

"Well, don't forget. I'm going down to the beach to talk with the fishermen when they come in with their boats."

Fifina rushed immediately into the house where her mother was working, but Popo didn't move. He was an obedient boy, but he regretted almost at once his promise to Papa Jean. Popo was anxious to follow his father down to the beach, to wander about and explore the neighborhood into which they had moved.

There was a tiny rum shop near the beach, and there a great many sailors and wandering men loitered. Popo heard their loud, heavy voices. He was eager to stop and hear what they said. One old fellow, a native of Santo Domingo, had a beautiful big parrot that sat on his shoulder. Popo thought it wonderful that a bird should sit on a man's shoulder; and he thought that bird with its large yellow beak, and its green and red and yellow feathers was the finest bird he had ever seen. What was more wonderful, the bird could talk. Popo wanted to stay longer in front of the rum shop, but there would be no time for that to-day; he would have to content himself with what he could see from his own yard. Maybe, if he were good, Papa Jean would let him run down to the beach another day, and wander through the streets of rickety houses even up into the main part of town.

"Run along," Papa Jean called back. "You mustn't let Fifina do all the helping."

Popo walked away slowly. Before he reached the door, he turned and saw his father walking with his hands in his pockets, smoking a cigar. Papa Jean was certainly a big strong man, but Popo could see that he was as eager to get to the beach as any child could be.

The little house to which Popo and Fifina had come with their parents was just a one-roomed shack with a tin roof. It had no windows, and only one door that was as rough and awkward as the door of a woodshed.

There were no steps to the house, for the floor was laid so near the ground that it was easy to walk directly in from the outside.

The yard was big. It contained a large mango tree and two banana plants. And next door there was a very tall palm.

When Popo went inside he found Mamma Anna and Fifina making a bed for Baby Pensia. They had already set up the big bed in which Mamma Anna and Papa Jean were to sleep, and they had fixed a straw pallet on the floor for Popo and Fifina. Now they were stuffing a gunny sack to make a bed for Pensia.

"What can I do?" Popo asked. "I want to help too."

"The beds are about finished," Mamma Anna said. "But we'll need some dry leaves to start the charcoal fire. You can get those for us."

That pleased Popo. He scrambled out of the house and ran across a sandy slope to a place where the brush seemed thickest and driest. Under the dead thickets he found leaves so dry and parched that they crumpled in his hands. That was the kind he wanted. He could tell when leaves were good for starting fires: he had gathered them before. So he quickly raked up a little pile with his fingers and took them into his arms.

When he returned, Mamma Anna and Fifina were in the yard. Mamma Anna had unpacked her little charcoal stove, and Fifina stood holding the kettle in which the food would be cooked.

The sun was sliding down the sky fast now. There would not be time to cook a kettle of beans and rice, the usual peasant dish in Haiti, so Mamma Anna simply boiled a few plantains—the huge Haitian banana that went with every meal. Then she warmed over a pot of meat they had brought from their old home.

While the fire burned and the pot sizzled, Mamma Anna squatted, resting her elbows on her knees. When she thought the food was warm enough, she filled Popo's and Fifina's small plates, which they carried a few yards away and placed on the ground.

Papa Jean was still down on the beach. Popo could see him standing beside the little boats, examining the catches of the fishermen, making motions with his hands as he talked, and evidently asking many questions. After a while, the fishermen started up a path to the road, and Papa Jean returned to his house.

Popo finished his plate and asked for more. Mamma Anna explained that she had no plantains left, but that she was about to boil some yams of which he might have a helping when they were done.

In the meantime Papa Jean reached the house with several fine fish that he had procured from the fishermen. Mamma Anna began at once to clean these. And when the yams were done she put the fish in the kettle.

If Mamma Anna had lived in the United States, she probably would have cooked her entire meal before she allowed her children to begin eating. But her stove was very small, and so she cooked one thing at a time—in no particular order. And her children ate what she cooked as soon as it was ready.

"I have arranged to go out with the other men," Papa Jean said, as he sat down to eat. "We must be on the beach before sunrise to raise our sails and leave the harbor by the first wind. In deep water we'll drop our nets. Then when the land breeze comes up in the afternoon we'll sail home with our catch. I'll get my share of fish and peddle them in the market—and bring some home to eat, too. It'll be a good way to begin life in this new town."

"H'm" his wife agreed. "And some day maybe you'll get a boat of your own?"

"Yes. I'll get a boat of my own. You'll help me to weave reed nets down on the beach. At night we'll hang them on that big tree to dry."

Papa Jean pointed to a huge rugged banyan tree growing near the water's edge. It had great gnarled roots that came out of the earth like immense serpents and curled up on the ground. The nets of many fishermen were drying upon its branches now.

"May I go with you then, Papa Jean?" asked Popo. "When you have your own boat, may I go out with you some time?"

"Of course," said Papa Jean. "You'll go with me many times. And some day we may even take Fifina and Mamma Anna and Pensia just for the sail. Who knows?"

"But it won't be easy to get a boat," said Mamma Anna. "We'll have to work hard."

"Yes," said Papa Jean. "We'll have to work and work and work."

"I am willing," Fifina said. "I am willing to help all I can."

"I too," said Popo eagerly.

"Well, the first thing you'll have to do will be to carry these pots and dishes to the fountain at the corner to be washed. Then, when you return, bring a kettle of fresh water. By that time it will be bedtime. We must rise early in the morning."

Popo and Fifina began collecting the few dishes and stacking them in the kettle. When they were finished they took the heavy kettle between them, each holding the handle, and started down the road to the public fountain. And Popo carried the hollowed-out shell of a round gourd to fill with drinking water.

On the way they stopped to look into the rum shop near the beach. It was a little out of their way, but Popo was so eager to see it again that he persuaded Fifina to stop a moment with him. The soft blue twilight was descending in the street like mist. Suddenly the lights of the rum shop came on. Music began playing. Popo and Fifina heard the happy voices of the sailors and wandering men; they heard their mugs and glasses rattling on the little wooden tables. The man with the parrot was still there, his parrot still talking in a strange language that Popo could not understand.

The street was full of happy noises and voices like music. It did not get dark soon; the twilight lingered. Popo was used to long blue twilights like that, but it was a new thing to hear the exciting voices of the city streets.

"Oh, I think the city is grand," he said to Fifina.

"Yes," she agreed. "I'm certainly glad we came. We must thank Papa Jean again for bringing us."

Running Water

The next day, in the heat of the morning, Popo lay in the doorway naked. There was no reason why he should wear his little dress-up shirt now, so he rolled in the dirt happily, and without fear of soiling a garment. He felt more comfortable than he had been since the beginning of their journey two days before.

At that early hour there was very little wind stirring, and there was almost no activity on the streets. The trees of the yard were still, their leaves powdered by white dust. The two burros were sleeping in their places at the back of the yard, and the usual tropical flies were buzzing their bright wings about the animals' heads.

Presently Fifina and Mamma Anna came to the door with their arms full of soiled clothes.

"We're going to wash to-day," Mamma Anna said to Popo. "You come with us, if you like."

Popo didn't really feel like moving at the moment. He was so comfortable on the warm ground he felt that he might have stayed there the rest of the day. But he managed to draw himself up and to roll his eyes at Mamma Anna's suggestion. After all, it might not be a bad idea to follow Mamma Anna and Fifina to the washing place. He might have a chance to play in the water. That *would* be a treat. Popo sprang to his feet.

"Yes, indeed, Mamma," he exclaimed. "I'd like to go very much. But where will you wash the things—at the fountain at the next corner?"

"Oh, no, son, not there. The fountain is all right for washing dishes or milk cans, or even for bathing babies like Pensia, but it is better to wash clothes in the stream that runs along the street." Then Mamma Anna put the clothes she was carrying in Popo's arms. "Here. You carry these. I'll go back and get Pensia."

Pensia, like Popo, wore no clothes at all, only a bead on a cord around her neck. She was a quiet and well behaved baby, and she seemed as delighted as any one to be going out for the morning work.

The stream along the street was no bigger than the stream in some gutters after a rain. But it was clean sparkling water from the mountain springs flowing in a little stone gully for the convenience of people who did not have private wells in their houses.

While Mamma Anna and Fifina washed the pieces of clothing, one by one, Popo and Baby Pensia played in the water. Popo took good care of his baby sister and seated her on the edge of the little stream where her feet could reach the water while he ran up and down in the middle of the stream splashing in every direction and having the time of his life.

Soon Popo noticed other women coming with their clothes to the little streams. They took their places farther up the street and began beating their garments in the water in the same way Mamma Anna washed. They took each garment, dampened and soaped it, then put it on the rocky edge of the gully and gave it a good pounding with a wooden stick while the soapy water ran out of it. Before long there was a line of busy women that reached almost the whole length of the street. Other youngsters like Popo were playing in the water, and other babies like Pensia were sitting with their feet in the stream. Occasionally a dog or a goat came to the stream to drink. The day that had seemed so dull and quiet a little while earlier was now full of sounds and movements.

There were by now, too, many people passing along the streets with bundles on their heads. Among them was one youngster who attracted the attention of Popo and Fifina—a little smiling black girl who carried a large wooden tray on her head and a small folding stool on one arm. She carried her burden lightly and happily, as if she had been used to balancing things on her head a long time.

All Haitian youngsters learn to carry burdens on their heads. Popo already knew the trick. He could go to the store for a bar of soap or a basket of fruit and bring it home on his head just as expertly as the little girl was carrying her tray. That was a fine thing for a playful boy like Popo, since he could forget the burden on his head and at the same time have his hands free to play.

But the little girl with the wooden tray and the broad smile was not out to play. She was on a business errand, and Popo could see that her tray was loaded with things to sell. When she was near enough, she unfolded her stool, put it on the ground, and set the tray upon it.

Popo's eyes popped, and his mouth began to water, for he was looking at a great collection of stick candy, large sugary peppermint sticks of pink and white. It was a soft crumbly kind of stick candy; it had a fine peppermint smell, and when the little girl removed the tray from her head she had to shoo the tropical bees and flies away. A whole swarm of them had been sitting happily on the sweet sticks as they traveled along the road uncovered in the sunshine.

"Will you have a stick of candy?" the little girl asked. "It's a penny a stick and awfully good. My mother just made it. Will you buy a stick?"

Popo turned to his mother with a pleading glance, but she was shaking her finger in the air. Fifina looked up eagerly. But pennies are scarce in Haiti. And Mamma Anna was not at all sure that she could afford to spend two or three of them that day for candy.

"Please, Mamma," Popo said softly.

"We haven't had a taste of candy for months," Fifina begged.

The mother paused, thinking.

"I don't know," she said. "Not now anyhow. But maybe when the morning's work is done, when the little girl passes here on her way home, you may each have a stick."

Popo clapped his hands and gave an excited leap in the water. Fifina showed her happiness by bringing the back of her hand across her open mouth in a little gesture. Then the girl gathered up her wares, folded her chair across her arm, and started down the street again. Fifina and Mamma Anna returned to their clothes, and once again Popo splashed and galloped in the water. Baby Pensia, who kicked her feet, gurgling, seemed also to understand.

When the washing was done, Mamma Anna wrung the clothes as dry as she could and stacked them in a large tin pan. The loaded pan she lifted quickly to her head. Then, leaving Fifina and Popo to attend to Pensia, she started off toward home, a great pile of whiteness balanced on her head.

At home Mamma Anna unfolded her clothes and spread them carefully on the grass around the house. There was no such thing as a clothes line in anybody's yard.

"Will there be anything for me to do?" Popo asked.

"Oh, yes," Mamma Anna told him. "I will need you to go down by the roadside and get me some soap weed to wash dishes. I used the last bit of bar soap on the clothes, and if you are to have your stick candy, I shan't be able to spend pennies for another bar. You will have to get me a good supply of soap weed."

"I'll go too," Fifina offered. "I know a soap bush better than he does."

The two youngsters went running down the path. And sure enough Fifina led Popo to a large clump beside the roadside. They tore off a few leaves to try it out. Rubbing the leaves between the hands produced a lather not unlike that from moistened soap.

"These will do," Fifina said. "Let's gather as many leaves as we can carry in our hands."

"All right," Popo went to work eagerly.

Ten or fifteen minutes later, when Popo and Fifina and Mamma Anna were at the fountain and Baby Pensia, getting a real bath, was covered with white suds that looked like wool, the little candy girl returned. Her tray was not empty, but it was plain that she had made sales since passing the family at the washing place. True to her word, Mamma Anna took two pennies from a pocket of her skirt and bought one stick for Fifina and one for Popo. Fifina's was white and Popo's was pink.

"Pensia can have a taste of each," she explained. "She does not need a whole stick."

"Glook!" said Pensia, crowing at the sight of the candy. "O—oo! Glook!"

IV

By the Sea

One afternoon, when there was no work to do and the day was bright with golden sun, Popo and Fifina went down to the beach.

Behind their house there was a gentle slope of about one hundred yards. At the end of the slope there was the large tree with the gnarled serpentlike roots curled above the ground. And a few feet beyond, along the water's edge, were the large rocks of the wave line.

Looking up and down the long curved coast, Popo could see that the harbor of Cape Haiti was shaped roughly like a horseshoe. He could see that almost all the way around mountains rose sharply out of the sea, rocks jutted out of the water itself, and almond trees grew among the rocks.

Popo and Fifina sat side by side on a large rock and looked out across the bay. Away out, some big steamships were anchored, and with them there were a large number of sailing boats.

"Aren't they fine!" Popo exclaimed.

"They are," Fifina agreed.

"But look at these tiny little boats pulling away from the shore. What are they?"

"They are sculling boats," Fifina said. "Those things behind them that the men wiggle like tails are what Papa Jean calls sculls. They are as good as oars, he says."

Popo was looking at a little craft no longer than a good-sized skiff. Three half-naked black men, standing at the end of the boat, were working the sculls back and forth, back and forth, very leisurely, very much indeed like tails. And somehow the motion of these tails sent the boat forward.

"Look," Popo said. "Look at that one near the shore. The men are wading in the water and pushing it."

"Yes," said Fifina. "But do you see what they are carrying in the boat?"

Sitting in the bow of the small craft was a boy about Popo's size. He was naked, and he held under each arm a game chicken. In addition to the boy with the chickens, the boat held a basket of mangoes, two bunches of bananas, and a tiny green parrot tied by the foot and sitting on one of the sculls.

Popo jumped to his feet and threw up his hands, waving at the other youngster. When he saw that the boy was looking at him, he called at the top of his voice, "Say, where are you going with the chickens?"

The boy smiled broadly.

"We are going out to the ships to sell them," he shouted back.

The men who had been pushing the boat out into the deeper water jumped aboard and began working the sculls; and promptly the little bark with its curious cargo drifted out into the blue bay.

Popo stretched out on the rock, rested his chin in his hand, and began daydreaming. He wondered what kind of boat Papa Jean had gone out in, and where he might be at that very moment. Was he selling things to the steamers anchored near the horizon? Or was he out beyond the harbor on the big tossing waves with his net cast in the deep water? Either of these seemed to Popo a fine occupation, and he longed with all his heart to be with Papa Jean. But some day they would have a boat of their own, Papa Jean had promised that, and then he would go out like the youngster with the chickens. Ah, wouldn't that be a life!

Meanwhile Fifina was hopping from rock to rock. Sometimes she stopped to look down into the shallow clear water. She would stand very still for a moment or two, and then she would start leaping and climbing again. Suddenly she came to a quick stop and called very loudly: "Popo! Oh, Popo, come here quick!"

Popo did not wait to ask what she wanted but jumped up and ran around to the rock where she was standing. The rock was under an almond tree that hung over the water, and it was so far out in the water that it could be reached only by stepping on another rock and making a little jump.

"What is it? What is it?" Popo whispered breathlessly as he stood by his sister's side.

"There. See." She pointed to the water near the base of the rock.

"Oh, yes!"

Popo slid down on his stomach, his head hanging over the edge of the rock. Fifina knelt beside him, supporting herself by her hands as she peered into the clear transparent water.

Down near the white sandy bottom they could see a host of lovely red, blue, and yellow parrot fish darting about excitedly. They looked as bright and pretty as sticks of candy, and neither Popo nor Fifina had ever seen any living creatures half so vivid.

"Do you think we could catch some of them?" Popo asked eagerly.

Fifina shook her head.

"We have nothing to catch them with," she said. "Besides, what would we do with them if we did?"

"We might have Mamma Anna cook them for our supper."

"It would be a shame to eat them," Fifina said. "They are such darlings."

Popo thought a moment and then calmly agreed. They were too pretty to eat. And maybe it would be just as well not to frighten them.

"You are right," he whispered.

"But we might catch a few crabs and carry them home with us," she suggested. "Mamma Anna loves them."

They climbed back over the rocks and came down to the water's edge at another place and began digging in the sand and scratching in the water with switches.

"Here, Fifina," Popo called presently. "I have the first one. And a beauty he is too. Just look."

He held up a large greenish-red crab, holding it carefully so as not to be snapped by its claws.

"Well, put a rock on him till I get one," Fifina said. "Then we can fasten their legs together so that they can't crawl away."

A few moments later, she caught a crab of her own, and they attached the claws together. Then they continued their search, digging separately. Soon the string of crabs was nearly a yard long, and Fifina suggested that they had enough for one day.

But before they started for home a boat slid up near the bank and Papa Jean with several other men got out and waded ashore. At first Popo was surprised. He had not supposed that it was time for boats to be returning. But here indeed was his father, and out in the bay were many other small craft, taking advantage of the land breeze for their return. Scores of small white sails flashed in the rays of the western sun. They were a sight to remember. And here was Papa Jean, standing with his bare feet wide apart, his pants rolled up to the knees, his ragged and sleeveless shirt hanging open in front, and a string of sparkling glasslike fish in his hand. The fish were hung on a switch that went through their gills.

"What will we do with so many fish?" Fifina asked as she looked first at Papa Jean's string and then at the crabs.

"Some of them we'll eat," he said. "Some of them we'll sell in the market. And if we have any left I'll carry them to your Uncle Jacques, who lives at the other end of rue Bord de la Mer. We have not gone to visit him since we moved to town, and I'd like to take him a present."

"May I go too?" Popo asked hurriedly.

"Not to-night," Papa Jean said. "It will be too late when I get back. But maybe another time. . . . Hello!" He suddenly noticed the string of crabs at his feet on the ground. "Well, just look at these! I see I have two bright children. Won't Mamma Anna be happy to see these! Some day I'm going to give you a treat. Maybe next Sunday I'll take you for a walk to the lighthouse."

Popo put his shoulders back. He felt as big as a man. And the promise of a trip to the lighthouse made him forget for the moment that he had just been denied the trip to Uncle Jacques's home. He followed Papa Jean and Fifina up the slope, dragging his string of crabs just as proudly as Papa Jean carried his sparkling fish.

V

A Trip to the Country

A few weeks passed and Popo began to feel that the family belonged in the town. He almost forgot that just a short time ago they had been strangers in Cape Haiti. But now he heard talk that took his mind back to the country. Mamma Anna was homesick for her relatives in the hills. She was anxious to see her mother, Grandma Tercilia, again. She wanted to be there in the house that always seemed like her real home; it was, in fact, the house in which Mamma Anna had been born. She was lonesome too for Aunt Marie and her large children. Mamma Anna had never before been away from her relatives, and it was natural that she should be homesick.

"You may go to the country then Saturday with the children," Papa Jean told her. "That will give you two days to visit. I will come for you late Sunday afternoon."

With that permission everybody became happy. Popo danced in the middle of the floor. Fifina clapped her hands. And Mamma Anna hid her face to keep from showing that her joy had made her cry.

Saturday! Oh, happy day!

Why don't you hurry and come, Saturday? Can't you see little black Popo sitting in the hut door waiting? Can't you see Mamma Anna standing silently with Pensia in her arms, waiting? Why don't you hurry, Saturday?

But Saturday was hurrying. Saturday came. Popo put on his little white shirt and felt very dressed-up. Fifina put on her cleanest dress and Mamma Anna gave Baby Pensia a good bath. And once again the little band started on a journey. This time the trip was unlike the last one they had made, in several ways. First they had left the burros in the back of the yard, for there were no large bundles to be carried. And secondly, Papa Jean was not with them. He had gone out in the boat as usual, for he could not afford to miss a day's work.

At the edge of the town they paused to notice the slaughterhouse. This was a concrete platform under an iron roof. Here every day sheep and cattle were killed so that the people of the town might have meat.

One might think that in a town as small as Cape Haiti it would not be necessary to kill animals every day. But in Haiti ice is very hard to

134

get. There are no ice boxes or big refrigerators; and since meat will not keep in so warm a climate, the animals must be killed every day. For that reason the slaughterhouse is always busy.

Mamma Anna paused a few moments to let her curious children get an idea of what was going on. There were a dozen bulls and sheep tied near by, and men were sharpening knives; but they did not wish to see the poor animals put to death, and so they soon turned their backs on the scene.

A little farther down the road they passed the only important factory of the town, where pineapples are canned and prepared for shipment to the United States. Here Popo saw many black men working. They did not move about leisurely, like other workers, and Popo thought he wouldn't enjoy working so hurriedly.

"Where shall we sleep to-night?" Fifina asked her mother.

"Perhaps with Aunt Marie," Mamma Anna said. "Grandma Tercilia hasn't so much space now. But at Aunt Marie's we may be able to spread mats on the floor for you children. She will have enough space."

"I'd rather sleep at Grandma Tercilia's," Popo said.

"I wouldn't," Fifina said. "Grandma Tercilia has that pig that runs in and out of the house all the time. He is a terrible nuisance when you have to sleep on the floor."

"The pig sleeps, too," Popo argued. "He would not be able to trouble us when he's sleeping."

"Well, anyway we'll sleep at Aunt Marie's this time," Mamma Anna said finally.

For the rest of the journey they walked in silence. They passed down a long road shaded by mango trees and banana plants, tall prickly cactus and high palms. And in the afternoon, tired and dusty, they came to the little by-lane through the coffee bushes that led up the hill to the huts of their relatives.

First they went to Grandma Tercilia's. Popo could see from a distance the tiny thatched house that he knew so well. He could see the great mango tree weighed down with fine fruit, beautiful ripe mangoes that were now orange and greenish—a charming sight. Certainly it was pleasant to be back, Popo thought. He could hardly wait till he reached the top of the hill. His mouth began to water when he remembered how sweet the mangoes from his grandmother's tree were. Surely not another tree in Haiti bore finer ones. He and Fifina broke away from Mamma Anna and scampered up the path.

Grandma Tercilia, an old wrinkled black woman with a pipe in her

mouth and skin that was parched like an autumn leaf, met them at the door.

"*Ah, mi cher, ti monde!*" she exclaimed. It was her most endearing expression, spoken in Creole French. It meant, "My dear little ones."

In a few minutes children came from every direction, from around the hut, from the banana trees, from the thickets, all of Grandma Tercilia's children and grandchildren who still lived at the family home came out to meet the visitors from town.

Grandma Tercilia and Mamma Anna began talking so fast and excitedly that Popo could hardly tell what they were saying. Then they fell upon each other's necks and embraced as if they had been separated for many years instead of a few short weeks.

A few minutes later the whole family came out in front of the thatched hut and sat on the ground. Popo and two or three other children climbed the mango tree and shook the branches. A rain of fruit fell. The children gathered them from the ground and passed them to the old folks. Then everybody began to eat.

The mango is a juicy and rather sticky fruit with a stone to which its meat clings. The skin is rather tough and is peeled back as the fruit is eaten. The meat of the mango is bright yellow, and to Popo it tasted good enough to repay all the trouble of eating it.

As the folks ate, they tossed the skins and seeds to a greedy little pig that ran from one to another, grunting and never seeming to be satisfied with what he got. Some fighting cocks belonging to big Cousin André pecked about, enjoying the fruit skins, too.

By and by, every one was through eating, and Fifina remembered her job. She went to the spring a short distance from the house, took the gourd that was left there always for convenience and brought it full of water for the old people to wash their sticky hands.

Popo followed her on the path and noticed the great bright-winged butterflies fluttering above the bushes along the way. His heart was light and happy, but he was beginning to feel sleepy. He had got up very early in the morning, and with Mamma Anna and Fifina had made a long and tiresome journey.

When he came back to the hut, he stretched out on the ground in front of the door and went to sleep. When he awakened, the sun was out of sight. Things were quiet around the house, and Mamma Anna suggested that it was time to start for Aunt Marie's place if they wanted to get settled before it was pitch-dark.

As they walked beneath the banana plants, Popo amused himself throwing stones at the dark lizards scurrying among the leaves and grasses on the ground.

VI

Drums at Night

This time Popo could not go to sleep. Baby Pensia, Fifina, Mamma Anna, and his Aunt Marie were all dreaming in the little hut. But Popo lay awake looking through the cracks in the door at the moonlight streaming down the mountain slope outside. He was listening to the drums in the valley below.

It was at least a half-hour's walk to the place near the main road where at night the drummers played and people danced the Congo. Popo had never been down there, but big Cousin André had gone there now, he was sure, because Mamma Anna and he had met him going down the path with some neighbor boys just after sunset. Popo wished he were a big boy so that he could go to dances, too. Indeed, as he lay on his little straw mat, listening to the drums, he felt sure he could find his way down the hill and up the main road to the place where the drums were. In the quiet night, they sounded quite near, booming deep and quick, in a lively sound that made your feet want to keep time. Through the wide door cracks he could see that the whole valley was a pool of moonlight. And the drums and the dancers were just at the foot of the hill.

Popo got up and went out. Two men were passing down the mountain path in front of his aunt's hut, laughing and talking. He knew they were going to the dance, and since André was there, Popo decided at once to go, also. What fun it would be, watching the drummers play! Maybe they would let him hit the big drum once. Anyhow, he would see. So down the mountain trail he started, not far behind the men.

The banana leaves were like long green fans in the moonlight. The wind made them sway languidly. Sometimes, on the way down, a palm tree would shoot up very tall, with its head against the stars. Once he crossed a gurgling brook that seemed to be in a great hurry to get somewhere. Popo knelt in the very middle and took a drink. How cool the water was on his knees and chin! He liked water so much that he would have lain down in it, if he had had time. But he had to hurry on to the dance.

As he came into the valley, the drums sounded louder and louder. The path was wider now, and the moon was bright overhead. The sky was full of stars. Several grown boys and girls were coming behind him, and

138

before he knew it, they were all on the main road, where there were huts and lights and many other people going to the dance. Nobody paid any attention to the little black boy walking along by himself. Popo didn't mind that, for children in Haiti are used to walking alone in the dark. He knew the night was as kind as the day. And near at hand were dancers, drummers, and drums!

Ahead was the flicker of many kerosene flares by the roadside. As Popo drew near, he could see under them the little stands of women with piles of candy to sell, white buns, hot fish and fried yams, and little pots of black coffee over charcoal fires at their feet. He wished he had a penny to buy a bun.

Popo wended his way into the grounds, where, under a thatched roof open on all four sides, many people were dancing, and at one corner, three black men were playing on tall drums of different sizes, swaying back and forth, their hands moving at a rapid rate, beating out the deep vibrant music.

The drums, as Popo knew, were made from the hollowed-out trunks of trees, one end covered with the dried skin of a cow or a goat, sometimes with the hair of the animal still left on the head of the drum. The tallest drum was about four feet high, just about the size of Popo. A huge young man held it between his knees, slanting the drum away from him, as he played it with a stick in one hand, while the fingers of his other hand brought forth a swift series of continuously happy booming sounds. The two smaller drums were played by men who used their fingers alone to make the music. Beside one of the drummers a boy squatted with a pair of sticks in his hand which he kept beating in time against the long wooden sides of the big drum. The three drummers, and the boy with the sticks who beat on wood, were all rocking gayly back and forth as they played, pleased to be making such grand music for the dancing people under the thatched roof.

Men and women were there dancing, facing one another but not touching, their feet scooting across the floor, heads up, hands out, and faces smiling under the oil lanterns that made the dim light. High over the thatched roof and the banana trees and the palms, the sky was bright with stars and moon.

Popo stood very close to the drummers, thrilled by so much noise and so many people. It was even livelier than the market at the Cape on a Saturday afternoon, for here everybody was moving in time to the music of the drums, laughing and dancing. Through the crowd Popo saw André dancing all by himself, twirling round and round, and crossing his feet in quick rooster-like movements. Popo tried it, too, but just as he began to get the steps right, the drummers stopped playing and the dancing ceased. Then the little boy ran through the crowd, calling, "Hello, André!"

His cousin seemed surprised. "I thought you were asleep," said André.

"I was, almost," Popo replied, "but I heard the drums."

"Well," said André, "you had better go back home before Anna wakes up, and finds you gone. She will be worried about you."

"I'll go when you go," Popo said.

"That will be soon," André replied. And before Popo had a chance to ask to beat the big drum, his cousin took him by the hand, bought him a cupful of peanuts from one of the roadside stands, and led him back up the mountain path.

"Little boys should be asleep," said André.

"And you, too," Popo replied.

André laughed.

All the way up the hill under the banana trees, and across the gurgling brook, they could hear the drums beating happily in the valley below.

VII

Play

One afternoon when Popo and Fifina were on the beach waiting for Papa Jean to return in his little boat, they noticed that the bright blue sky was full of kites. The kites were flying high and smoothly, like a flock of sea gulls on a gentle wind. Some of them were square, and others were triangular, and still others had long tails such as were never seen on real birds.

"Oh, Fifina!" Popo cried. "Did you ever see anything like them?"

"Never," Fifina said. "Look at that big one like a box. What a strange kind of kite!"

"And the little one without a tail—isn't it a beauty?"

"But where are the strings? And who is flying them?"

They searched the beach with their eyes, looking up and down as far as they could see; but they could see no one. The kites seemed to have no anchoring strings. They seemed indeed to be as free as the tropical birds of Haiti which they resembled so closely.

A large white cloud hung above the horizon like a puff of smoke. It was a fine sight. Water lapped the clean sand of the beach and ran to where Popo and Fifina stood—a long green tongue of water licking the sand and wetting the feet of the children.

Suddenly Popo shouted:

"There they are, Fifina. See, on that big rock away down the beach. See the boys holding the strings. They are the ones who are holding the kites."

"Yes, yes. I see."

"I'd love to have a kite, Fifina."

"Maybe Papa Jean will make you one."

"Do you really think so, Fifina?"

"I do," she said. "I think he will gladly make you one if you help around the house and give Mamma Anna no trouble."

Popo bowed his head and began to think. He was very anxious to be helpful and to make a good impression on Mamma Anna. He knew that if Mamma Anna approved of his having a kite Papa Jean would be much more likely to grant the request. So he wrinkled his brow and wondered how he could help his mother.

"Let's go home, Fifina," he said finally. "I want to see what I can do for Mamma Anna."

"We might go to the fountain and help the milk women with their cans. They may give us a penny, and if they do we can take that home with us. That would be a good thing to do. Mamma Anna needs money."

"That's fine. You are almost as smart as a grown person, Fifina."

She shook her finger before her face playfully.

"You are teasing me, *petit monde,*" she said affectionately. "I don't always think of smart things."

They ran up the slope to the rue Bord de la Mer. Then they turned toward the public fountain and began walking in the middle of the street. Popo kicked his feet in the soft dust and scampered off ahead, but Fifina was like a little lady. She walked sedately, swinging her arms.

Sure enough there were two women at the fountain with their milk burros. These were the animals that carried their cans. On each burro's back there was a grass mat like a blanket. And on either side of the mat there were large pockets into which the milk cans fitted.

The women had evidently finished their day's rounds and had come to the fountain to rinse their milk cans with clear water before carrying them home. They followed their tired little beasts up to the water spout and began removing the large empty cans from the pockets of the mats.

Popo stepped up very respectfully.

"Help you wash the milk cans, ma'am?"

The tall strong woman looked down at the tiny black youngster at her side. She smiled a little.

"Why, son, you are not as big as one of these cans."

"But I think I could wash them for you," he insisted. "I know how to wash things. Mamma Anna always lets Fifina and me do her pots and pans."

"I am tired of walking," the woman mused. "I have been on my feet since early morning and I could enjoy a little rest all right." She looked down at Popo again. Then suddenly she made up her mind. "Well, go ahead and try it. If you wash them well, I'll give you a penny."

Popo did not need a second invitation. Quicker than you could say it he had turned the huge can over on its side and was inside it, head and shoulders, with a handful of sand scrubbing its sides. Popo certainly knew how to scrub things at the fountain. His little naked body wriggled like the hind legs of a frog as he twitched and worked with his hands. Popo was a sight.

In the meantime Fifina had gone to work on the cans of the other woman. She did not tip the can over on its side as did Popo. Neither did she crawl into it with her head and shoulders. Instead she reached down with her arms, as a grown woman would have done. By standing upon the little concrete step in front of the fountain she was able to reach nearly to the bottom.

While the children worked, the two women sat across the street beneath a tree. They dug the toes of their bare feet into the ground, kicked up dust, and stretched their tired legs. A moment or two later they were both smoking black cigars and chatting happily together. Popo caught a glimpse of the pair when he came out of his can for a fresh handful of sandy dirt. He saw their heads wag as they laughed, saw their pearly teeth flash.

Perhaps they were talking about the new hats they hoped to buy when they had saved enough money from the milk business. Or perhaps, he thought, they were laughing at the fat man across the street. He had just tipped his hat at them. And such a hat it was! A high silk topper such as old-fashioned coachmen used to wear. And the funny thing was that the rest of the fat old fellow's clothes were pitifully ragged. The milk women hid their faces with their hands when he stared at them.

When the four cans were clean and shiny inside and out, the women gave each of the children a penny as they had promised, and Popo and Fifina set out joyfully for their home. The sun was slipping down the sky fast now. The tide was coming in, and little white breakers were splashing on the rocks along the water front. Out on the clear green water there was a line of silver sails. All the dozens of small fishing boats were quietly returning with their day's harvest of fish. The fishermen of Cape Haiti were bringing in the harvest of the sea. Their sails flashed in the sunlight like white wings.

"There's a pretty sight," Fifina said, pointing out across the water.

"Yes," Popo agreed, "but where are the kites, the pretty kites we saw before we went to the fountain?"

"I guess they have been taken down. And I suppose the boys have gone home for dinner."

"Already?"

"It's late," she said. "The sun will be down before you know it."

"Well, if I had a kite I would not take it down so soon on a fine afternoon like this. I'd leave it up as long as I could see."

"You had better not talk like that to Papa Jean or Mamma Anna. They might not be so anxious to make you a kite if it's going to keep you out when you should be home having your supper."

Popo thought for a minute. That was an idea. A little boy could not always tell all the things that came into his mind. Old people had so many strange ideas. But Fifina understood them all. She was certainly a great help.

"Oh," he said finally, "I see. I won't tell them how long I'll leave it up."

The New Kite

Papa Jean rubbed his chin with the back of his hand. His forehead wrinkled. He was thinking about Popo's kite. What chance would a busy fishing man like Papa Jean have to bother with a kite? But, on the other hand, how could he refuse? There were Popo, Fifina, Mamma Anna, and Pensia all looking him in the face and waiting for him to say yes.

"They have been fine children to-day," Mamma Anna said. "You should make a kite to please them, Papa Jean."

Papa Jean threw up his hands in despair.

"All right, all right," he said finally. "Just leave me alone, and I'll make you a kite. If I don't, I know I'll never have another minute's peace. When you wake up to-morrow, you will find your kite finished and ready to fly."

Popo sprang up from the dirt floor, kicked his feet in the air.

"Oh, Papa Jean, Papa Jean!"

Fifina clapped her hands and danced.

"Oh, Papa Jean, Papa Jean!"

Mamma Anna smiled. Pensia cooed.

Oh, Papa Jean, Papa Jean! How happy you have made Popo and Fifina! A real kite! Just think of it. A beautiful red or yellow or green kite, like a bright bird of Haiti. A lovely delicate kite to soar in the clouds— like a wish or a dream. Oh, Papa Jean, how do you expect Popo and Fifina to sleep to-night.

The next morning the children were up at daybreak. And sure enough, there was the big handsome kite Papa Jean had promised. It was red with trimmings of yellow and green paper. Beside it was a large ball of strong cord. Popo examined everything carefully. This kite *was* a dream.

"It's all ready to fly, Fifina."

"Yes, Popo," she said. "And we couldn't have wished for a better one."

They carried the treasure out between them. They walked slowly, carefully down the slope to the beach. When finally they stood upon the clean white sand, they paused to make sure that all was well overhead.

No, not quite ready. Popo shook his head. There was a tree limb a short distance away, and he did not care to take a chance. He had seen many a fine kite hung in the branches of a tree. And he did not care to lose his in the same way.

"Let's move a little farther down the beach," he suggested.

"All right."

Fifina helped him bear the kite beyond danger.

"Now," he said. "You hold it up while I let out the string. Hold it lightly, and when I tell you to, let it loose. See?"

"I understand," she said. "Hurry up and unwind your cord."

Popo let out about fifty yards of the string. Then he looked behind himself to make sure there was a clear running space. Everything was clear.

"Ready," he cried. "Let her go."

At that instant Fifina released the kite. And at the same time Popo began to run.

Almost immediately the lovely bright thing began to climb up into the air, a big scarlet star rising from the seashore. How wonderful! Up, up, up, steadily it climbed. Popo began letting out more cord. He had a large ball, and he could afford to let it out generously.

Fifina ran to his side, but she did not speak. There was nothing to say. What could anybody say who saw a great red star rise from the white beach in the daytime? It was just beautiful to look at, and the less you tried to talk about it the better you could enjoy seeing it. But Fifina knew that Popo's kite was not a real star. It just looked like a star and made her think of one.

Across the harbor the tiny sailing boats could again be seen. Another day of toil had begun for them, another day on the tossing water. In one of them stood Papa Jean. He was leaning with one arm against the little mast and the other arm waving proudly in the air. As he stood there, the wind went through his ragged shirt flapping it like a bullet-torn flag. His naked arms and shoulders flashed like metal in the early sun.

Popo knew that Papa Jean was as proud as anybody of the kite. And why shouldn't he be? Hadn't he made it?

Soon all the little boats were out of the harbor. The bay became still and the round copper sun mounted the sky steadily.

"How is the kite pulling?" Fifina asked.

"Fine," Popo said. "The wind is still good up there, I guess."

"H'm. I guess it is. Does she hum?"

Popo put the cord to his ear. His face brightened.

"Hum?" he cried. "Hum? Why, this kite sings."

"Let me hear."

Popo held the string to his sister's ear. "How's that for singing?"

"It's good. Let me hold the string awhile."

The two youngsters walked down the beach to a place where some stones jutted out into the water. There they sat down to rest, and held the string of the kite in turn, feeling the steady firm pull and vibration, listening to the soft purring hum of the string. It was great fun.

Presently Popo looked up and saw that there was another kite in the air. When had this second kite risen? Who was flying it? And what did the stranger mean anyhow by cutting in on Popo and Fifina? There were other places to fly kites. But the strange kite, a dull brown thing, rode the wind just as gayly as did Popo's. It ducked and darted about so wildly that Popo feared it would become entangled with his own string. It reminded him of a hawk swooping over a smaller bird.

A moment later something happened. The big brown hawk-kite got across Popo's string, and began ducking and darting more than ever. About that time Popo caught sight of the boy who held the string. It was clear that the fellow was very proud of his rude misbehaving kite. He was jerking the cord and plainly trying to saw across Popo's string and cut it loose. It was an old game, and Popo knew something about it. Mischievous boys often cut the strings of innocent youngsters, causing them to lose their kites in the sea. But Popo had confidence in the kite Papa Jean had made him. He believed his big red star-kite was a match for any hawk. He started jerking vigorously on his cord. Back and forth, back and forth. Then suddenly something happened. Popo's heart stood still.

A cord snapped. Popo could feel it go. But it was not his cord. His kite pulled and sang as steadily as ever; but the other one, the hawk, was falling to the earth like an evil bird with a broken wing. Down, down, down it sank. A moment or two later it dropped into the ocean. Popo's big red star climbed the sky proudly, a true conqueror.

IX

A Job for Popo

A few nights later Papa Jean and Mamma Anna sat in their doorway calmly smoking pipes. The children were still on the beach flying their kite. For three or four days they had done almost nothing but fly that kite, and Mamma Anna had begun to wish that she might have them at home more. Often she had little things to do, but when she called, nobody answered. Realizing that they were not in the yard she would go to the door and look into the sky. When she spied the big red kite, she would shake her head in despair. That meant that they were half a mile down the beach, and probably would not come home for hours. It meant that Mamma Anna would have to go to the fountain herself for water. In the evening Papa Jean would look about for someone to go with him to the market and help him sell his fish, but he would see no one. His children were not to be found. But in the sky he could always see the red star-kite he had made them.

As the parents sat in their doorway smoking, the voices of the young-sters suddenly rang out above the waves, and a moment later they came up the slope, tired, sleepy, exhausted, but happy. They never seemed to get enough of flying that kite. Once again they had kept it up till the night was dark.

Coming toward the house, Popo heard the voices of his parents. They were talking very softly, very calmly, but in the still night air their words were perfectly distinct.

"All play and no work makes Jack a dull boy," Papa Jean was saying.

"H'm," Mamma Anna agreed. "That's an old foreign saying, but it is very true."

Popo knew what they meant. He realized that for several days he had done nothing but play, eat, and sleep. He had been wonderfully happy. He had forgotten all about work. These words made him remember.

"Well," Papa Jean said, changing the subject quickly, "did you fly the kite again to-day?"

"Did we?" Popo swelled with pride. "Tell him, Fifina."

"We let out all the string to-day," she said. "We had it so high it looked like a tiny speck."

"Ah, that's good."

"H'm," Mamma Anna said. "That's the way to fly a kite."

"And how it pulled!" Popo exclaimed.

"H'm, and how it sang!" Fifina cried.

"That's very good," Papa Jean said.

"Very good," said Mamma Anna.

"But I've been thinking." Papa Jean rubbed his chin.

"We've been thinking," said Mamma Anna.

"I've been thinking that maybe you have flown the kite enough for a while. Maybe a little work would be a change."

"H'm," said Mamma Anna. "A little work would be a change."

For a moment no one spoke. Popo sat on the ground in the moonlight, his kite across his knees. Fifina sat beside him holding the ball of cord. Down at the bottom of the slope the waves were beating against the rocks.

"What can we do?" Fifina asked humbly. "We like to work and help."

Popo said nothing.

"That's a good girl," Papa Jean said. "What about you, Popo?"

"Oh, yes," he said quickly, "I like to help."

"Well, to-morrow we'll leave the kite on the shelf."

Popo brushed a tear away.

"All right, Papa Jean," he said.

"Fifina will help Mamma Anna in the house. Popo is growing fast. I think it is time for him to have a real job."

Popo felt his heart leap. He had not guessed that he would be going to work like that. He had thought that Papa Jean and Mamma Anna only wanted him to run errands around the house.

"Will you take me with you in the boat?" he cried.

"No, son, not yet. I am going to take you to your Uncle Jacques's cabinet shop. You can stay there and learn the trade. It will be better than fishing. That is, it will give you two trades. You can learn the fishing later, any time. I can teach you that."

Mamma Anna kept nodding and humming as she agreed with the things Papa Jean said. H'm, h'm, h'm-m. It was almost like some one singing.

"You will have to be up early in the morning," Papa Jean continued. "I shall have to take you to the wood shop before I go out in the boat. So you had better be getting to bed."

"All right," Popo said.

He and Fifina went into the house. A moment later Mamma Anna came in and lit a flare that filled the room with a soft yellow light. And almost before you could say the word, they were tucked in their sleeping places in the corner.

The next morning Popo and Papa Jean walked nearly a mile down the rue Bord de la Mer. At the end of their walk they stood in the entrance of a small woodworking shop that smelled pleasantly of fresh-cut wood. There were several workbenches in the room and a number of large saws and tools for cabinet-making. Against the rear wall was piled the rough sweet-smelling wood.

Work had not yet begun in the shop, and only an old frail man was there. This was not Popo's Uncle Jacques, but Uncle Jacques's helper, old man Durand. The wrinkled old fellow was very ragged. He was stiffened with age and rheumatism and got about almost as slowly as if he had been actually lame. With his toothless gums he chewed on the stem of a cob pipe, and at the moment that Popo and Papa Jean came to the door he was busy moving things about, getting ready for work. He looked around when he heard the visitors enter the door. He was very friendly, and when he smiled his old face split up like a pie into which some one had punched his fist.

"Is my brother here yet?" Papa Jean asked.

"He was here," old man Durand said. "He has gone back home a minute to drink a cup of coffee."

"I'm in a hurry," Papa Jean said. "I suppose I'd better go to his house and call him."

"Not at all," old man Durand said. "Just stay right here. I will get him for you in a minute."

The old man went out into the street and started down the block. The sun was not yet up, but a pearly gray light hung along the horizon. Smoke was coming from the windows and little chimneys of some of the houses. The air was full of the fine odor of fresh coffee.

Soon old man Durand came hobbling back, followed by another man, a tall strong fellow who was much like Papa Jean in the face. This was Uncle Jacques. And trotting along behind him was a small boy. This was Popo's cousin, Marcel.

The two brothers greeted each other. Uncle Jacques was older than Papa Jean, and their resemblance was more nearly that of father and son than that of brothers. Marcel and Popo stood behind their respective parents. Though they were cousins and had heard of each other, they were timid at their first meeting.

"I've brought Popo to put him to work," Papa Jean said.

"Fine," said Uncle Jacques. "My Marcel has just started to work, too.

They can learn together. I had two other boys, but I let one go last week to make a place for Marcel. I will let the other one go to-day. One has to favor his kinsfolk."

"Thank you, brother. I'm leaving Popo in your care. See that he works hard and learns the trade. He will be yours till he has learned enough to earn money at woodworking."

"Fine!" Uncle Jacques said, putting his hand on Popo's shoulder.

"Now I must be gone. It is time the boat was getting under sail."

"Don't worry, Jean. Popo will be at home here."

Uncle Jacques threw his hand into the air as Papa Jean disappeared down the street. The sun peeped over the horizon.

Old Man Durand

Popo stood beside his workbench smoothing a board that was to become the top piece of a little table. Uncle Jacques had shown him how to put his sheet of sandpaper around a block of wood and then use the block as if it were a plane. The thing worked like magic. It slipped easily over the surface of the rough board, and wherever it touched it left the surface smoother. Popo was happy. He was helping to make a table—little Popo helping to make a table for the front room of some well-to-do family of the town. And what he was doing to the table was important too. Why, what would a table look like without a fine smooth top?

While he was working, and thinking these thoughts, he did not pay much attention to the youngster who was working at the bench directly in front of him. But a moment later, when Popo stopped to put another sheet of sandpaper on his block, he saw that the other boy had paused a moment also. Marcel was looking at Popo with a pleasant smile.

"Well, how do you like it, cousin?"

"Oh, fine," Popo said.

"That little table you're working on isn't much. Anybody can make a table. But it's fun when you learn to make really pretty things."

Popo didn't like what Marcel had said. It sounded as if Marcel had no respect for the simple, easy things that Popo could work on.

"Maybe I can only work on tables now," Popo said sharply, "but I'll learn as fast as you. I'll make things that are as pretty as anybody can make when I have had a chance to learn."

Marcel laughed out heartily.

"Sure you will, cousin. I mean it's not much fun when you are just beginning, when you have to just sandpaper boards and do trifles like that."

"It sounded as if you were making fun of me."

"Never, cousin. Come here a minute—I'll show you something."

Popo went around to Marcel's workbench. Before him lay a beautiful serving tray carved from a single piece of wood. Marcel held it up so that Popo could look at it to advantage.

"It's a beauty," Popo exclaimed.

"Oh, it's just plain," Marcel said modestly. "You see, I haven't been here so long myself. This is the first pretty thing I have tried to make."

"And shall I make things like this?"

"Surely, cousin. You'll make a tray like this in a week or two. Trays are easy."

"But all that little fancy business around the edge and by the handles—isn't that terribly hard?"

"That is about the hardest part, but Papa Jacques will help you do that on the first one. He helped me with this one."

Popo fixed his eyes on the careful designs carved by hand in the wood. There were flowers, leaves, and stems. The handles were twisted like the coils of a vine.

"Does Uncle Jacques have another tray, a finished one, that he goes by when he makes a new one—a pattern?"

"No," Marcel said. "The trays are all made alike, but each design is different. So the old patterns would not be much good. If a lady wants to buy a tray, she does not want it to look exactly like the one her neighbor has. So each one has to have its own design."

Popo went back to his own bench and worked on his board.

Sunshine flooded the little workshop. Uncle Jacques looked very tall and dignified working near the door. His forehead was wrinkled as he leaned over the strips of woods that he was fitting together. And as he worked, Popo noticed, he whistled or hummed a tune.

Old man Durand kept hobbling around, moving things and smoking his pipe. He was making a stool. But old man Durand was forgetful like many other old people, and he could never remember where he had laid his tools. This kept him constantly busy. So during the course of a day, old man Durand did not get as much done as Uncle Jacques—although he was really just as good a worker.

One thing was not clear in Popo's mind. How could a person make designs on a tray without a pattern? And how could he get new designs for each tray? It was hard to figure out. He wanted to make all the fine pieces of furniture that Uncle Jacques and old man Durand made, but he was afraid it would take him a long time even to make an attractive tray. Later in the afternoon he went over to Marcel's bench again.

"Marcel," he said quietly, "tell me this: How can anybody make a design without a pattern, and how can he make a new design every day for every new tray he works on?"

"That's a hard question, cousin. I've wondered about it myself. Let's ask Papa Jacques."

They went over to Uncle Jacques's bench.

"Uncle Jacques, tell us how you make designs without a pattern, how you make a new design each day, a new one for each new tray."

"That's a hard question, boys, very hard. Ask old man Durand."

Old man Durand was pounding on his chisel with a wooden mallet. When the boys stood in front of him, he looked up and wiped the perspiration from his forehead. His face split up in a great smile. He took his pipe from his mouth and held it in his left hand.

"Old man Durand, tell us this: How do you make a design without a pattern, and how do you make a different design every day?"

"That's a hard question, boys, very, very hard."

"Yes, old man Durand, but you must tell us. We want to know."

"Well, boys, it's like this: you have to put yourself into the design."

"Ah, you're teasing us, old man Durand. That's a riddle. How can a boy put himself into a design?"

"Ah! It's a riddle indeed, but I'm not teasing you. If I walk down by the beach on my way to the shop in the morning and see the tiny boats putting out to sea, that makes a picture in my mind. If I see a hungry beggar, that leaves a picture too. Some pictures make me glad to be living. Some make me weep inside. Some make my heart sad. And when I'm glad to be living, trees and birds and leaves look one bright color to me. When I weep inside, they look different. Well, I don't think about this when I sit down to make my design, I just sing or whistle a tune and carve away with my knife or chisel. But what I am inside makes the design. The design is a picture of the way I feel. It sounds strange, but it is just like that. The design is me. I put my sad feeling and my glad feeling into the design. It's just like making a song."

"It's wonderful," Popo said.

"It sounds just like old folks, but I like it," Marcel said.

"And when people look at your design," old man Durand went on, "when people see the picture, they will just see trees and boats and flowers and animals and such things, but they will feel as you felt when you made the design. That's the fine part. That is really the only way that people can ever know how other people feel."

"There is nothing in the world like making designs!"

"Nothing is finer," old man Durand said.

"That's true," Uncle Jacques agreed. "Old man Durand has told you a beautiful thing and a very true one. I hope you understand him."

"I am sure I do," Popo said.

"I too," said Marcel.

"To-morrow, Popo, you shall start on a tray of your own," Uncle Jacques smiled.

"To-morrow!"

"Yes, to-morrow. You are a bright boy, and I think you can begin one right away."

Popo was so excited and happy that he could not speak again. To-morrow he would make a tray, a beautiful tray with a design on it. And there would be nothing but happiness in that design.

Popo's Tray

With his hands stuck proudly into the pockets of his new breeches, Popo walked to work like a man. He felt like a man too. The morning air was fine. People were in the streets. Some were going to the fountains; others were starting out for their jobs. Popo was glad to be among them. He too was going to a job. He was going to a job he loved.

On the sidewalk he saw a group of men sitting beside some small tables that had been placed outside in the sunshine by the proprietors of a café. The men were playing an odd game of cards, in which the losing pair had to wear clothes pins on their noses. When they began winning, their opponents had to wear the clothes pins. Popo thought it very odd for old men to wear clothes pins on their noses while they played seriously at cards. But he could not stop long to watch them. He was in a hurry.

Old man Durand was already in the shop. The old fellow had swung the big door open and was getting things in order.

"You are early, Popo," he greeted the boy.

"Yes," Popo said. "I came early to work on my tray—the one Uncle Jacques started me on—I want to finish it to-day."

"I am sure you will," old man Durand said. "And I think it will be a mighty fine one too for the first you ever made."

"I hope so," Popo said. He tried to talk so as not to show how eager he was to make a success of his first tray.

Old man Durand lighted his pipe and set to work at his own bench with a mallet and chisel. Popo began sanding his tray. A little later Uncle Jacques and Marcel came in. Popo looked up and greeted them pleasantly, but he did not stop working. He was making a picture of a sailboat in the bottom of his tray and all around it he had drawn curves to represent the waves of the ocean.

The hours passed. Still Popo worked. Soon it was lunch time. Popo took only a few minutes off. Then he hurried back to his workbench. He would have to hurry to finish his tray by evening, and he needed every minute for work.

That afternoon, while they worked in the shop, Uncle Jacques told a few stories to amuse the boys. Popo did not stop work for a minute, but he heard what Uncle Jacques said. That is, he heard it in snatches;

and he remembered the pictures Uncle Jacques drew as he remembered dreams. Uncle Jacques could tell stories well.

It seemed that the grandfather of Uncle Jacques and Papa Jean had lived to be more than a hundred years old. Before his death he had told his grandsons some things he remembered. He had told them how the great stone fort called the Citadel of King Christophe came to be on the high, far-away mountain overlooking the town of Cape Haiti. For old Grandfather Emile, as a boy, had seen it built.

Away back in those old days many heroic things were done. Grandfather Emile had seen the black workingmen drag large bronze cannon through the streets to the foot of the mountain. Later he had seen them drawn up the steep sides of the hill by an army of half-naked people who tugged and pulled like animals. Grandfather Emile had told about men who left their homes to work on the Citadel and remained away for ten or twelve years at a time without returning to their families for a single holiday. Once, he had seen the great black king who was responsible for this huge structure. He had seen King Christophe pass through the town on a white horse, surrounded by bodyguards in flashing uniforms.

That was wonderful, Popo thought. It was a pretty story. But somehow it made Popo feel sad. He could see the ruins of the Citadel from the door of the workshop, and it made him sad to think how hard people had worked to build it. He could not forget those poor men who dragged the heavy cannon up the mountain, or those others who went away from home and could not get back for ten or twelve years.

But as Uncle Jacques went on with his story, Popo began to understand. The Haitians had once been slaves to the French. They had freed themselves, fighting. Then they had built that fort, the Citadel, as a protection, so that the French might not come and make them slaves again. And that was why the men worked so hard, and stayed away from home so long.

Popo began thinking about his tray again. He must not waste any time. He must hurry if he wanted to finish it by evening. He thought of what old man Durand had said about a design being a picture of how you feel inside. And Popo wondered if his tray would show that he felt sad as a result of Uncle Jacques's story about the men of old. He hoped not, for it was his plan to have nothing but happiness in his first tray. He wanted everybody to know how glad he was to make something with his own hands.

Soon twilight began to creep into the workshop. Popo put the last touches on his tray of wood and held it up with a cry of joy.

"It's finished, Uncle Jacques. It's finished, Marcel. It's finished, old man Durand. Just look. All finished."

"Ah! That's fine," said Uncle Jacques, noticing the pains Popo had taken.

"Ah," said Marcel, looking at the sailboat in the center, "that's fine!"

"Fine!" said old man Durand, gravely.

"I'm happy," Popo said. He felt as if he could cry, but he was too big for that. Besides, what was there to cry about?

"Since that is your first," Uncle Jacques said, "you may carry it home and give it to Mamma Anna. Tell her to take good care of it. Tell her to remember that it was your first piece of work in my shop. When you are older you will make many beautiful things, many much finer than this tray; but there will never be another first one. For that reason the first one is precious."

"Thank you, Uncle Jacques," Popo said. "I'll tell Mamma Anna what you said."

"And remember the riddle about putting yourself into your designs," old man Durand said with a grin.

"I'll try," Popo answered.

XII

Making Plans

One day, after he had been in the shop several weeks, Popo said to Marcel:

"Have you ever gone to the lighthouse, cousin?"

Marcel looked up from his work with a sad expression.

"No, Popo, I have never been out there. It is a long walk, and my mamma never lets me go that far from home by myself."

"Mamma Anna would not let me go alone either," Popo said. "But Papa Jean has promised to take Fifina and me soon. I wish you could go with us."

Marcel's eyes sparkled a moment, then they became dark again.

"I'd love to," he said. "I'd love it better than anything, but since I'm working in the shop here I may not have a chance to get away. You see, I'm going to take first communion next Sunday, so what chance have I?"

Popo's eyes opened wide.

"First communion!" he whispered. "We were planning on Sunday; but if you are going to take your communion, I'd rather stay home so as to see you in the procession."

Popo knew that he could not hope to be in a first communion procession. He did not have a pair of shoes. Papa Jean was too poor to buy him any. And of course, no boy or girl would ever take first communion without shoes. But just the same he did not intend to have his trip to the lighthouse spoiled by the fact that Marcel was going to be confirmed.

"Listen," he said after a long pause. "Wouldn't Uncle Jacques let us go on a week day—if we worked very hard till then?"

"Maybe." Marcel gave a little shrug of his shoulders to indicate that he was not at all certain.

"Ask him," Popo urged.

"You come with me," Marcel said. "He might not be so apt to say no if both of us ask him."

"All right."

Uncle Jacques was bent over a low bench, with his knee on a strip of board to hold it rigidly in place. His shoulders were rising and falling with a regular motion, for he was sawing and he seemed to be deeply absorbed in keeping his line straight.

The boys waited till he had finished. Seeing them at his elbow, Uncle Jacques looked up.

"Well?" he said, half surprised.

Marcel lost his courage. "You tell him, Popo."

"Papa Jean promised to take Fifina and me to the lighthouse next Sunday, and I wanted Marcel to come. But he is to take first communion then. Couldn't we go on a week day if we work well till then?"

Uncle Jacques rested his saw on the bench and put his hands into his pockets. He walked to the door and looked out at the quiet street.

"To the lighthouse," he mused.

"We have never been," Popo urged.

"No, we have never been," Marcel repeated.

"Are you sure my brother Jean could take you on a week day? You know he fishes every day except Sunday, the Lord's Day. I wonder if he'd want to lose a day."

Popo could not answer. He stood digging his big toe into the dirt floor of the woodworking shop. Marcel showed his disappointment. Uncle Jacques looked down at the youngsters, and after a moment or two his lips parted in a smile.

"There now!" he said. "Don't feel disappointed so soon. I'd like you boys to have a trip to the lighthouse. It is worth seeing. In fact, I have just been thinking that if Jean is willing we might all take a trip out there. He could stay home from his fishing, I could leave the shop to old man Durand, and then every one could go—your Mamma Anna, my wife, every one. A regular picnic. The womenfolk might fix something to eat."

Both boys looked up happily.

"I am sure Papa Jean will be glad to go," Popo said. "He promised to take us on the Lord's Day, and when he finds that Marcel will be in the procession, I know he will want us to stay home to see the sight."

"Well, you ask him to make sure," Uncle Jacques said, picking up his saw again. "Day after to-morrow will suit me all right."

When Popo went home that evening, he immediately told the glorious prospect to Fifina.

"Oh, Fifina," he fairly sang. "I've got a thing to tell you that'll burn your ears. I've got a thing to tell that will make you laugh and cry at once, but part of it isn't known yet."

"How is that, *petit monde?* What do you mean by that riddle, little world?"

"Uncle Jacques will take a day off if Papa will do the same. Uncle Jacques will take his family for a trip to the lighthouse day after tomorrow if Papa Jean will do the same. We can have a picnic if Papa Jean is willing to have it on a week day instead of Sunday."

"Let's tell Mamma Anna."

"Yes, let's do."

"Oh, Mamma Anna," they sang together. "I've got a thing to tell that will burn your ears, burn your ears."

"Tell me, *petit monde,* tell me."

"Uncle Jacques will take his family for a trip to the lighthouse day after to-morrow if Papa Jean will do the same. We can have a picnic if Papa Jean is willing."

"There he is on the beach," said Mamma Anna. "Now he is coming up the slope. Let us ask him."

"Oh, yes, let's do, let's do!"

Papa Jean came into the yard and stood outside the door with his string of glistening silver-green fish. He was tired but apparently happy. His shoulders were wet with perspiration and shiny like metal.

"Oh, Papa Jean! We've got a thing to tell that will burn your ears, burn your ears, burn your ears," the three sang.

"It's a riddle, little world. Tell me, tell me."

"Not exactly a riddle, Papa Jean. Uncle Jacques will take a day off if you will do the same. Uncle Jacques will take his family to the lighthouse day after to-morrow if you will do the same. We can have a picnic if you are willing."

When they had calmed down, Papa Jean said:

"Of course I am willing. I promised you that. But why not go on Sunday as we first planned? Why must I lose a day? I am a poor man."

"Marcel is going to take first communion next Sunday, Papa Jean. He could not come; Uncle Jacques's family could not come. And besides, we want to see Marcel march in the procession to the church."

"Oh, I see."

Papa Jean bowed his head. Popo watched him closely. Above the man's shoulders the youngster could see the bright colors of the sunset.

"Say yes, Papa Jean. Please say yes," Popo urged.

"Please say yes," Fifina said.

"Please say yes," Mamma Anna whispered.

When Papa Jean looked up, he was smiling pleasantly.

"Yes," he said softly. "We will go."

XIII

A Grand Trip

The day for the picnic came. Popo got up early and went to the fountain for a pail of water. Fifina took care of Pensia while Mamma Anna prepared a lunch, and Papa Jean walked around the house smoking his pipe. The sky was clear and blue, but there were a few rosy clouds near the eastern horizon. Popo skipped for joy on the way to the fountain. When he had filled his pail, he placed it carefully on his head, balanced it so that it would not fall, and started home. He could carry a pail of water on his head quite easily now that he was becoming a big boy. He had practiced, and now it was not hard to do. Being so happy about the picnic made it seem easier.

When Popo got home, Uncle Jacques, Aunt Melanie, and Marcel were sitting on a bench in the yard. They had brought a large basket of mangoes and bananas and were ready to start the journey.

"Hello, cousin," Marcel called as Popo came into the yard. "When did you learn to carry water on your head?"

"A long time ago," Popo smiled modestly. "Mamma Anna taught me."

"Yes," Mamma Anna joined in, "now that he is getting to be a big boy, he must learn to do things."

"You are right," Aunt Melanie said sadly. "Marcel could learn a lesson from Popo. I like to see boys help their mothers."

Uncle Jacques and Papa Jean walked down to the water's edge while they waited. Soon, however, Mamma Anna called to let them know that she was ready, and immediately they started up the slope. As they walked, they talked together in quiet, subdued voices.

"So we're all ready!" Papa Jean said.

"Yes," said Mamma Anna. "You men will have to carry the lunch baskets. I shall have Pensia in my arms, and Aunt Melanie is not feeling so very strong. She had better not try to carry a load."

"Well, all right," the men agreed. "Come along then, we don't want you weaklings to lag behind." They laughed indulgently.

Uncle Jacques and Papa Jean led the way, still talking quietly. They turned into rue Bord de la Mer in the direction that led out of town and toward the entrance to the harbor of Cape Haiti. Popo and Marcel and Fifina came scampering behind them, while Mamma Anna and Aunt Melanie brought up the rear.

They walked steadily for about a mile above the sea, passing houses, trees, and hills on one side. On the other they passed a number of boats tied up to the shore, and nets stretched out to dry on the low trees. There were several small beaches too. One of them belonged to the American Marines. Their bathhouses were built near the water, and the water itself was fenced in to keep the sharks away from the place where the Marines bathed.

Beyond this were the beaches where the people of Haiti bathed. These also were protected from sharks—but not by wire fences built in the water. They were protected by natural reefs, and the seaweed, that was so thick a short distance out from the shore, could be clearly seen from the hillside path as Papa Jean and Uncle Jacques with their families began the descent to the ocean's edge.

In one place the children stopped to look at a group of teachers from the Catholic school in Cape Haiti as they bathed in the surf. The spot which they had selected was very rocky. The mother superior sat on a stone on a little hill away from the water. She shielded the teachers from view and helped them while they changed their black robes for white bathing gowns. Then she let their hair down for them. These women all white-clad and looking very much like angels, walked slowly and solemnly into the water and bathed sedately among the big rocks that jutted up out of the sea. It was a beautiful sight. The water was still and blue-green. Where it washed against the stones, it threw up a bit of white foam. The teachers went out where the water was deep enough to reach their shoulders. Their hair floated on the water. And all the while the mother superior watched them lovingly from her rock on the hill.

Popo and the others walked a little farther and then set their lunch baskets on the sand.

"What shall we do first?" asked Uncle Jacques.

"Let's stay here till after dinner," said Mamma Anna. "It will be better to bathe now and then go to the lighthouse after eating. You know, it is not good to swim right after a meal."

"Yes," said Aunt Melanie. "That is the best way."

The plan pleased the children. They were all anxious to see the lighthouse, but they were also eager to bathe in the ocean; and they did not mind putting off the visit to the lighthouse for a few hours. They quickly squirmed out of their clothes—none of them wore more than two pieces—and dashed out into the surf. Uncle Jacques and Papa Jean also got ready for a swim. Mamma Anna and Aunt Melanie sat on the sand near a flat rock and played with Baby Pensia.

All the children were at home in the water. They dived in and easily swam out to the reefs. Then they returned to where the water was not too deep and began playing in the seaweed. They found long beautiful switches and garlands of green weed and drew them out of the water. But they soon saw that the seaweed was not nearly so pretty out of the water. It felt slimy and was a dull brown color when held up to the sun.

"Leave it where it ought to be—in the water," said Mamma Anna.

Fifina came up on the sand to rest. A little later Popo and Marcel heard her calling.

"Oh, see what I have found, Popo! Come and see, Marcel!"

She had found a fine sea shell, rosy and pink inside, and almost the color of silver on the outside.

"That *is* a beauty," Marcel said.

"Yes, indeed," said Popo.

Papa Jean and Uncle Jacques were swimming along the far reef with long powerful strokes. Two or three hours passed, and the sun climbed the sky steadily. In a short time, it was overhead.

Mamma Anna and Aunt Melanie spread the baskets of lunch on a flat rock and called their children and husbands. The children came leaping out of the water like young animals, but the two brothers took their time. They swam reluctantly to the shore and walked slowly up the beach.

The food tasted good after so much exercise. Popo got his mouth smeared and sticky with the sweet juice of the mangoes. He licked his fingers. It seemed to him that nothing had ever tasted so fine before. Fifina liked bananas best, but Mamma Anna would not let her eat more than three. Too many bananas might make a small child sick.

After dinner the men and the children put on their clothes and started for the lighthouse. The women stayed behind, playing on the sand with Pensia.

The lighthouse path led up a hill and under the overhanging branches of almond trees, tropical oaks, and the long dangerous arms of giant cactus. Occasionally it came out of the shadows, and Popo could see the water farther and farther below, at the foot of high steep cliffs. The waves looked smaller, and the ocean seemed smoother. But he did not have much time to notice the view. The lighthouse was still a good distance ahead, and Papa Jean and Uncle Jacques were walking steadily.

Suddenly Uncle Jacques, who was leading, called over his shoulder: "Look out for the snake. Don't hurt it."

That sounded very strange. Most people would have said, "Don't let the snake hurt *you*." But Popo knew exactly what he meant. A moment later he saw the thin green thing, beautiful and delicate, hanging across the path like a twig. Its head was in the bushes on one side of the path, and its tail was in the bushes on the other side. Popo had always heard his father say that the slender green snakes would not hurt any one. He had also been told that it was wrong to kill them. They had for years been regarded as sacred by the people of Haiti.

The little group passed through the ruins of two or three abandoned forts, in secluded parts of the mountain side. They had been built long ago, Uncle Jacques said, when Haiti was still a French possession. Old rusted guns pointed up out of the crumbled stonework. These forts reminded Popo of the sad story about the Citadel.

"Well, here we are!" Uncle Jacques cried.

Popo had been so busy thinking that he was amazed to see the lighthouse just a few steps ahead. And what a view! The great Atlantic!

The lighthouse was a tall, round white structure with big lenses near the top, like huge eyes.

"That is where the light comes out at night," said Uncle Jacques. "When everything is dark, that light flashes far across the water to warn passing ships of the dangerous rocks on our coast. These ships carry grains, meats, sweet woods, ornaments, and all manner of treasures. They go to France and Germany and England and the United States, and they must not be wrecked on our rocky coast. Sometimes ships come to us bringing cloth, shoes, canned foods, and wine. They must not be lost, either. They must bear their cargoes safely. When they arrive in the middle of the night and see our lighthouse, they know that they have reached their destination. So they drop anchor and wait till morning to be piloted into port by our own men who understand the passages and the reefs."

"It's a wonderful light," Popo said.

"Indeed," said Marcel.

"How beautiful the sea is from here!" said Fifina.

"Yes," said Papa Jean, "but do you see the sky?"

All the others looked up at the same moment. Sure enough, the west was covered with black heavy clouds.

"It's going to rain," said Uncle Jacques.

"H'm. We'd better hurry back," said Papa Jean.

Popo took one more look at the wide sea where the great ships pass. Then all turned and started down the hill quickly to get Mamma Anna, Aunt Melanie, and Pensia before the storm.

The sky became darker and darker, and a wind came up. It went through the tropical trees like music. Birds hid in the thickets and cried. The bathing beaches were deserted, and only Mamma Anna and Aunt Melanie were left on the sand. They had their baskets ready, and Mamma Anna had Pensia in her arms.

When the group came down on the sand again, the first drops fell.

"We must hurry," said Mamma Anna.

"Yes," said Aunt Melanie. "This is the first rain of the season, and I'm afraid it will be a heavy one."

The men took the baskets and started out in the path. The youngsters followed close. Behind them came the mothers with Pensia. There was no loitering this time. Everybody was excited. Everybody was anxious to get home.

"We must hurry," one said.

"We must hurry," another repeated.

That was all Popo heard. That was all Fifina heard. Everybody was saying, "We must hurry."

A few more drops fell, and the sky got blacker and blacker. The wind whistled. It blew through the trees like heavy music, like horns and drums. The poor frightened birds in the thickets cried louder and louder.

Suddenly the storm broke. A peal of thunder rattled the roof of the sky. The clouds were so low that Popo could not see the tops of the mountains. There was a flash of lightning and another clap of thunder. Then the rain came, a great sheet of warm white rain.

The sea became noisy. The waves boomed, and the long green tongue of the water licked the white sand. The sky boomed, and water poured down.

The little group walked faster and faster. But Popo was not afraid. He was used to the water, so he did not mind getting wet. But just the same it would be good to get home, to be in the house and to put on a dry shirt.

Back in town the rain was still pouring and the gutters were streaming. Popo and Marcel waded in them, splashing the water with their feet. The two brothers, walking ahead, did not mind the storm either. They had seen many storms. They talked together quietly while the thunder rattled over the hills.

A little farther on, a small goat was standing alone in the street un-

sheltered from the rain. His back was turned to the wind, and he was drenched. He looked very poor, very helpless there in the heavy downpour all by himself. Popo wondered what he could do to help the poor creature.

"Look at that poor goat," he said to Marcel. "I wish I could help him."

"There are thousands of goats in this town," Marcel laughed. "Would you like to help them all? There are more goats than there are people."

"I'm not making fun," Popo said seriously. "He looks so pitiful out here alone."

"That shed over there is his house," Fifina said. "Why don't you make him go inside?"

"I will," Popo said eagerly.

He ran to the goat and tried to push him toward the shed. But the goat was blinded by the rain and did not seem to understand that Popo was trying to help him. Suddenly, the confused creature turned around abruptly and butted Popo in the stomach. It was not a very hard butt, but it caught Popo off balance; and over he went into a mud puddle.

When Popo pulled himself out of the mud, he heard loud laughter. He was surprised and frightened but not hurt.

"That goat doesn't know what's good for him," he said sadly.

"That's the trouble with most goats, Popo," Papa Jean said. "They don't know what's good for them."

The little group started on again, and very soon they were home.

"Come in and stop with us till the rain is over," Mamma Anna told Aunt Melanie.

"Thanks, but we may as well go on," Aunt Melanie said. "We're all wet, anyway."

Papa Jean stood a long time in the door watching the downpour. He seemed to enjoy the rain. Then, suddenly, he said:

"Popo, this is the beginning of our long rainy season."

"Yes," said Popo. "That's what Aunt Melanie said."

"There won't be much kite-flying from now on, son. You will have to spend your spare time around the house with Fifina and Mamma Anna and Pensia, if you're not at the shop."

"I am willing to stay when it rains," Popo said.

"That's a good boy," said Papa Jean. "This summer perhaps you will go with me sometimes in the fishing boat. You will be big enough by then."

Popo was happy to hear this. Fifina too was happy. She thought Popo deserved to go out in the fishing boat and fish like the men.

"That will be fine," she whispered in his ear.

But the summer seemed a long way off. Popo thought that he would indeed be a big boy by that time.

Outside, the rain fell harder and harder. The gutters overflowed. The streets were flooded. A little water began to drip into their house, *tap, tap, tap* on the floor, but Mamma Anna put a pan under the leak.

Popo could not see the beach, the rain was so heavy. He could not even see the tree with the gnarled roots a few hundred yards away. The whole world was wrapped in rain, but the thunder had ceased.

In a little while the storm passed, the sky lightened, and there came a rainbow over the ocean. The world brightened. Fifina put all their wet clothes outside to dry, Papa Jean went off down the street, and Mamma Anna began cooking supper.

"We certainly had a grand trip to-day, even if it did rain," Popo said.

"Yes, indeed," answered Fifina and Mamma Anna together. And even Baby Pensia seemed to agree. "We had a grand trip."

Black Misery

Illustrations by Arouni

(1969)

Misery is when you heard on the radio that the neighborhood you live in is a slum but you always thought it was home.

Misery is when the teacher asked you who was the Father of our Country and you said, "Booker T. Washington."

Misery is when your pals see Harry Belafonte walking down the street and they holler, "Look, there's Sidney Poitier."

Misery is when your white teacher tells the class that all Negroes can sing and you can't even carry a tune.

Misery is when you learn that you are not supposed to like watermelon but you do.

Misery is when the kid next door has a party and invites all the neighborhood but you.

Misery is when your very best friend calls you a name she really didn't mean to call you at all.

Misery is when you call your very best friend a name you didn't mean to call her, either.

Misery is when nobody told you the floorwalker would stop you from riding up and down the escalators 16 times when mama is shopping.

Misery is when somebody meaning no harm called your little black dog "Nigger" and he just wagged his tail and wiggled.

Misery is when your mother said considering the kind of family your new friend Leroi has even if he is white you can't play with him.

Misery is when you have always heard the old folks say Mississippi is a place to be away from, and on your first day in a new school the kids ask, "Are you from Mississippi?"

Misery is when you start to play a game and someone begins to count out "Eenie, meenie, minie, mo. . . ."

Misery is when you can see all the other kids in the dark but they claim they can't see you.

Misery is when you find out your bosom buddy can go in the swimming pool but you can't.

Misery is when the taxi cab won't stop for your mother and she says a bad word.

Misery is when you find out Golden Glow Hair Curler won't curl *your* hair at all.

Misery is when the colored actor on the late, late show bucks his eyes at the wind shaking the shutters as if he really believes in ghosts.

Misery is when you first realize so many things bad have black in them, like black cats, black arts, blackball.

Misery is when your own mother won't let you play your new banjo in front of the *other* race.

Misery is when Uncle Joe gave you a button-up sweater and you wanted a slip-over that bunches at the bottom.

Misery is when you go to the Department Store before Christmas and find out that Santa is a white man.

Misery is when the only man on the bus who is drunk and talking out of his mind is black.

Misery is when you wish Daddy hadn't named your dog Blackie.

Misery is when you start to help an old white lady across the street and she thinks you're trying to snatch her purse.

Misery is when you come back from the beach proud of your suntan and your pals don't even know you've got one.

Misery is when you see that it takes the whole National Guard to get you into the new integrated school.

The Pasteboard Bandit

By Arna Bontemps and Langston Hughes

Contents

Chapter 1

The Man with the Rabbit Whiskers

He was only six inches tall, and there were many people who hadn't even noticed him at the fair. But that did not matter to Tito. He knew that by and by somebody would come along and pay attention to his big white sombrero, his shaggy hair, his bushy black whiskers and his little round eyes. Somebody, he was sure, would admire the way he clinched his tiny fists and held one hand in the air, making a strong gesture.

Tito was willing to wait. Of course there were many pasteboard men at the fair. Many of them were much larger than he. Some wore brighter clothes. Some had bigger sombreros. All this Tito knew. Even on the shelf where he stood under the bright awning there were tall figures who tried to push in front of the brave little bandit so that he could not be seen. Yet Tito was not impatient. He felt sure that his time would come.

The sun was bright that day. Many people had come to the plaza. Some were shooting firecrackers. Some were eating candy. Some were throwing rings and guessing numbers at the prize booths. And some were just sitting on the benches. All of them seemed to enjoy the day.

The Indian woman who kept the booth where Tito and the other pasteboard toys stood wore a cherry-colored waist and a skirt like a pumpkin flower. Her hair was braided into two long ropes that hung down her back. Her husband sat on a stool with a bright red serape thrown across his shoulders. His face was the color and shape of a brown pottery jug. They had no children. That is why the woman looked so happy when a small bright-eyed boy came up to the booth and began looking at the figurines.

"How do you like my pasteboard toys?" she asked him.

He shrank away a little, for he was very shy, and answered so softly she could scarcely hear what he said.

"They're fine."

"Would you like to buy one?"

He didn't know how to answer that. He wanted one very much, but he had only a nickel in his pocket and he hated to spend it for a thing that looked like a doll, even though it was actually a bandit and dressed in bright clothes. He intended to buy candy with his big copper coin.

"I don't know," he said.

The Indian woman leaned across the counter and took his hand.

"What is your name?"

"Juanito," he told her. "Juanito Pérez."

"Where do you live?"

The boy turned and pointed to some houses high on the side of the hill. One, a very small one, was painted bright green.

"There," Juanito said. "My papá is the man who paints gourds and pottery to sell at the fiestas."

"Yes, yes, I know. Well, are you a good boy, Juanito?"

Again he bowed his head and shrank away shyly. Of course he was a good boy, but he couldn't say he was. Fortunately, a man who sat nodding on a nearby stool opened his eyes at that moment and answered for him.

"Certainly he's a good boy, Consuelo," he said. "Don't you see how polite he is? Give him a toy if he wants one."

Juanito's heart beat hard. Did the man mean he would give him one *free*? Had he understood the man?

"All right," the woman said. "Which one do you like best, Juanito? Look at all of them and tell me which one you like."

Tito, from his shelf, heard the last words very distinctly. This was his chance, he thought. He looked down at the little brown boy and tried to think how it would feel to belong to such a polite little fellow. Tito couldn't move, but he tried to look as important as he could, tried to clinch his little pasteboard fists even tighter, but it did no good. There was a big fat man beside him, a man who seemed much more impressive in his brick-red suit, his lavender sombrero and his glossy pointed whiskers. On the other side there stood a huge stupid-looking fellow with a long nose and a funny little yellow jacket. Tito was sure he would not be seen between two pasteboard men so much larger than himself. Yet, he *did* like that little boy named Juanito. It would be fine if—

Ah, the little boy was looking straight at Tito, looking straight into his bright round eyes. And, yes, he was smiling.

"I think," Juanito said, pointing his finger, "I think I like that small one with the blue coat and the bushy rabbit whiskers."

"Oh, the little bandit," the brown woman said. "Well, I think that's a good choice. He seems to be such a brave little man. He is yours, Juanito. Show him to your father when you go home."

"Thank you," Juanito said, taking the pasteboard figure in his hands.

"Thank you very, very much."

He started down the road, passing the other booths and the places where games were being played, forgetting about the candy he intended to buy, paying no attention to the merry-go-round on the corner. He was thinking that maybe he and Tito might become good friends.

People with suitcases were getting out of the bus at the next corner, people who had come to Taxco from Cuernavaca and Mexico City, but Juanito did not stop. He had promised the señora in the booth that he would show Tito to his father, and he intended to keep his word.

When he was halfway up the hill, he paused to catch his breath and look down on the dense green plaza. He could still hear the music of the merry-go-round, still hear the voices of people standing in front of the tall church and of others playing games at the fair. But the things down there did not seem to matter so much now that Juanito had Tito. With no brothers or sisters of his own, a friend like Tito could make a lot of difference. Juanito was almost out of breath when he reached the green house on the hill, but he knew he was one of the happiest little Indian boys in Taxco that afternoon.

Chapter 2

Juanito Makes a Friend

At first Tito felt like a stranger in the small green house on the side of the hill, a house belonging to real people. He had never been in a house before, and here there were no other little pasteboard men to keep him company.

The inside of the house, too, was something of a disappointment at first. The furniture was very simple, just a table in the center of the living room and a few chairs around the wall. Tito could only peep into the other rooms from his place on the table, but he could see that they had in them no more than was absolutely necessary for rooms to have. He began to think that maybe Juanito's family was very poor. But, of course, he knew that that did not matter if they were kind and polite.

There was no clock on the wall, so Tito began to wonder what time it was. There were voices in the kitchen. What was going on? Tito couldn't even tell whether it was night or day. But a few minutes later somebody opened the kitchen door and he found out. Señor Pérez, his wife and his little son, Juanito, were at breakfast.

They did not talk much as they ate, and when they spoke their voices were soft.

"Well, Juanito," the father said, "what will you do with yourself to-day?"

The boy bowed his head and thought a long while. Then he said, "There is a strange American family in the red house down the road. Maybe I'll walk down there and say hello."

"Strangers, you say?"

The mother put another tortilla on his plate.

"They just came yesterday," she said. "They seem to be artists."

"Artists, artists, artists. Taxco is getting full of them," exclaimed the father.

"Aren't you an artist, Papá?" Juanito asked.

"Well, yes. But not the same kind. Artists are fine, I only mean I'm afraid there are too many of us in this little town. Maybe, though, you'd better not bother them if they're busy painting."

For a few more minutes Juanito ate in silence. His mother, who was barefooted, went outdoors and returned with a cup of cool water from the well. When she came back she sat down and began eating the egg on her plate.

"I wouldn't bother the people any if they're busy," Juanito said. "I only thought maybe I'd show them Tito."

The two older people laughed softly. Tito heard it all from the front room. That Juanito, his mother and father thought, he was surely some boy. There he was wanting to show that new American family a little pasteboard bandit that didn't cost more than a nickel. Juanito—what a boy he was—thinking little Tito worth showing to those tourist people who had just come to town.

All this talk made the tiny bandit himself feel very sad. Why, he wondered, was it so funny for Juanito to be proud of his toy? Why did they think people would not appreciate a brave little man like himself?

"Tito is a fine little fellow," the father said. "But he's just a toy."

"Maybe," Juanito suggested timidly, "maybe I could show him to the little boy."

"They have a little boy?"

Juanito and his mother both assured the father that the new family did have a little son, and a bright looking one, too.

"Well, now, maybe that's different," Señor Pérez smiled.

Tito began to feel much happier. It was good to know Juanito appreciated his worth, if nobody else did. Now perhaps the little American boy would see tiny brave Tito; perhaps—if Tito made a very, very good impression—even the mother and father might take him into their house, hold him in their hands and examine his little blue coat, his red girdle, the white buttons down the side of his pant legs, his furious little rabbit beard. What an experience for Tito!

Breakfast was over and the doors and windows were thrown open to let in sunlight and a fresh breeze. Little Tito saw the fig trees in the yard, saw the chickens scratching just outside the door, and he could hardly wait for Juanito to take him visiting. He clinched his tiny fists tighter and tighter. Then he began to think.

Surely this was no way to behave. A little toy bandit could not make time fly faster by clinching his fists and working himself up. No, he should always be patient. "I must learn to control myself," he said. "I must not fly into a temper. My time will come. Juanito has not forgotten me."

And Tito was right. Juanito finished helping his mother in the kitchen and came into the front room for his little friend. Carrying him carefully, he went across the patio, out the front door, and down the narrow little street on the side of the hill.

The morning was fine. The plaza was greener than ever. The fair was still going on, but there were not so many people there today. Once more an automobile bus was unloading in front of the church. The cathedral seemed taller than ever against the clear blue sky. Juanito passed many small poor houses, passed a few large fine ones and came to a red one that was neither small nor large, neither poor nor fine, but something in between. A small American boy was standing in the door.

Looking very solemn, feeling very shy, Juanito bowed his head, scraping his bare toes in the dirt. When he looked up he saw the strange child coming toward him, so Juanito took a few more steps. Tito understood. He began to feel quite happy. When they were facing each other on the path, the little blond stranger pointed to himself and whispered, "Kenny."

"Juanito," the little Indian boy answered.

"Come," said Kenny, starting up the path.

"*Vamanos,*" Juanito said, following him.

Then both boys paused and Kenny pointed to the little pasteboard bandit. There was a question in his eye.

"Tito," Juanito said.

The little bandit could almost feel himself puffing out with pride.

Kenny's father and mother left their easels and came to the door with their paint boards on their arms, their buff-colored smocks smeared with finger marks. The father could talk Juanito's language. He said good morning in Spanish.

"*Buenos dias,*" Juanito answered.

The mother smiled and said something in English that Juanito did not understand. But Tito knew that it was, "What a nice little Mexican boy! He will be a fine playmate for Kenny."

And Tito agreed with that.

Chapter 3

Tito Tumbles

Then for a handful of days Tito stood on a shelf in Juanito's bedroom, half-forgotten. Dust collected on the brave little man's shoulders. A tiny speck of paint peeled off one of his clinched fists. But time passed rapidly, and one day Juanito came into the house from his play, stood in a chair and took Tito down from the shelf.

Kenny was in the patio waiting. The two boys were now able to talk pretty well, using a little of Juanito's language and a little of Kenny's. But since Tito could understand both languages, it made no difference at all to him.

They sat beside the well, with Tito between them on the low stone fence.

"*Abeja!*" said Juanito as a fierce little creature came zooming over the wall of the courtyard.

"A bumble-bee," Kenny said.

But as quickly as he had come, the bee was gone. Tito felt a trifle nervous, standing there on the well-stone, looking down into the water. A bee darting about so fast in the patio, not noticing where he was going, might accidentally zoom right into little pasteboard Tito. It was too horrible to think about. That bee might knock him off the stone fence and into—oh, it would be better not to think about it at all.

"Where is your father?" Kenny asked. "I thought he was going to paint his pottery vases this morning."

"He's in his room," Juanito said. "He's waiting for the man who brings the pottery. See," Juanito pointed to the corner of the courtyard where his father usually worked, "he has nothing else to paint, no bowls or jars or dishes, nothing. Not even a gourd."

"Will the man come soon?"

"Maybe today, maybe *mañana*," Juanito said. "*Quién sabe?* I don't know."

Just at that moment something bumped against the swinging doors of the patio. Then, as they flew open, a little calf ran in from the street. He had no business there, as he did not belong to Juanito's father.

The boys left Tito on the well-stone and began chasing the frisky young animal round and round the courtyard. As they ran the calf bounded about, kicked up his heels and circled the well dangerously near Tito, passing the gate and making circles again.

Once Juanito got his hands on the little fellow and held him by one ear, but the calf was anxious to frolic, so he jerked away and kicked up his heels again. Then, abruptly, something happened. Tito saw two big dark eyes looking directly into his small bright ones. The calf was looking mischievously at the tiny brightly clad bandit and was coming directly toward him.

Of course, the little calf didn't mean any harm. He only wanted to play and maybe to touch the brave little fellow with his nose. Juanito saw what was about to happen, but he couldn't get to Tito in time. Kenny saw, too, and tried to catch the calf by the tail, but that did no good. The young animal kept looking straight into Tito's eyes and prancing stubbornly toward him.

Tito clinched his fists. His whiskers bristled furiously. Then—woe, woe, woe—he felt a blunt wet nose against his. He saw a black tongue come out to lick at his paint. And he felt himself shoved backwards, tumbling head over heels down, down, down into the well!

"Now see," Juanito shouted. "See what you've done?"

The little calf only kicked up his heels again and bounded out the gate and down the street.

"What'll we do?" Kenny whispered worriedly. "The water'll spoil him, won't it?"

Juanito was almost crying, but his mind worked fast.

"The bucket," he said. "Maybe we can save him with the bucket."

Juanito's mother came running out of the house.

"What's happened? What's happened?"

The boys told her how the calf had come into the yard, scampered round and round till he was tired and then tried to lick the little bandit's paint off. Yes, and he had pushed Tito backwards into the well.

Señor Pérez had now come to the door in his white pajamalike clothes, a red Indian blanket over his arm. He had heard some of what the others said.

"Well, what are you waiting for?" he called. "Drop the bucket down. See if you can't bring him up before the water spoils the pasteboard."

Juanito let the rope slip through his hands as the bucket went down into the well. Looking over the stone fence, he tried to see the white hat, and the furious whiskers of his tiny bandit on the water far below. There was something, but Juanito couldn't be sure what it was. Perhaps it was just a shiny glint on the face of the water. At any rate, he aimed his bucket as well as he could, let it sink into the water, then began drawing it up to the surface.

Kenny put his hand on the rope and helped him pull. Juanito's father and mother were both standing beside the well now, looking over the low wall.

Suddenly the mother's eye caught sight of a bobbing object in the pail.

"Oh, there he is! Easy, Juanito. Don't shake the bucket. There he is! Easy now. You might splash him out. . . . Now."

She leaned far over the stone railing and snatched the little man from the water.

"Is he spoiled?" Juanito cried. "Is the paint running off? Is the pasteboard soft?"

"The paint's running just a little, but he isn't spoiled, though," his mother said. "Here, let's stand him in the bright sunshine. This flower pot will be a good place. He floated on the water, but he didn't really get wet through and through."

"I'm glad of that," Kenny said sympathetically.

Señor Pérez looked at the little fellow carefully.

"No, he's not quite spoiled," he said. "But that was a close call. Don't stand him on the well-stone any more if you don't want to lose him."

"I won't," Juanito said.

And Tito, having no love of water, was glad to hear him say it. He knew that the little boy meant what he said.

"If Uncle Diego gets in from the country with that load of pottery, come down to the cafe and get me," Señor Pérez said to Juanito.

Then he threw his bright red serape across his shoulder and went out the wide gate into the street. Tito watched him from his place in the flower pot.

"Come with me," Juanito's mother said to the boys. "Let me give you some pennies. I want to send you for some *camotes*."

"Sweet things," Juanito whispered when he saw Kenny didn't understand.

Both of them were eager to go for her.

Chapter 4

Dry Soup

It was afternoon when the man came with the pottery. Tito was still standing in the flower pot on the wall, and Juanito and Kenny were sitting on the well-stone teaching each other words.

"House," Kenny said.

"*Casa,*" Juanito answered.

"Boy."

"*Muchacho.*"

"Thank you."

"*Muchas gracias.*"

Tito wasn't very much interested. He knew what people said no matter what language they spoke. But soon he saw a country fellow standing at the patio gate. He was very dusty, a brown man with loose-fitting clothes and a broad straw sombrero. He wore sandals, and behind him Tito saw the face of a faithful, patient, sad-eyed little burro. A moment later the man swung the gates inward and the little pack animal, heavily loaded, trotted into the courtyard.

The clear afternoon sky made a lovely blue dome over the green patio. Soft big clouds strayed across the sky like great silvery sheep in the meadows of heaven. Both boys rose to greet the newcomer. Kenny didn't know who the man was or what the animal carried in the great straw-lined rope bags that bulged like balloons on either side of the burro's back, but Juanito knew right away.

"Papá's gone to the cafe," he said. "I'll run and get him."

"No hurry," Uncle Diego said. "It will take some time to unload all this pottery. Every piece has to be handled carefully."

Kenny persuaded Juanito to wait till he had seen how the earthen jugs and vases, jars and dishes were packed, then they started toward the gate together. Hearing a new voice in the patio, Juanito's mother came to the door and stood in the archway without speaking. Heavy braids of hair hung down the sides of her face. She had been cooking and she dried her hands on her apron as she watched the man unload the burro.

A cool breeze was beginning to stir. Uncle Diego had said there was no need to hurry, but the two boys began running almost as soon as they were outside the gate. It was easier to run down the hill than to walk.

They reached the plaza, crossed a cobble-stone street and entered the cafe where Señor Pérez so often sat with his good friends and talked.

"Papá," Juanito said, "the pottery has come. Uncle Diego's unloading the burro now."

"So soon? Well, now, that uncle of yours is not as sleepy as he looks. I'll be right along."

He raised his glass to finish the soda he was drinking. The boys did not wait but walked along ahead.

When Señor Pérez got home, he showed the boys how to help him place the pottery pieces some in one place and some in another, grouping them according to shape and size in the corner where he did his painting. Both boys helped willingly, and soon the great bags were empty and there was nothing left in them but the straw in which the pottery had been packed.

Uncle Diego went into the house and passed a few words with his sister Carmen, who was Juanito's mother, and then came back to the well and drew a bucket of water for his faithful burro and one for himself. When they had both drunk all they could hold, the quiet country man unfolded his serape and put it over his shoulders by sticking his head through a hole he had cut in the middle.

"There's a cool wind blowing," he said.

"Won't you stay and have a bite to eat, brother?" Juanito's mother called from the doorway, her face perspiring from standing over the charcoal stove in the kitchen.

"No, thank you," he answered. "I must buy some things before the shops close, and then I'll have to start home. My family expects me tonight, and it's a long way to walk. I'll be leaving now."

Señor Pérez paid his brother-in-law for bringing the pottery and stood at the gate waving good-bye as the copper-brown country man and his mouse-gray burro went down the road. Juanito and Kenny were still busy looking at the various pieces of earthenware Uncle Diego had made and brought to Señor Pérez to be decorated with brightly colored birds and flowers.

Poor little Tito had been blown over by the afternoon breeze and lay on his back in the flower pot, seeing nothing but the great dome of heaven and the fleecy clouds like mammoth sheep.

Señora Carmen was in the door again.

"Well, your food is ready, little men and big man," she said kindly.

Tito almost rolled out of his flower pot. He thought at first she was talking to him. But in a minute he understood better. She was calling the boys little men.

"This is the day you promised to eat dinner with us," Juanito said, turning to Kenny.

"*Gracias,*" Kenny said, using his new language easily. "I told my mama and papa you had asked me and they said all right."

They drew some water to wash their faces and hands. Señor Pérez washed out of doors, too. Then all took big drinks of water and went inside to the dining room.

The table was set with two bowls of chili sauce and a large dish filled with a paste of avocados with chopped onions and tomatoes. There was also a big pile of hot tortillas wrapped in a cloth. When they were all seated, Juanito's mother brought in four brown cups full of delicious clear soup, and into these each one squeezed the juice of half a lime he found beside his plate.

Taking her seat, Señora Pérez uncovered the tall pile of thin tortillas and handed a few to each one at the table. On these she spread the avocado paste for Kenny, who didn't seem to understand, and twisted each one into a tight little roll with the delicious green paste running out of each end.

The next course (for even the poor people in Mexico serve each item of food separately) Juanito's family called *sopa seca* or dry soup. This consisted of a big platter of tender dry rice colored with red from tomato sauce and chili. It had been prepared in such a manner as to make each grain stand out from the others, and Kenny thought this one of the finest dishes he had ever eaten.

"Dry soup, you call it?" he asked.

"Yes, *sopa seca,*" Juanito answered.

The others smiled. It did sound a little funny.

"What kind of egg will you have on your soup?" the mother asked Kenny.

"Fried," the boy said.

The others chose to have theirs fried, too, so Señora Pérez left them a few moments while she prepared the eggs over her charcoal stove in the little adjoining kitchen.

Guisado followed, a meat stew highly seasoned with chili peppers, which, like much of the other food, burned Kenny's mouth. The tortilla was used as a spoon in eating this, but since Kenny had a hard time, Señora Pérez got him a fork. While she was up, she brought in the salad, chopped lettuce with a radish nearly a foot long lying across the plate.

They ate quietly, and Juanito knew why Kenny's eyes got large when the mother brought in the *verdura*, the green vegetable which today consisted of squash cooked with carrots. She smeared more avocado paste on another tortilla for him, and rolled it up. Kenny ate it all, but his eyes did get big. He was wondering how he could ever hold so much.

"Does the chili burn your mouth?" Señor Pérez asked, smiling as he saw Kenny reach for the water.

"Just a little," Kenny said.

"Wait a minute. I'll get you something sweet and cool for that," the man said.

The father went out the front door. When he returned in a few moments, he was carrying a large wide-mouthed jug filled with ice-cold pineapple juice. He got pottery mugs from a cupboard, filled them one by one, and placed them beside the plates. Kenny drank all of his at once, and Señor Pérez refilled it promptly.

Kenny thought he had never eaten so much in his life, but the food was so good he didn't want to stop—even though the chili peppers were hot.

Señora Pérez cleared away their plates, went into the kitchen again and returned with a large earthen pot of beans that had been simmering on the charcoal stove a long time and was all blackened on the bottom. She set it on a red straw mat and began serving all the plates very generously. She took a spoon and dipped chili sauce for every plate except Kenny's. She could see that some of the food had been burning him so she decided he had perhaps eaten enough chili for one day. It didn't seem hot to them; they were used to it.

The fruit followed, mangoes, oranges, pomegranates, and figs. Kenny looked at the heaping basket and decided he'd try a mango, since he had never tasted one before. He was full, but he was sure it was a good fruit.

He was so full he had no taste for the dessert, which was guava jelly served in large squares. It seemed to him too sweet. But he tried to eat a little to keep the others company. He couldn't understand how Juanito's mother and father could take coffee, too, after eating so heartily for about an hour and a half.

"I think I should go home now," he said to them, drowsily.

"Already?" Juanito said.

"Stay for supper," said the mother. "We'll have enchiladas and chocolate tonight."

"I'd like to, but I'm afraid mama and papa—"

"Well, *mañana*, maybe? Perhaps some other day?"

Kenny smiled, going out the door into the courtyard. He was so full that when he walked he waddled.

In his flower pot, neglected and forgotten, Tito heard the gate swing, shivered in the cool afternoon breeze and wondered if he was to be neglected the rest of the day. Would Juanito leave him out in the evening dew to get his paint all spoiled, his pasteboard softened? Oh, there were so many things for a little figure of a bandit to worry about. His rabbit whiskers bristled furiously. He clinched his fists—and just lay there.

Chapter 5

Locked in a Mine

The next day the boys watched Señor Pérez paint lovely birds and flowers on some of his pottery in the corner of the courtyard. After a while Kenny persuaded Juanito to come to his house, and it was then they remembered Tito, whom they had left in the flower pot the previous afternoon.

As a result of his fall into the well, the little fellow had been badly damaged. Spending the night in the flower pot and being wet by the dew perhaps did him no good either. At any rate, he was now a sorrowful sight. His paint had run. His little blue coat had faded. His bright red girdle [waist shash] had disappeared. He had lost all the white buttons on the sides of his pants. His dashing white sombrero was now as brown and ugly as a gunny sack. His cheeks were as pale as chalk and tears had run out of his eyes, streaking his face.

Nothing had happened to his furious little beard, however; the thatch of hair above his forehead was as bushy as usual, and his tiny brave fist was still clinched and raised indignantly. Yet Tito was a pitiful sight. Juanito felt sorry for him. It made his heart tender to see the little fellow so marred.

"Poor Tito," he said to Kenny, holding the small papier-mâché figure in the palm of his hand.

"He's still well and strong," Kenny said, "even if his paint is spoiled."

"Yes, but he doesn't feel the same. You see, Tito loves bright clothes. He's proud."

"If he were a doll, you could have your mama make him some new things."

"I wouldn't have him if he were a doll," Juanito said petulantly. "He'd belong to some girl, and she could look after him the best way she could. But Tito's a regular fellow."

"Bring him along," Kenny said.

They left the patio in the bright morning sunshine, went out the gate and started down the road toward the red house that was neither small nor large. Tito's heart thumped. He was a great one for going places. Every time Juanito went out the gate, he began to feel excited.

Kenny's mother and father, Mr. and Mrs. Strange, were not at home. Concha, the Indian woman who kept the house clean for them, said they had gone up on one of the higher peaks above the town. They had worn their buff-colored smocks and navy blue berets and carried their easels, so she supposed they had gone to paint.

"We can find them," Kenny said. "Let's go too."

Juanito was willing and Tito was more than pleased.

After a long walk on a winding path, they reached a high point and saw the two artists working at their easels on a twin peak that was not more than a block away. Kenny called to them cheerfully and both stopped and waved their brushes. The boys reached their hill and saw what they were painting.

Down below the town of Taxco looked magical. The red clay tops of houses, the little green patios with wells or fountains in the centers and yellow flowers growing, scarcely seemed real. In the center was the plaza, dense with trees and deep green. In front of it stood the cathedral, very tall, very grand. Around the plaza were shops and booths, most of them ornamented with crepe tissue paper and paper cut-outs. . . . And this was the picture each of the artists was painting on his canvas.

"What are those piles of dirt over there?" Kenny said to Juanito after a while.

The Indian youngster turned to see where he was pointing.

"Oh, mines," he said. "Old silver mines, no more good. Want to see them?"

Kenny said that he did.

"Be careful," said the mother, squeezing a little dab of paint out of a tube.

"I say as much. Don't get lost," the father said without looking up from his work.

The boys went down a slope, pausing now and again to pull at leaves or to throw stones. The mines were further away than they had seemed from the peak where Blyth and Myrna Strange were painting.

The boys examined two or three of the old abandoned shafts, venturing inside a few feet, peeping cautiously to see what was back in the black holes, then came to one where a great beam ran across the entrance, supporting some other boards overhead.

"I wonder what's back inside," Kenny said, pulling a big loose stone out from underneath the beam.

"Let's find out," Juanito suggested.

Tito quaked with fear. What kind of black hole was this that they wanted to enter? What might happen to a little pasteboard man in such a dismal shaft? Were there animals back there, badgers, wild cats? Oh, it was a fearful moment for Tito. He was brave enough for his size, but, you know, that wasn't much. And Tito had just suffered a bad accident the day before, so you couldn't blame him for being quite nervous—if you didn't want to call him really scared.

"What about Tito?" Kenny asked.

"He does look scared, doesn't he?"

"I'll say he does. Is he trembling or is that the wind blowing his whiskers?"

Both of them laughed.

"I'll just stand him here on this rock," Juanito said. "If I dropped him back in the dark, I might not ever find him. We might step on him and mash him up."

"Yes," Kenny said. "This stone is a good place for him. He can be a look-out for us. There, stand there, little bandit."

Tito was happy. It made him proud to be stood at the entrance of the mine shaft and given such an important job. He made up his mind to do the best he could, even if he was a pretty wretched sight with all his gay clothes ruined, his painted eyes running.

"Watch out for us," Juanito said.

They left the little bandit and started back into the black hole in the mountain side. Back, back, back they went. It was terribly dark. It was quiet and still. The walls were damp, and now and again a bit of gravel fell. Occasionally a drop of water splashed on a stone. Once Kenny looked back. The entrance seemed a long way off, but it was easy to see though it looked small now. Ahead—blackness. This was going to be a real adventure. On they went.

Outside on his stone little Tito kept guard. The afternoon sun moved steadily across the sky and began slipping down toward the rim of the earth, behind the beautiful line of hills. Why were the boys staying so long, Tito wondered. Time was passing. Didn't they know that? Tito was beginning to feel worried when suddenly he heard an awful jolt at the entrance to the mine.

Dear, dear, dear! What could that be? Tito could have cried for fear. His little painted eyes were not so good, but now he could just dimly see that the great beam had suddenly fallen across the door of the mine. Some of the boards had fallen, too, and some of the rocks and dirt, and the entrance was barred. Juanito and Kenny were inside!

Tito was so distressed he wanted to tear his hair. Something horrible had happened, but what could a little pasteboard bandit do? The boys had told him to be look-out, but how could he help now? How were the boys ever going to get out of that black hole with such a heavy beam across the entrance? Oh, woe! woe! woe! thought Tito. He clinched his tiny fists; his whiskers bristled. If he could only move! Run for help! Shout and call!

Chapter 6

Tito Becomes a Hero

Blyth and Myrna Strange finished their painting and folded their easels. It was getting late, and they were sure Concha would be waiting with supper for them. Where were the boys, Kenny and Juanito? Where was that little bandit, Tito?

"Kenny should know better than to wander so far away and stay so long," Blyth Strange said, wrinkling his forehead.

"I'm getting worried," Myrna added, looking far across the hillside.

They waited a little longer, searching with their eyes for their son and his little Mexican companion.

Neither of them had entirely completed the picture on which he was working, but on each canvas, from slightly different angles, there was a fine reproduction of the little town viewed from the hill. Each had caught the vivid warm colors of the houses; the brick-red roofs, the patches of cucumber green, the gray cobble-stones, and pumpkin-colored walls were all there.

"Well, we can't go home without Kenny," Mr. Strange said. "And that little friend of his—why Juanito's mother and father will feel terrible if we don't send him home soon."

"What shall we do, Blyth?"

"Stay here," he said to his wife. "Keep these things. I'll go look for them."

Myrna kept looking across the hillside at the old abandoned mines in the distance and at the heaps of slag piled near the openings of the holes. After a while she began shaking her head slowly.

"No," she told him. "I'm going, too. These painting things will be safe here. I'm worried about Kenny. I'm going, too."

"Well," Blyth said slowly. "All right."

They went down one slope and up another. They crossed a level place and crept along a high ledge. They passed one mine, then a second mine. Each time Blyth Strange went to the mouth of the shaft and called at the top of his voice.

"Kenny! Kenny!"

There was an echo of his words deep in the heart of the earth, but no answer came. Surely Kenny was not back in one of those dangerous holes, they told each other. Surely he and Juanito knew better than to do such a thing. But, just to be quite sure, they thought it would do no harm to call. Blyth Strange called, and then his wife, Myrna, called.

"Kenny! Kenny!"

The second shaft was just like the first. He was not in it either. There were footprints where the boys had come to the entrances and peeped in, one little barefoot boy and one with New York shoes, but there were also prints showing that they had come back to the path again and continued up the hill.

The sun was quite out of sight now and the sky was a soft bandanna handkerchief of rose and gold. It was past supper time and they knew Concha was waiting to put the food on the table, but where was Kenny? Where was his little friend, Juanito?

Presently they came to a third mine. Their hearts began to beat rapidly. They were so excited and troubled by now that at first neither of them noticed a little pasteboard fellow standing on a stone, clinching his tiny fists.

"What!" Mr. Strange said. "Isn't this that little toy Juanito showed us?"

"Why yes," his wife said. "Oh, dear, he must have gotten wet. His paint is all spoiled. But what does this mean?"

Her husband caught sight of the heavy beam that had fallen across the entrance to the mine. He wrinkled his forehead and looked at the other boards that had fallen, too, partly covered with loose earth.

"It means that our Kenny is in that horrible hole," he said. "It means that he and Juanito left this little fellow here while they went inside to explore. And it means that that beam has fallen and locked them inside!"

"Oh, no, no!" Mrs. Strange began to cry softly. "What shall we do? Do you think they're hurt, Blyth?"

"We'll have to be calm," her husband said, throwing off his smock and going to work furiously.

Tito began to feel better. He wondered if he had done his work well, just standing there on guard. Had he not shown the mother and father of Kenny where the boys were? But the main question now was whether or not the boys were hurt and how they would get them out.

Mrs. Strange climbed up on a heap of dirt that had fallen with the beam and called through an opening above.

"Kenny! Oh, Kenny!"

Her husband stopped tugging at the beam and listened.

Tito listened, too, straining his little pasteboard ears.

Then, very faintly, he heard something. It said, "Mother! Mother!"

Blyth Strange found that he could not make much headway trying to move the big beam. He would have to remove the fallen dirt and rocks first. His wife helped him. It was hard work, and they began to perspire. But Kenny was inside. And with him was Juanito. A shovel would have made things easier, but they had none and they couldn't wait to get one. The sun was gone, and it was getting darker and darker.

Finally, with great effort, Mr. Strange began to move the heavy beam. He had cleared a way that enabled him to drag the thing two or three feet. Then he put his head in the new opening and called, "Kenny! Kenny!"

Tito listened for the answer with all his ears.

"Yes, Daddy," Kenny's voice said. "We're right here. I think we can get through."

They came wriggling out of the dark, first Kenny and then Juanito. The mother and father were so happy to see them that they forgot to scold the boys for what they had done. Instead, Myrna Strange said, "Hurry, both of you. Juanito's mother and father will be wondering where he is, and Concha is waiting with supper for us. It'll be dark and we won't be able to find our painting things. Hurry, both of you."

"That's true," her husband said, "but we don't want to forget Tito, do we?"

They all turned around at once, for there was the tiny fellow about to be left on his stone.

"No, indeed," Myrna Strange said. "Tito saved you naughty boys! He stood on that rock and let us know where you were. We couldn't leave Tito. Here, take good care of him, Juanito."

"Thank you, I will," Juanito said.

Tito's little chest nearly burst with pride. It was the biggest moment of his life. Perhaps, he thought, as they hurried down the mountains in the dusk, he had saved Juanito and his little friend from starving to death locked in that horrible mining shaft. He had been on guard and had pointed the way for the rescuers.

Chapter 7

Cousins from the Country

Tito was standing in his flower pot again. High on the side of the patio wall he felt the cool December breeze blowing through his bushy whiskers and through his thatch of rebellious rabbit hair. Poor Tito's eyes were not so good now. Most of the paint had run down the sides of his face and he could scarcely see. His little painted coat, his girdle and shirt, his pants with the white buttons were getting worse and worse, too.

Yet the little fellow was not unhappy. Juanito and Kenny came and spoke to him affectionately almost every day. They would never forget how he had saved them from that mine by standing guard and letting Mr. and Mrs. Strange know where the boys were. Tito always liked to have people praise him, especially Juanito and Kenny, whom he loved.

In the courtyard Señor Pérez worked faithfully at his decorating. Christmas was not far away, and he wanted to get a good amount of pottery painted so that he might sell it and have money to invite his friends to his house for a celebration of the holidays.

One day Juanito came through the gate from the street and stood watching his father work for a long time. Tito watched too, but his eyes were dim. The father painted in silence. Finally he finished the bowl on which he was working and stood up to stretch the kink out of his back.

"Well, Juanito, what's my young man thinking about?"

The boy paused a moment before he answered. Then he said, "Tito's clothes are bad, papá. His eyes are almost washed out."

"Well, now, I'm not a tailor, son," the man said smiling. "And Tito is not exactly a doll."

Juanito put his hands in his pockets, thinking. A bird circled over the patio, perched on the corner of the stone wall near a spot where the plaster was falling, then flew away. A barefoot country man passed the gate with a huge pile of chicken coops on his back, all of them tied together and a chicken in each one. He called, "*Gallinas, pollos, pollitos!*" A woman passed, going the other way, with a wide round basket of fruit on her head: pomegranates, oranges, limes, melons, and bananas neatly piled on shiny greens to make them look pretty.

Juanito waited till she had passed before he spoke again to his father.

"Couldn't you paint Tito some new eyes and another coat and girdle and put some more buttons on his pants?"

"That's an idea," Señor Pérez said, turning. "Where is he? We'll dress him up for Christmas."

Juanito went to the wall, climbed up on a stone that jutted out and took the little bandit from his high flower pot.

Señor Pérez examined the small cardboard figure carefully, turning it over and over in his hand.

"Wouldn't you rather have me buy you a new toy?" he asked.

"No," Juanito said promptly. "I'd rather have you paint Tito some new clothes."

"Well, if that's your wish—of course, I haven't much time. But run along and play and meanwhile I'll see what I can do."

Juanito went to play with Kenny. They wandered through the town and found an old house that had grass growing in the cracks of the stones and at the corners of the roof. It was so old it had hardly any plaster left, but the house was still strong and the stone walls looked as if they would stand a good many more generations.

When they returned to Juanito's house late in the afternoon, they found Mr. and Mrs. Strange visiting in the courtyard, talking to Señor Pérez and watching him work. Tito was drying in the sun, dressed in new painted things from head to foot. He felt like a new person. His bright new eyes were round and shining, and he was finer looking than ever.

"Did you have a good walk?" Mrs. Strange said as the boys came through the gate.

"Yes, fine," Kenny told her. "Look at Tito."

"He is dressed up for Christmas," Juanito cried happily. "My papá, he did it. Look at Tito now—my banditito!"

Mr. and Mrs. Strange came and inspected him.

"Isn't he darling," said Mrs. Strange. "Just see how he stands there under that geranium. Wouldn't he make a cute picture, though? I think I'd like to paint him, Blyth, just as he is there, bright and brave."

Tito's little pasteboard chest filled with pride. Did this American lady mean she wanted to paint his picture? The picture of little Tito?

"He fell in the well and spoiled his clothes," said Señor Pérez, "so Juanito persuaded me to make him some new ones."

"We saw him before," Mr. Strange said. "But he did not look nearly so fine as he does now."

"May I take him home in that flower pot and paint him standing there under the geranium?" Mrs. Strange asked Juanito. "I'll take good care of him."

Juanito smiled and said yes.

"Thanks, so much. I'll borrow him after Christmas—and paint him life size, as big as a real man."

That was almost too much for Tito. He reeled, and nearly tumbled out of the flower pot. Life size! Like a real man! A picture of Tito by an artist! It was certainly worth waiting for to have this happen to you.

The afternoon passed and the Strange family had to be going home. Before they went, however, Señora Pérez left her cooking, came to the door wiping her hands on her apron and asked if the whole family would not come to celebrate Christmas with them. There would be Uncle Diego's family from the country, too, and they would break piñatas every night for nine nights at their *posadas*.

Mr. and Mrs. Strange and Kenny did not know what a piñata was, but all of them were eager to come to the Christmas fun, and to find out.

"We'd love to accept," said Mrs. Strange, standing at the gate.

"We'll expect you then," Juanito's mother said.

When the visitors left, it was time to lock the gate and go in to supper. Señor Pérez pulled the gates together and fastened them with a strong chain, as he always did at night, then put a prop against them for extra protection. Juanito took Tito down carefully and carried him into the house.

At the supper table the family talked about nothing but Christmas. Even Tito became excited and began to feel that he couldn't wait for the holidays to come.

"Never mind," Señor Pérez said to Juanito. "You will have to be patient. The *posadas* are still a week off."

But three nights later, when the gates were locked and propped, when the family was at the supper table eating enchiladas, Juanito heard a great banging beyond the patio and the voices of many children calling him.

Everybody got up and hurried through the courtyard.

"Hello," the voices called. "Hello, Juanito. Hello, Uncle Juan. Hello, Aunt Carmen. Hello, little Juan. Hello. Hello."

They unhooked the gates and let them swing open. There in the blue twilight stood Uncle Diego beside his faithful burro; with him were Aunt María, Grandma Lupe and Juanito's five cousins, Luana, Angelina, Carlos, Aurora and baby Paco, whom they often called Paquito. They had all made a long journey, but they were laughing and cheerful. They had come to visit their relatives in town and to stay till after Christmas.

"*Qué milagro! Qué milagro!* How wonderful," Señora Carmen kept saying.

The little crowd swept through the patio gate and filled the courtyard with the music of their voices and their laughter.

Little Tito, standing on the shelf in Juanito's room and hearing all the excitement, thought that Christmas had started already. Tito didn't know much about things like that, but he was happy, too.

Chapter 8

Nine Days Christmas

Juanito's mother told Kenny that there would be nine days of Christmas parties. She called them *posadas*. They would be held at the different houses of their friends, and the last one would be at Juanito's house on Christmas Eve. Kenny must be sure to come, he and his mother and father, she explained.

So the night before Christmas, Blyth and Myrna Strange and their son left their little red house that was neither large nor small and went out into the cool Mexican evening and up the rocky little streets of Taxco until they came to the Pérez home, where the soft sound of Christmas carols came floating out the gate to meet them. The Pérez family and all the children and the guests and their children were marching slowly around the courtyard, singing about the first Christmas in their high clear Indian voices.

"How beautiful!" said Myrna Strange, stopping at the entrance to the courtyard. Blyth Strange and Kenny stopped, too. The singers did not see them until they had finished their song.

Juanito saw them first and came running over to greet them. His father and mother followed him. And then all of Juanito's little cousins came to welcome the Americans who had come to their party. They were led into the courtyard and introduced to everybody.

There were dark young men, and lovely young brown girls in soft, bright-colored dresses, and old ladies, some in black silk waists with high collars, black shawls thrown about their shoulders or over their heads. There was a nice old man with a leather-brown face and a very white beard. Almost all of the grown-up guests had on shoes, but some wore sandals, and most of the children were barefooted, dancing happily about the patio.

But what most attracted Kenny's attention, and indeed that of his mother and father, too, was the large life-size figure of a jolly Mexican-doll character named Mamerto copied from the funny papers, a gay fat fellow here made of cardboard and tissue paper with a huge potlike stomach and enormous mustaches under his wide sombrero. An enormous doll, he was swinging overhead from a rope strung across the patio.

Juanito explained to Kenny why his stomach was so big—because it was made of a big round pottery jar, that was why, covered with a tissue paper shirt. And it was filled with good things, that stomach, gifts and fruits and nuts for children, so Juanito had told him. Later in the evening it would be broken.

"How do you like our piñata?" Señor Pérez asked.

Kenny was too interested to say a word, but his mother answered, "Why, I've never seen anything like it! It's the jolliest doll I've ever seen. But tell me, why is it hung so high up that nobody can reach it?"

"Wait," said Señor Pérez. "You will see."

Just then Uncle Diego, who had brought his guitar in with him from the country, began to play and sing. He sang a very long half-gay half-sad song with a great many verses, and everybody joined in the choruses, even little Juanito.

They sang several songs, and after that one of the little girls from the country recited a poem about selling flowers in the market place. Juanito said a poem, too. And then everybody began to call on the Americans to do something.

"Say your little verse for them, son," Blyth Strange told Kenny, "the funny one about the cow."

"It's not in Spanish," Kenny explained, but everyone said that made no difference. So he stood up and recited:

> I never saw a purple cow,
> I never hope to see one,
> But I can tell you, anyhow,
> I'd rather see than be one.

Everybody applauded and laughed as Kenny bowed. Then Blyth Strange borrowed Uncle Diego's guitar and began to play and sing:

> Oh, Susanna,
> Don't you cry for me,
> 'Cause I'm going out to Oregon
> With my banjo on my knee.

Then he and Myrna Strange sang together the old American song called "Listen to the Mocking Bird," which all the people at the party liked very much even if they didn't understand the words.

But it was getting late now and the children were all anxious to break the piñata, to see what was hidden inside the stomach of this gay fat fellow swinging in the evening breeze there in the center of the patio, his tissue paper arms waving, his blue legs dangling and blowing in the wind.

Kenny wondered how this ceremony that Juanito had told him so much about was to take place, but he did not have to wonder long. Amidst much laughing and joking, the chairs were moved back and plenty of room made in the center of the patio.

"Who wants to be the first to break the piñata?" Señor Pérez asked, as the guests grouped themselves against the wall.

"I do," said a tall young man stepping up. But everybody said no, he would never do! He was too tall, he could almost reach the piñata and pull it down.

Señor Pérez had a big white handkerchief in his hands, and when the first person was finally selected, a little girl named Luz, he put the handkerchief around her head and blindfolded her so that she couldn't see anything. Then he gave her the long pole that they used to prop the door shut every night.

"She must try to break the piñata with the stick while she is blind-folded," Señor Pérez explained to Blyth and Myrna Strange. "It's lots of fun watching people try to find Mamerto blindfolded."

Juanito and his cousins took the little girl by the arms and led her beneath the swinging figure, so that she could touch it with the pole when she waved it above her head.

"You see where Mamerto is?" they asked the little girl, laughing.

"I feel him," she said, poking him gently with the stick.

"Then find him again and try to break him open," they said slyly as they led her away toward a corner of the courtyard. There they turned her around and around until she didn't know what direction she was facing when they stopped. Then they just left her standing there blind-folded with the long stick in her hands.

"Try and find Mamerto now," everybody teased and laughed. "Where is he?"

"Here I come," said the little girl, as she advanced haltingly, step by step, waving the pole. But the funny thing was that she wasn't going toward the piñata at all. She was walking blindly right toward the people grouped near the sides of the house. Everybody scattered laughing.

"Watch out, or she'll drop the pole on you," everybody cried.

"Run, Kenny," Juanito yelled, laughing, "or she'll bring the stick down on your head."

The little girl, realizing she was going the wrong way, turned and went in another direction, walking slowly and waving her stick in the air, trying to find the tantalizing hanging figure that she wanted to break open.

"You're getting warm," somebody cried.

"There he is now, hit him," yelled Juanito.

The little girl brought her pole swishing through the air—but she didn't hit a thing! She was two or three yards away from the piñata, so everybody roared with laughter. She laughed too. And after one or two more trials, she gave up. When Señor Pérez untied the blindfold, she found that she had wandered way over by the well, and was nowhere near the gay funny little man whose clay shell of a stomach was full of gifts.

But she was good-natured about it and didn't mind that everyone laughed loudly.

The next to try his luck was a young cousin of Juanito's named Carlos. Once blindfolded, Carlos dashed madly toward what he thought was the piñata, and brought his stick slicing through the air with full force. But what he hit neither cracked, nor broke nor moved. He hit the wall!

Everyone screamed with laughter as he tore the bandage from his eyes to discover that he was standing with his back to the swinging doll and his face to the wall.

"Let Kenny try," everyone said.

"Yes," said Juanito and his father both at once. "Let Kenny have a chance at it."

So they blindfolded Kenny, gave him the long pole, and turned him around and around near the gate. Then they left him to find his way toward the piñata as best he could.

"Watch out! You'll fall in the well!" his father called, but Kenny knew Blyth Strange was only teasing him.

"You're near," Juanito yelled when Kenny kept getting farther and farther away.

"No, you're not," a little girl cried. "Don't believe Juanito."

Kenny was not sure which way to turn, but he kept searching step by step, his eyes blindfolded and his stick waving above his head.

People kept screaming and laughing and teasing. But Kenny noticed now that everyone was really excited, and shouting more than ever.

"You're warm!"

"You're near him!"

"Now, hit it!"

Kenny struck once blindly with the long stick. An excited scream went up. He realized that he had not missed the stuffed little man by much. He swung again. This time he felt the stick strike a tissue paper leg. He heard the paper tear, as everyone laughed and screamed in excitement.

"If I could only see," thought Kenny, "I'd split that piñata wide open. But I'm almost sure I'll hit it this time anyway."

He took the pole in both hands, leaned back with it raised above his head, and struck a furious blow through the air. And sure enough, he hit Mamerto squarely in the stomach! The swinging doll's fat clay girth broke into a hundred pieces, and all the gifts and fruits, candies and nuts, fell into the patio amidst the delighted shrieks of the onlookers.

Kenny tore off his blindfold just in time to see all the youngsters scrambling on the stone floor for the prizes that had fallen to earth.

Kenny began to scramble, too, on his hands and knees. Everybody was good-natured, laughing, and polite about it. And several children ran to their parents, or older brothers and sisters, to offer them handfuls of peanuts they had picked up, or an apple, or an orange; or to give them a little straw-horse to hold, or some other simple gift that had fallen from the now broken body of the piñata.

Kenny gave his mother a handful of candy and nuts he had gathered. And to his father he gave several pieces of sugarcane.

"Wasn't I lucky to be the one to break the piñata?" he asked proudly.

"You certainly were," said Blyth Strange. "How could you find it?"

"I couldn't see him," said Kenny, "but I felt him with the stick."

"I wouldn't say you *felt* him," said his father. "I'd say you socked him one."

Kenny laughed as he looked up at the cardboard head with the few strands of paper left hanging from it, that had once been Mamerto's body. On the ground lay the bits of cracked clay that had been his round fat stomach full of Christmas cheer.

The grown-ups were being served cakes and wine and pineapple juice now while the children still scampered about picking up peanuts or cuts of sugarcane that might have rolled into cracks and corners of the courtyard. But shortly it was time for the party to break up, and everyone began to say goodnight.

"What a delightful Christmas Eve," Myrna Strange said, as they went down the starlit street toward their house that was neither large nor small.

"Yes," her husband answered, "very jolly, indeed."

"A piñata's almost as good as a Christmas tree," Kenny said sleepily, "except that it hasn't got candles."

Chapter 9

All the Toys March

Juanito saw that things were not the same, but he couldn't imagine what had made the change. He was still lying on the floor where he had fallen asleep, but the other people had left the patio, and for some reason the courtyard was brighter than at midday. Something was wrong with Tito, too. He didn't look the same.

In a moment Juanito realized what the change had been. The little bandit was not clinching his fist in the air. He had his hands in his pockets, in fact! And as Juanito stared at him he began to smile behind his bushy rabbit-hair whiskers. For the first time Juanito saw his teeth.

Then—more astonishing still—he heard the little pasteboard fellow's voice. Tito spoke!

He said, "You're asleep, Juanito."

"Yes," Juanito answered. "People stayed so long and we played so hard I couldn't keep my eyes open any longer."

"I know. You were tired. It's a fine Christmas, though."

Just then another strange little voice spoke in the corner of the patio.

"You're right, Tito. I never thought it would be so grand."

Juanito looked up and saw a straw horse trotting across the courtyard with a little straw rider bouncing in his saddle. The rider swung himself to the ground and hooked his arm in the horse's bridle. He and Tito shook hands and laughed together. Juanito gave them each a handful of peanuts.

Now that the visitors were all gone, he thought he might just as well get his playthings together, so he began to walk around the well. Where was his new bank—the monkey on top of the cucumber?

He found the cucumber in a corner where one of his cousins had dropped it, but the monkey was gone. Juanito almost cried. Somebody must have broken the clay monkey off the cucumber bank.

"Don't worry," a gay voice called from a flower pot. "I'm all right, Juanito." And sure enough, there on the wall was the little brown monkey with his red cap.

"Well, don't forget where you belong," Juanito said, much relieved. "You're the most important part of the bank."

"I won't," the tiny monkey said. "But it is tiresome just sitting on a cucumber all the time."

"Oh, I don't mind if you run and play," Juanito said politely, "only I don't want to lose you."

Two or three pasteboard men who had fallen behind a chair got up and began brushing the dirt from their bright clothes.

"I wish there was something *we* could do," one of them said.

"Why not march around the well," Juanito suggested, "everybody."

The suggestion seemed to please them. Tito, and the straw rider of the straw horse and the monkey, came around and joined the others. A painted pig, very fat and funny, came waddling and grunting as fast as he could travel.

"I'm the leader," Juanito said. "Follow me."

All of them sang as they marched round and round the well, making fancy turns and figure eights. And just then Juanito noticed his father and mother in the doorway of the house, their backs against the light. Uncle Diego and all the youngsters were standing behind them smiling. Evidently they thought the parade was very amusing, for several times they laughed aloud. Then Juanito noticed his mother saying something, so he paused to hear what she said.

For some reason she did not mention the parade at all. Instead she said, "Poor child. He's so tired."

"Yes, he's had too much Christmas," his father said, looking down.

He came over and took Juanito in his arms, and the little fellow began to realize that his eyes were heavy and the patio was dark. "Perhaps," he thought, "perhaps I'm falling asleep!" Was that it? Or was he just waking up a little? Anyway, he was happy in his father's arms.

The man took him into the bedroom and in a few minutes Juanito was tucked under the covers, smiling.

"He must be dreaming," his mother said, as she kissed him goodnight and closed the door.

Chapter 10

Shooting in the Plaza

Another handful of days passed and many things happened.

Everywhere Kenny and Juanito walked in the village there were people selling flowers, baskets of orchids, handfuls of roses, armfuls of lilies, cart loads of pinks.

"It must be spring," Kenny said.

"Yes, nearly," Juanito answered. "But here we have flowers all the year round anyway."

A man came through the streets driving a flock of turkeys. The fowls were so glossy, their heads so red, they seemed to have been enameled. The turkeys trotted along tamely, a big herd of them, guided by the old man with a long stick.

Men sold ice cream in the street, rolling their small white wagons over the cobblestone roads; and almost every day the two boys got pennies from their fathers and bought little cones in front of the cathedral. Kenny was delighted because there were many new flavors like mamey, tamarind, and melon that he had never tasted before.

Some days they bought *buñuelos* instead, large wafflelike cakes with powdered sugar sprinkled over the top. They were more than a foot across, but when Kenny started eating them he found that they were just crust expanded by air and not really so big as they seemed.

"What is the next holiday?" Kenny asked.

"Easter," Juanito told him. "You'll like it. Easter is fun. Firecrackers and everything."

"I'll be glad of that. I've been feeling lonesome."

"That's because Tito's not here. He's so busy having his picture painted."

They both laughed. They did miss Tito from the patio. But, of course, it was fine to know he was being so highly honored by Kenny's parents.

Then a few days later some workers began suspending lights from tree to tree in the plaza. Shopkeepers began hanging out new decorations. Long paper streamers were tacked to the walls. Other people erected new booths on the square and on the side streets of the village. Some brought little charcoal stoves and set up food stands, stretching blankets overhead to protect themselves against the sun. Things were preparing to happen.

Here and there a firecracker popped. Many of the booths offered a variety of fireworks for sale, Roman candles, sparklers, giant crackers and the like. Some youngsters couldn't wait for the fiesta and lit a few of theirs ahead of time, but mostly the people were waiting for the Saturday before Easter to shoot off their fireworks.

On Good Friday the town became quiet. A steady stream of people went in and out of the cathedral. The next day the celebration became noisy.

Blyth and Myrna Strange left their painting for a few hours and came down the hillside to see the excitement. Kenny and Juanito met them in their smocks and berets walking arm in arm and seeming to enjoy the spectacle greatly. Then the boys lost the couple in the crowd. At another time they saw Señor Pérez and his wife entering the cathedral. But they did not follow this pair either because of the crowds.

The air was burdened with the odors of foods frying or steaming or boiling on little charcoal stoves: *buñuelos,* tacos, tamales, enchiladas. Candy lay in pretty displays on counter after counter in the open air: fudge, taffy and candied fruits—oranges, sweet limes, sliced pineapple, pears. And now more and more children were lighting little firecrackers.

Kenny and Juanito walked till their legs were tired.

"They're going to burn Judases pretty soon," Juanito said.

"What's that like?"

"Well, they're pasteboard Judases they burn. Something like Tito only big as a real man, with lots of different shapes, sometimes a cowboy, sometimes a clown, or a fat man, or a lady, all covered with firecrackers. They hang them up in the trees or in front of the shops and light the firecrackers, and they all go off and the Judas is burnt up."

"We'll see that, won't we?"

"Yes, by and by."

They walked around the plaza again, when suddenly they heard a loud burst of explosions, a whole series of explosions right in front of them. Boom-boom-boom-boom-boom-boom! A cloud of smoke arose amidst the trees and people started suddenly to run in all directions. The noise was just on the other side of the square. What could it be, so sudden and so loud?

The boys were both frightened. Where were their mothers and fathers now? Hadn't they better start toward home? People were running every which way. Someone knocked over a basket of fruit. A young woman spilled a pail of pineapple juice that she had been selling. An old man bumped into a counter and tipped over a tray of candied pumpkin. Everybody was running.

"Are they burning Judas?" Kenny asked as he ran.

"No, no," Juanito answered. "I don't know what this is. It sounds like trouble! Like a revolution! Shooting is dangerous. We'd better get home."

Down the street they went. At the first corner they turned and dashed up a hill to a narrow cobblestone lane. Down a block and then up again. Still they could hear that frightful boom-boom-boom-boom, a great roaring and crackling, like a war. They were both out of breath when they reached Juanito's house and sat down to rest in the patio.

Señor Pérez and his wife came home about an hour later.

"Didn't you boys see them burn Judas?" Juanito's mother said.

The youngsters shook their heads.

"We left when the shooting began," Kenny said. "We didn't want to get hurt."

"The shooting!" Señor Pérez said as the two older people began laughing. "That's good! So you thought it was shooting, did you?"

"What was it?" Juanito asked.

His father was laughing so hard he couldn't explain. Señora Pérez had to tell them what had happened to cause the excitement. A firecracker booth had caught on fire and all the giant crackers and little crackers and Roman candles and fire-wheels had all gone off at once, causing a great commotion in the plaza. Nobody was hurt, but a good many other people had evidently thought it was shooting, too, but perhaps they had not run so far before they learned their mistake.

"That's too bad," Kenny said.

"Why?"

"Well, we didn't get to see them burn Judas."

"No," Señor Pérez said, still laughing. "But you heard the shooting. Isn't that enough for one day?"

"We heard it running," Juanito said.

Chapter 11

Serenade

The fiesta lasted for several days after Easter, and often in the evening musicians played in the plaza. Juanito's father brought his guitar and joined four or five friends who had brought their instruments, too: violins, guitars, and a cello. In the starry night you could hear them up to the very tops of the hills that surrounded the town.

Juanito sat with his mother in the patio tonight.

"It's been a long time since we had such music in the plaza," the woman said. "When your father was young he was always playing his guitar like that. He used to come and serenade me beneath my window."

"I hope Kenny and Tito hear the music," Juanito answered.

"Of course they do, if they are not too busy packing up. Tomorrow they go away."

"Don't you think it would be nice if the musicians serenaded them tonight then," Juanito asked, "if Papá and the others went to play beneath their windows?"

"It's just the thing, Juanito," she said. "Let's go ask Papá."

"All right. I want to see Tito's picture, too, if we go to the house."

"Of course we will. We must tell Mr. and Mrs. Strange good-bye."

She drew her shawl tighter around her shoulders and wrapped one end about her neck and head as they went through the patio, opened the gate, and hurried down the steep street.

They walked very quietly through the dusk, but they lost no time. Their bare feet slapped the cobblestones briskly with every stride.

Soon they were passing the booths and shops of the plaza. Food was still frying on the charcoal stoves. The displays of candy were not all gone, and there were even a few fragrant flowers left in the baskets. The vendors were offering them very cheaply, now that evening had come.

"We'll carry some flowers," Señora Carmen said.

"That will be fine," Juanito murmured.

They crossed the plaza toward the cathedral. A circle of people had surrounded the musicians, crowding as close as they could get to them. Juanito and his mother waited for their song to end. Then they pushed up to Señor Pérez and whispered in his ear.

"Listen, Papá. Mr. and Mrs. Strange and Kenny are packing up tonight to leave Taxco. Couldn't you have the musicians come serenade them after they have finished playing here?"

"I'll ask the men," he whispered. "I'm sure they'd be glad to do it."

He went to each of the players, speaking softly. Then when he had spoken to all, including the cellist who stood at the far end of the group, he returned to his wife and Juanito.

"They say they'll be happy to do it," he said. "Will you both come?"

"We'll go along ahead if you don't mind. We want to see the painting of Tito Mrs. Strange has made. And we are going to carry her some flowers."

Señor Pérez thought that was a fine idea, so he slipped some pennies into Juanito's hand and a few brighter coins into the hand of his wife. By that time the musicians were ready to play another song. Juanito and his mother left the group and walked around the plaza looking for flowers that pleased them.

The night was warm and starry and full of music. And the little flares that lighted the street stands sometimes looked like twinkling stars that had fallen down to earth.

Juanito filled his arms with carnations and his mother bought a basket of yellow roses at the corner of the plaza. A few minutes later they knocked at the door of Kenny's house and Concha let them in.

Everything was topsy-turvy. Suitcases were lying open in the middle of the floor. There were two enormous bags that had been packed but not locked. There was a box of painting materials and a stack of pictures ready to be packed.

Juanito and Kenny sat together on a box kicking their feet against the sides. The older people told each other how much they hated to part, and the Stranges kept saying they liked Taxco and did not wish to leave. Mrs. Strange put her face in the basket of roses, trying to take in all their sweetness at once. Her husband pinned a carnation in his wife's hair and one in the glossy black coils of the Mexican women, Concha and Señora Pérez.

After a while Juanito's mother said, "We were anxious to see your picture of Tito."

"Oh, I must show it to you," Mrs. Strange cried. "Dear, brave little Tito."

She looked through her canvases quickly and brought out a frame about four feet high. She placed it on a chair in the far corner of the room and turned the light so that it would show the picture as well as possible. There painted in oils as big as a real man stood the pasteboard bandit! His rabbit whiskers bristled magnificently. His little fist was raised as if to strike. His huge sombrero sat proudly on the back of his head. His startled eyes were as round as saucers. Everybody looked at it with admiration, saying nothing. It was a fine picture of Tito, bright and beautiful, and very jolly.

In the corner of the room, however, standing beside the red geranium in his flower pot, Tito thought of himself and imagined things that none of the others could possibly imagine. Sometimes, when he was very, very happy, he was inclined to think that he'd rather be a tiny pasteboard bandit than a real man. And that is what he was thinking tonight, having had his portrait painted, and such a fuss made over him.

"It's a wonderful picture," Juanito said.

"We have fallen in love with Tito," Mr. Strange said. "We can scarcely bear the thought of leaving him when we go."

"He is yours," Juanito said quickly. "I want Kenny to have him. Maybe—how do you say it?"

"Oh, I know what you mean," Mrs. Strange said. "You mean he'll make us think of you. Isn't that it?"

Juanito was too shy to say any more. He bowed his head.

"Thank you," Kenny said in Spanish, "*Muchas gracias,* Juanito."

Just then there was a burst of music in the street outside. Everyone paused a moment. Then the American family realized that they were being serenaded, and they all ran to the windows and out onto the balcony to listen.

There in the steep cobblestoned little street stood five or six Mexicans, their serapes thrown over their shoulders, their clothes very white in the soft darkness. Their heads were back and the sweetest of music came from their instruments as their voices were lifted in song, an old, old Mexican song.

When the singing ceased, Myrna Strange exclaimed, "How beautiful!" Then she threw them a rose, a rose for each man.

They played and sang several more songs there in the street.

Then the Americans invited the men in and offered them refreshments. For the third time everybody began to say how sad it was to part, and how much Taxco would miss them, as Juanito and Kenny sat on a box drinking fruit juice from large earthen mugs and kicking their feet against the sides. Tito stood beside them, looking across the room at his picture.

The next morning Kenny and his mother and father caught the bus in front of the cathedral. Their bags were piled on top, and they went away, waving good-bye from the windows.

"*Adiós!*" Juanito shouted as the bus departed. "*Adiós,* Kenny! *Adiós!*"

Chapter 12

Washington Square

The bus carried the Strange family to Mexico City. There they caught a train. Throughout the journey Tito stood at the car window and looked out. He had never traveled before and everything he saw was new and wonderful. In one field there was a loaded ox cart, in another a group of children chasing butterflies. On a country road a man was carrying a bag of charcoal bigger than himself, and in a tiny crumbling village a little girl was sliding down a stone banister as the train whizzed by.

Tito noticed that the country was mostly mountainous, with dizzy slopes, deep valleys and high peaks. He noticed that the train skirted many towns rather than going through them, and this deprived him of some of the sights. Yet he did see a few villages close up. He got a good look at the narrow streets, the high adobe walls, and the flower pots in tall grilled windows. It was a great experience for little Tito, who had never known any town but Taxco.

Whenever the train passed a village station, he saw country people lined up along the tracks. Some were sitting on horses. Some waved their big sombreros. All of them seemed happy watching the train. But what little Tito thought was that they had all come down to the tracks just to see him!

Poor little Tito, he had been praised so much since he saved the boys from the mine! He had been so flattered by having his picture painted as big as a real man that he thought all this waving of hats and serapes was just for him. He clinched his fist as tight as he could. Was he making a good impression? Of course he was!

At mealtime the train usually stopped and the passengers got out to stroll along the platform and buy tamales, enchiladas, or tacos. Some of the travelers sat down on little stools and ordered dinners at the out-of-doors tables beside the tracks when they had time.

There was much to see and Tito's bright little eyes missed nothing on the road till finally one afternoon, while Kenny was asleep, Mrs. Strange decided that the small pasteboard man had been at the window quite long enough. He was getting all dusty so she took him and tucked him away in a suitcase. That ended his fun, and the rest of the journey was hot and tiresome.

When the train crossed the border at Laredo and entered the United

States, a customs officer opened the suitcase, and Tito thought for a moment that he was going to get out. But the man only unwrapped the paper enough to take one peep at the little bandit. Then he put him back in his place and locked the suitcase.

Tito didn't know how many days passed. But when he saw daylight again, he was in New York. Kenny and his mother and father were in their big studio on Washington Square with a circle of friends. Many strangers took Tito in their hands and admired his bushy whiskers and his bright clothes, as they talked about Mexico.

The next day Kenny carried the little fellow to the front window and stood him where he could look down on the Square. Later Tito heard the boy's feet on the stairs. He wondered where Kenny was going. In the street below there were many cars and taxicabs and trucks. On the sidewalks there were many people passing. In the Square there were pigeons near the fountain and children on the walks and old people on the benches. It was almost like a Mexican plaza, except busier, and there were no palm trees.

Suddenly Tito saw a familiar boy on a scooter. The boy stopped at the fountain and looked up at the window where Tito stood. He waved his hand. Yes, it was Kenny! Tito felt perfectly happy.

He knew that he would never get tired of looking out of that window with so many people below, with so many things to watch. But he couldn't help wishing that Juanito, too, had been there among the youngsters in the Square. It was really too bad that Taxco was so far from New York, he thought. And in another country, that you had to cross mountains and rivers to reach.

But one day Tito heard Blyth and Myrna Strange tell Kenny that they were going to publish a book about Mexico and put the big painting of him, Tito, in it in full colors.

"And I'll send the book to Juanito," Kenny said, "for a present."

As Tito heard this he could have laughed for joy, except that a little pasteboard bandit cannot laugh—that is, not out loud. So he just remained quiet and smiled to himself.

Once Kenny thought he caught him smiling, but then he noticed that the window was open a little and the wind just seemed to be tickling his mustache.

"Good old Tito!" Kenny said, picking him up. "Maybe next year we'll go back to Mexico again—all the way to Taxco to see our friend Juanito. How would you like that, heh?"

"Fine," Tito said—to himself.

"First" Books

The First Book of Negroes

(1952)

For advice and helpful guidance in the preparation of this book, the writer is especially grateful to Arna Bontemps, author of *Story of the Negro;* Charlemae Rollins, Children's Librarian at the Hall Branch Library in Chicago; Ellen Tarry, author of *Hezekiah Horton;* and to Mary Bird Piel, Librarian of City and Country School in Manhattan.

A Brave Explorer

A black man in faded knee pants and a velvet hat that had once had a sweeping plume in it stood on a high mesa in the blazing sun and looked across a golden desert. In the distance were only purple mountains. But the man Estevan, called by his friends Estevanico, was looking for the Seven Cities of the Indians that he had heard were built of gold. The Indians who guided him into the Southwest simply shrugged their shoulders, wondering what this strange man was seeking and why he had come into this desert country.

Estevanico, whose Spanish nickname meant Kid Steve, was a strong, very dark Negro born in Morocco. He became an explorer, fearless and full of the spirit of adventure. More than four hundred years ago he sailed from Spain in a group of five hundred men seeking new lands beyond the seas. They landed on the coast of Florida where hostile Indians and strange diseases killed half of them in less than three months. They set sail again. This time their ship was wrecked on the Florida reefs, and only the Negro, Estevanico, and three Spaniards escaped death. All the rest were drowned.

For more than eight years these four men wandered across the country living with the Indians. Estevanico learned to speak many Indian languages and so became very helpful as a guide. He traveled as far south as Mexico City where he entered the service of the Spanish Viceroy. But he did not like to stay in one place long. When in 1539 Friar Marcos de Niza organized an expedition to search for the fabulous Seven Cities of Cibola, which no white man had ever seen, Estevanico joined the expedition, and they set out northward over the mountains and across the plains of what is now the state of Texas.

The summer was very hot, and before it was over the good Friar Marcos and his Spanish companions were near exhaustion. They asked Estevanico if he would go ahead with a group of Indian runners. If he found rich lands or golden cities beyond the horizon, they told him to send back word and they would join him. Since the Indian runners could not speak Spanish, Estevanico worked out a simple code for his messages. He told Friar Marcos that he would send back a cross every few days to indicate by its size how far he had gone and the importance of what he had found. If he had no news to report and had made no interesting discoveries, he would send back a little wooden cross the size of the palm of the hand which he would make from a couple of twigs. But if he found rich cities or rare treasures, he would cut from a tree larger boughs and send back a bigger cross, as a message of success.

At first the Indian runners brought back to the camp of the Spaniards only very small crosses, for Estevanico was traveling across a rough and dangerous land where nobody lived. Heat, sand flies, mountain lions, chill nights, and blazing days slowed his progress. Coyotes howled and grizzly bears scooted up the rocky passes. On the prairies there were a great many snakes. Sometimes a blue racer darted across his path, or a diamondback rattled in an angry coil. Sometimes a herd of buffalo thundered across the dry earth in a cloud of dust. Gophers and horned toads scrambled into their holes. Vultures and eagles soared overhead. But Estevanico kept on across the sands, beyond the purple mountains, searching for the gold and treasures of the rich land he hoped was just ahead. Meanwhile, in their encampment the Spaniards waited.

One day two Indians, sweating and tired, staggered into camp with a cross as tall as a man. Then Estevanico's fellow explorers knew that he had found somewhere in the desert a wonderful land. Perhaps he had found even the Seven Cities of Cibola! Quickly the Spaniards broke camp to follow the Indian runners toward the new country which the Negro explorer, Estevanico, had discovered for them.

The Spaniards did not find any golden cities, but they did find great Indian pueblos with houses made of stone, sometimes as high as four stories, whose doorways were decorated with gleaming turquoise. And they found what is now the American state of Arizona—a rich and beautiful country of mountains, desert, gold, copper, cotton, and flowers. Friar Marcos followed the trail of the crosses, but he never did see Estevanico again. The Zuñi Indians had killed him outside the walls of Hawaikuh. The Indians had become fearful that other strangers might follow Estevanico into their land and take it away from them. And that is exactly what happened in the end. The Spaniards claimed it in the name of the King of Spain, and it became a part of the New World—now Arizona and New Mexico—discovered by Estevanico, a Negro.

Songs of Freedom: The Spirituals

Eighty years after Estevanico blazed the trail to Arizona, a Dutch sailing ship dropped anchor in the harbor at Jamestown, Virginia. It brought from Africa a cargo of men and women, who were sold as slaves to the planters. Other ships from England and elsewhere brought to the New World white men and women to work as slaves, too. These were called "indentured servants." Most of them were people who had been in some kind of trouble in the Old World. Maybe they had a debt they could not pay and had been fined by a court. So they had to work for nothing until they had paid the fines and bought their freedom.

But most of the slaves in America were black men and women. Soon it became a very profitable business to capture Africans and bring them to our shores to sell. Because the Africans had only spears or bows and arrows for defending themselves, it was easy for slave dealers to force them into the holds of ships, chain them, and sail away across the Western Ocean. In America the Africans were sold to work on rice, sugar, and cotton plantations all the rest of their lives for nothing.

Not only did these slaves toil in the fields, but some became fine builders, brick masons, carpenters, and ironsmiths. Most of the beautiful wrought-iron balconies and grilles in old New Orleans, Charleston, and other lovely cities in the South were made a long time ago by Negro ironworkers who were slaves. Slavery lasted almost two hundred and fifty years.

When Abraham Lincoln declared slavery ended, there were about four million colored people in the United States. Not all of them were in bondage, for some had run away, some had bought their freedom, and some were born free. But most of them were slaves until the Civil War. Then more than two hundred thousand colored soldiers fought for their freedom in the Union Armies. The day when freedom came in 1863 was called Emancipation Day. Freedom! For a long time the Negroes had sung a song:

> Oh, Freedom!
> Freedom over me!
> Before I'd be a slave
> I'd be buried in my grave
> And go home to my Lord
> And be free!

This was a song the slaves made up, but they would be beaten if they were caught singing it. They made many such songs called "spirituals." One was based on a Bible story about the Hebrew people in an ancient land, but the song was really a song about American slaves wanting to be free.

Go down, Moses,
Way down in Egypt land,
And tell old Pharaoh
To let my people go!

Now people everywhere love these songs because they are so beautiful and because they are about hope and freedom.

Negroes in America Long Ago

The first highway from the Atlantic to the Pacific was built by Negroes and Indians under Balboa's direction.

History says that thirty Negroes were with Balboa when he discovered the Pacific Ocean in 1513.

Some say that when America was discovered one of the pilots with Columbus, Pedro Alonso Niño, was a colored man.

The first wheat in the New World was planted by a black man who came into Mexico with Cortez.

A Little Boy in a Big City

Terry Lane is a little boy whose skin is brown as a walnut and whose hair is black and beautifully crinkly. He lives in Harlem, a section of New York City where many colored people live. It has been the home of famous folks like Joe Louis, world champion boxer; Adam Powell, pastor of the largest Baptist Church in the world and a member of Congress; and of many musicians like Duke Ellington, maker of happy music.

Terry does not know these famous men, but he knows the "A" train on the subway, about which Duke Ellington wrote a song. The "A" train rushes full speed underground through a long tunnel. Sometimes Terry's father and mother take him downtown on the subway to Broadway or Radio City where some of the tallest buildings in the world are. They take Terry to a show or into a fine restaurant or to see the ice skating at Rockefeller Plaza.

If Terry lived in the South where his great-grandfather was once a slave, he could not go into a downtown theater or restaurant, since it is against the law in Southern cities for colored people to sit next to white people or eat with them in public. Negroes must ride on the back seats of busses and streetcars, and they must sit in a separate train coach unless they are rich enough to afford a Pullman. This is legal segregation, but Negroes call it "Jim Crow," and they do not believe it is legal because it does not follow our Constitution or the Declaration of Independence which says all men are free and equal.

Such divisions of the races in the South come from the time when Negroes were slaves and white people were free. Now the division lies in what people can do and where they can go. There are many things in the South Negroes are not permitted to do. For example, in many towns a Negro cannot read a book at the public library, and if he is sent there on an errand he must go in the back door. This is true of railroad and bus stations, too, where the entrances to the barren rooms set apart for Negroes are usually at the back or on the side.

If Terry lived in the South he could not go to school with white children, nor could they go to school with him. That is one reason why Terry's father and mother prefer to live in New York where children go to any school. Some of Terry's teachers are white and some are colored. Some of his classmates are white and others are as brown as Terry. Some are Puerto Ricans who are just now learning English, since their island home once belonged to Spain and they spoke Spanish. But all of these children are good friends, learning and playing together.

Perhaps Terry's great-great-grandfather was an explorer who came to America from Portugal or Spain. Perhaps Terry's great-great-grandmother was an Indian who married an explorer. Maybe another great-great-grandfather was a slave, perhaps another was a free Negro. Like most Americans, Terry's ancestors had the blood of many races in their veins.

African Negroes are almost all very dark people, handsome in their blackness, but American Negroes are of many colors. Some American Negroes are ebony, some a warm cinnamon brown, some tan, some the color of ginger, others golden as peaches, and some are the color of ivory. Some are coffee-and-cream. There is a reason for such differences in color. A long time ago the Indians, the French in Louisiana, the Spanish, the Negroes from Africa, and people from many other countries met in the New World and their children's children became the American Negroes of many colors and types today.

Grandmother's Stories

Terry's grandmother grew up in the South. She remembers a great many funny rhymes and stories she heard there when she was a child. Some of them are about animals:

> A sheep and a goat
> Went a-walkin' through de pasture.
> Said de sheep to de goat,
> "Can't you walk a little faster?"
> Said de goat to de sheep,
> "My foot am sore."
> "Oh, 'scuse me goat,
> I did not know your foot am sore."

Sometimes Terry begs his grandmother to recite:

> What a wonderful bird the frog are!
> When he sit he stand almost,
> When he hop he fly almost.
> He ain't got no sense hardly.
> He ain't got no tail hardly neither
> Where he sit almost.

Terry's grandmother graduated from Fisk University, so she does not say "ain't," or use bad grammar, except when she is reciting folk poems or telling stories, like the one about the old man on a farm who sent his son out early one frosty morning to hitch up the mule.

The boy came back and said, "Pa, when I went to put the harness on our mule, I said, 'Get over, John!' And, you know that mule answered me back and said, 'What do you mean, "Get over, John?"'"

The old man said, "Son, you're just imagining things. You know my mule can't talk."

So the old man himself went out to hitch up the mule. When he got inside the stable, he said, "Get over, John!"

But the mule just rolled his eyes and said, "Here you come, talking about 'Get over, John!'"

This frightened the old man so badly that he lit out running lickety-split. Just as he got to the kitchen door, he ran over the cat. The cat jumped up and cried, "What do you want to step on me for?" This scared the old man more than ever, so he kept on through the house, out the front door, and down the road as fast as he could toward town. Finally he could run no longer, so he sat down beside the road. His little dog, who was right behind him also sat down.

The old man said, "I'm tired."

The little dog said, "Me, too!"

Terry always wanted to know what the old man did then. His grandmother says, "I don't know. It is only a story and that is the end."

So Terry says, "Tell me another one."

His grandmother says, "Say 'please,' young man!"

"Please, tell me another one."

The Kings of History

Sometimes Terry's grandmother tells him true stories out of history about the brown kings and queens in ancient lands. She says the Queen of Sheba, whom King Solomon loved, was an Ethiopian. She read to Terry from the Bible how Sheba "came to Jerusalem with a very great train, with camels that bore spices and much gold and precious stones. . . . And she gave the King a hundred and twenty talents of gold, and of spices a very great store, and precious stones. . . . the Queen of Sheba gave to King Solomon." From the Song of Solomon she read, " 'I am black but comely, O ye daughters of Jerusalem,' " to show Terry that black people were well known in Biblical times.

Certainly two thousand years before Christ was born Ethiopia had a civilization famous throughout the world—great writers, men who studied the stars, and kings who loved music and painting. This civilization spread into Egypt where brown-skinned Pharaohs were building gigantic pyramids, and where they carved out of stone an enormous figure, half-animal, half-human, called the "Sphinx," still there today, its paws stretched out in the dry sweep of desert sand.

Besides Egypt, there were other great kingdoms in Africa, too, such as Mandingo, Ghana, and Songhay. Timbuktu, in West Africa, more than four hundred years ago had a great school called the University of Sankoré, where scholars from all over the ancient world came to study medicine, geography, literature, or law. It was the Africans who first learned how to smelt iron, and from Africa the results of their learning traveled to Europe.

Historians know that civilization flows in great streams. One great stream started in Africa, then traveled northward into Europe. It did not flow south all over the African continent because there were strong barriers—great rivers, deserts, mountains, and jungles. Later, when the Europeans began to go all over the world with new inventions and scientific knowledge, they were until recently more interested in conquering people than in teaching them. So, many Africans have not yet learned to build factories or make gunpowder, but have remained hunters, fishermen, herders of cattle, and farmers.

The shortest men in the world and the tallest men in the world live in Africa. The short men, called Pygmies, inhabit the heart of the jungle. The tall men are of the Watusi tribe of the plains and hills. They are giants over seven feet tall. They are very great athletes, running, jumping, and dancing from early childhood. Some of them can leap with ease over a bar that is at least eight feet high.

The Watusi raise cattle with very long horns. These tall night-dark men and women dress in beautiful garments of hand-woven cloth. They also use the soft furry skin of the leopard, the panther, and the antelope for clothing. When they have dances, they wear lions' manes on their heads and bracelets made of little bells on their ankles. At their fairs, they adorn their beautiful cattle in wreaths of flowers and ornaments of shells.

In Africa there are long wide rivers: the Nile, the Niger, and the Congo. Along their banks live many different peoples, speaking different languages and dressing differently—farmers, pottery makers, basket weavers, artists, wood carvers, seamen, students, lion hunters, dancers. In the big cities and in the port towns now many people dress as Americans do, but in the heart of Africa, where it is very hot, people wear almost no clothes at all. In some parts of Africa there is as yet no written language, and messages are sent from village to village by drum beats that can be heard for miles. But in large cities like Accra and Lagos, today Africans are publishing their own newspapers, presiding as judges in the courts, and helping to run their local governments.

Large portions of Africa are governed by European countries. But Ethiopia is an independent country ruled by an emperor, Haile Selassie. And Liberia is a republic founded over a hundred years ago by American Negroes. Liberia, with its rich iron-ore mines and large rubber plantations, has many business relations with our country. Liberia and America are friends.

Negroes around the World

From Africa long ago Negroes came not only to North America but to the palm tree islands of the West Indies and to South America. With them they brought their songs, their dances, and their drums. Throughout the Caribbean, on islands such as Cuba and Haiti, drums are played by hand much as in Africa. The tall drum that stands alone is called a "Congo drum." The little double drums held between the knees are "bongos." In the West Indies, as in Africa, drums are still sometimes used for sending messages, as well as for dancing and religious ceremonies.

Some of the islands in the West Indies have had a very exciting history—a history of pirates, explorers, invading armies, and revolutionists. The slaves of Haiti freed themselves long before American slaves were freed. They freed their country from the French and eventually set up the first Negro republic in the world.

History tells us that the French planters in Haiti had been very cruel to their Negro slaves, working them sixteen hours a day. They thought it was cheaper to work a young slave to death than to allow him to get old and have to feed him when he was too aged to work. The planters gave their slaves very little to eat, so bands of hungry field hands took to roving the hills at night like animals in search of food. These slaves grew to hate their masters. So when an old coachman named Toussaint L'Ouverture decided to lead them to revolt, they did not mind dying for "the cause that makes all men brothers—freedom." They set fire to the cane fields and burned the mansions of their masters. From Europe Napoleon sent an army to crush them, but the slaves fought with sticks, stones, and pickaxes until they had captured enough guns to make an army of their own. Napoleon sent gunboats and heavy artillery. But the slaves put their arms into the very mouths of the French cannons to try to pull the cannon balls out. Of course, they were blown to bits, but hundreds of others rushed up to take the cannons away from the French and use them to drive their former masters out of Haiti forever. Thus they were freed.

At first they had an emperor named Dessalines, then a king, Christophe, and then they chose their first president. But the noble old coachman, Toussaint, who had been their leader, before the revolt was over had been lured into a French gunboat under the promise of peace, then seized, chained, and taken off to France to die there in a cold cell far from the palm trees of his native land.

After the French had gone, the Haitians under King Christophe built a mighty fortress on top of Monte Ferrière overlooking the harbor of Cap-Haitien. This fortress, called the Citadel, "the first wonder of liberty," still stands today after more than one hundred years. For its walls men had to drag each stone up the steep mountain trail. It took weeks to pull the three hundred heavy cannons up the sides of the mountain. But when the Citadel was finished, with its great arches and deep underground corridors, it could house fifteen thousand soldiers and stock enough supplies for a year. Today it is a very beautiful building rising like the prow of a ship from a mountain peak sometimes hidden by clouds. It is a monument to all the slaves who once turned Haiti into a battleground for freedom where Toussaint, the gentle old coachman, dropped the reins of his carriage to become a warrior.

A Negro Saint

In South America an even gentler Negro lived almost two hundred years before Toussaint. He will be remembered forever as Blessed Martin de Porres. Born in Lima, Peru, in 1579, little Martin was baptized a Catholic in the Church of San Sebastian by the same priest who baptized South America's first saint, Saint Rose of Lima. As a boy the brown-skinned Martin was, like Saint Francis, so kind to the little creatures of the earth, birds and animals, and so helpful to the sick and the poor, that the good fathers of the church took an interest in him. When Martin de Porres grew to be a man, he became a Dominican lay brother and devoted his life to healing and helping people. He could not bear to kill any living creature. In the monastery where he lived, instead of setting a trap for mice, Martin fed them.

This kind Negro brother became so famous for the sympathy and understanding that he had for all the troubles of men that, when he died, pilgrims came from all over Peru to pray at his shrine. The Catholic Church declared Martin de Porres blessed, and today all over the world there are churches, hospitals, and schools named after this good Dominican of old Peru, whom people think of as a saint.

In most of South America little, if any, distinction is made between peoples because of color. White and black people live in the same houses and their children go together to school. Negroes are in more governmental positions in South America than in North America. In South American history many Negroes have become famous. Today a large number of colored people live in Venezuela, Uruguay, and Brazil. Sometimes a Brazilian naval cruiser comes into a North American port on a Good Neighbor visit. Then we see fine-looking Negro officers serving along with white ones, and dark sailors who do not speak English, visiting our shores. Brazil has no separate white and colored units in the army or navy.

The Brazilians speak Portuguese. In Cuba, Negroes speak Spanish. In the Caribbean island of Martinique they speak French. Along the coast of the Gulf of Mexico in Yucatan and Vera Cruz, Negroes now speak the Indian languages. On the Black Sea in Russia there is a settlement made up of the descendants of slaves who escaped long ago from the Turks. These Negroes speak Russian. Guiana Negroes speak Dutch.

American Negroes

Outside of Africa, there are more Negroes in the United States than in any country in the world. Our country has fifteen million colored citizens—more people, for example, than there are in Australia, Denmark, Israel, or Ireland.

The Negro citizens of the United States have many beautiful schools and churches, hotels, large newspapers, and businesses. This was not always true, for, when freedom came to them, less than a hundred years ago, most Negroes did not own anything. In slavery they were paid no wages and had no chance to acquire property. Starting with nothing, the Negro people have worked very hard to buy the homes and buildings they own today.

Booker T. Washington, who built a great school in Alabama, worked as a young boy in a coal mine. One day he quit and walked more than fifty miles to a school for Negroes and Indians in Virginia called Hampton, but he had no money to pay for an education when he got there. The New England white woman who ran the school said, "Let me see how well you can clean a classroom." She gave Booker T. a broom, a mop, a pail, and a dust-cloth and left him alone in the room. When she returned, it was so spotlessly clean that she rubbed her white handkerchief around the corners of the room and her handkerchief was still white! She told Booker T., "I will admit you to the school."

When he graduated he founded his own school, Tuskegee Institute, to teach all sorts of trades, such as carpentry, brickmasonry, printing, horseshoeing, and farming. It was one of the first schools for practical education in America, and people came from all over the world to study its system and to build schools like it in their own countries. Booker T. Washington became a great leader and speaker and wrote a famous book called *Up from Slavery.* He was a friend of President Theodore Roosevelt, who invited him to dinner at the White House, in Washington.

Another great man who was born a slave was Dr. George Washington Carver. He had a laboratory at Tuskegee. From the red clay of Alabama he made paints, and from the peanuts that grew there he made peanut oil, peanut milk, cheese, face cream, liniment, dyes, and many other things that had never been made from peanuts before. He used only things growing around him. From cornstalks, Dr. Carver made wallboard for houses, and from sweet potatoes he made flour, rope, and rubber.

His science was called chemurgy, which means chemistry at work, and his laboratory became famous throughout the world. Yet, when he went traveling about his country to make speeches, there were many hotels where he was not allowed to stay because Dr. Carver was a Negro. But his great discoveries he gave to America out of love, not for profit.

Another Negro whose name is known everywhere today and whose grandparents were slaves is Dr. Ralph Bunche. He was the man who brought peace in a bitter war between the Arabs and the Jews in the land of Palestine now called Israel. At the skyscraper United Nations headquarters in New York Dr. Bunche is in charge of all the problems relating to colonial countries ruled by people who do not live in them, such as Nigeria in Africa, which is governed by the English who live far away. In 1950 a famous honor, the Nobel Peace Prize, was awarded to the American Negro, Ralph Bunche. Terry's father tells him that he must study hard so he can grow up to be a wise and helpful man like Dr. Bunche, of service to his country.

Famous American Negroes

Frederick Douglass was a slave who ran away to freedom and became a great orator, newspaper publisher, writer, and the United States Minister to Haiti.

Paul Laurence Dunbar was an American poet born in Ohio, the son of slaves. He became world famous for the charm and humor of his verses.

Thurgood Marshall is a brilliant lawyer. He heads the legal staff of the National Association for the Advancement of Colored People and has won important cases before the United States Supreme Court.

W. C. Handy wrote an American song famous around the world, "The Saint Louis Blues," and founded a music publishing company.

Terry Goes South

Terry Lane lives on a hill on Convent Avenue in a tall, modern apartment house. On the corner is a beautiful Negro church with arched cloisters, and a charming park slopes down the hill to lower Harlem. From Terry's front window he can see City College nearby, and farther downtown the great Empire State Building surrounded by other mighty skyscrapers. Not far from Terry's house is the Hudson River where sometimes American warships anchor and the deep horns of oceangoing boats can be heard. Along the Hudson below Riverside Drive is a long stretch of parkway with green grass, trees, baseball fields, and tennis courts where Terry goes to play. His playmates are children of all nationalities, for New York City is full of people who come from everywhere on earth, some born in America, and some in Europe or Asia or Africa where Terry's great-great-grandfather came from. All of these different people get along all right, and in New York their children play together.

But sometimes Terry's parents take him South to visit relatives in Alabama. There people do not work together if they are not of the same color, nor do colored and white children go to the same schools. On the train Terry's father and mother have to ride in a separate car set aside for colored people. In the South, Negroes cannot eat in the railroad station restaurants.

In Alabama Terry noticed that the drinking fountains in the public squares were marked WHITE and COLORED, and that if you were a Negro you could not drink from a WHITE fountain because it is against the law and a policeman can arrest you. Also the benches in the park in front of the courthouse in the town where Terry's relatives live were marked WHITE and COLORED. If you were not a white boy, you could not sit on a WHITE bench. There were even public parks where Negroes could not play, and colored children could visit the zoo only on Mondays. This seemed very silly to Terry.

Terry's grandmother explained to him that the WHITE and COLORED signs in the South were a holdover from slavery almost a hundred years ago. But, she said, there were many white people in slavery times who did not believe it was right to buy and sell human beings. In 1837, Lovejoy, a white newspaper editor in Illinois, wrote in his paper against slavery, so a mob burned his plant and killed him. But other white people who did not like slavery continued unafraid to write against it. Harriet Beecher Stowe wrote a book in 1852 called *Uncle Tom's Cabin* that showed how wicked slavery was. Another woman, Julia Ward Howe, composed a great song called "The Battle Hymn of the Republic" to whose mighty melody Union soldiers marched in the Civil War that ended slavery. White abolitionists helped Frederick Douglass escape from bondage to become a great leader, a friend of Lincoln, and eventually American Minister to Haiti.

So, Terry's grandmother said, there have always been white people in America who wanted Negroes to live happily and have the same rights as other Americans. No one has yet been able to wipe out *all* the ugly leftovers of a bad time in our country, but good citizens are trying, and someday there will be no more WHITE or COLORED signs anywhere.

The Story of Harriet Tubman

Many Negroes in the days before the Civil War did not like to be slaves so they ran away to the North, and to Canada, and freedom. But some were not happy to be free themselves while their brothers remained slaves. One person like this was a very dark woman whose front teeth were missing because a slave master had hit her in the face with his fist when she was a child. She never forgot this. So when she was old enough, she ran away from his plantation in Maryland and headed North. But she could not live at peace, free, while her relatives and friends were still slaves.

In secret by night, disguised and alone, she went back to the plantations of the South to rescue others. Her name was Harriet Tubman, and she became known as "the Moses of her people," leading slaves to freedom. Because runaway Negroes had to travel by night to keep from being caught, whipped, and enslaved again, this secret way of escaping was called the Underground Railroad. Harriet Tubman became a "conductor" on the Underground Railroad. Many kind white people, especially the Quakers, helped her by providing "stations" in their attics or haylofts where runaway slaves could hide on their way to the North. To these fleeing Negroes they gave food and money. Sometimes they transported them in closed carriages or in wagons that had false bottoms, so they could hide from the slavers who pursued them with bloodhounds and guns.

Harriet Tubman could not read or write, but she had a great sense of direction. She could find her way alone through the streets of strange cities, across swamps, or through thick woods at night. She was very brave. Once free, she made up her mind never to be captured again, so she carried a pistol hidden in the folds of her dress. Because of her success in helping slaves escape, many all over the South got the idea of trying to run away. She was a dangerous example for others, so the slave owners offered a reward of forty thousand dollars for Harriet's capture. But no one ever captured her.

Harriet would walk two or three hundred miles from the North into the slave country, sleeping in hiding by day, walking, walking, walking by night. When she located the slaves she wanted to rescue, she would set a time for them to be ready. Then she would stay hidden in a swamp or beneath a corncrib until Saturday night when she would gather them all together in some secret place in the heart of the woods to start their flight. On Sunday slaves did not have to work in the fields. So, if they ran away on Saturday night, they might not be missed until the new week began.

With Harriet Tubman in front, all night these barefooted Negroes with no lanterns walked across fields and through woods. They did not dare show a light or travel the main roads. When dawn came they would hide underneath haystacks, in caves, or wherever they could until the sun had set. Then they would start walking again, following the creek beds as much as possible, since in running water bloodhounds smell no tracks. On clear nights the freedom seekers were guided by the North Star. On dark nights they felt the bark on the trees as they went along, searching for the moss that often grows on the north side of tree trunks. If there were no trees or no star, failing to find any other guide, Harriet prayed, trusting God to lead them in the right direction.

Her band of runaways had to travel silently to escape being captured. If babies cried, they gave them medicine to make them sleep, so that no one would hear any noise. If some of the travelers grew weak or weary or became afraid, Harriet would not let them stop for fear they would be caught and cause danger for the others. Sometimes, when a person thought he could not walk any further, she would take out her pistol and say, "If you stop, I will have to shoot you, because we cannot leave you here to be captured alive."

Nobody stopped, so none of Harriet Tubman's band was ever captured. They gathered strength, lived to travel on, and to thank her later for having brought them to freedom. In a speech once Harriet Tubman said, "I never ran my train off the track and I never lost a passenger."

She made nineteen dangerous trips into the South to rescue first her two children, her sister, her old father and mother, and then many of her friends. During the Civil War she helped to recruit troops for Abraham Lincoln. If they had taken women into the army in those days, no doubt Harriet Tubman would have joined the Union soldiers, so bitterly did she hate slavery and so much did she love freedom. But she did not love freedom for herself alone. She helped as many slaves as she could to be free. That is why people said Harriet Tubman was like Moses, for freedom in those days was like the Promised Land, and it was hard and dangerous to be free.

Well-Known American Negro Women

Ethel Waters is a great actress.

Dr. Ruth Temple is a well-known physician.

Marian Anderson is a famous concert singer.

Charlotte Hawkins Brown, speaker and educator, is founder of Palmer Memorial Institute, a preparatory school for boys and girls.

Charlemae Rollins is a distinguished librarian.

Golden Trumpets

Terry likes jazz music. He and his father have a big collection of records. For fun in the school band, Terry plays a horn. Once Terry's father told him the story of Louis Armstrong, who is one of the great hornblowers of the world.

When Louis Armstrong was a ragged little boy in New Orleans, he followed through the streets the colored bands that played for funerals. They played sad music going to the cemetery and gay music as they marched back to town when their work was done. In those days bands were often hired to play for lodge parades, picnics, and dances too. Best of all the instruments, little Louis loved the loud clear notes of the trumpet, and the golden way a trumpet shines in the sun when a man lifts it to his lips. He could hear a trumpet miles away, and when it played happy music it would set his feet to dancing. When it played blues, it would make him feel as if he wanted to cry.

The blues were a sad kind of music, but a funny kind of music as well, with words that made people laugh. Sometimes a man would sing:

I wonder if a matchbox will hold my clothes?

Then everybody would laugh because, even if a man's clothes were limited to a pair of socks, he could not get them into a matchbox. In New Orleans the blues were usually songs about trouble. But the music had a rhythm that kept driving trouble away, and the words often had a sudden humorous twist:

> I'm going to the railroad,
> And lay my head on the track,
> Going to the railroad,
> Lay my head on the track—
> But if I see the train a-coming
> I'm gonna jerk it back!

That's the way the blues were, full of surprise endings with the kind of music that kept marching on.

Little Louis Armstrong loved the way a trumpet lifted its blues melody up above all the other instruments and sent it soaring through the air for blocks. Louis longed for a golden trumpet. But when he first puckered his lips to the mouthpiece of a borrowed horn, not a sound came out. He puffed his cheeks and blew into the horn. Finally he was able to make an ugly squeak. Then a squawk! But that was all.

Some of the bandmen took an interest in helping him, so after a while Louis began to make notes. But he had to practice a long time before the notes he made became round and full and beautiful and golden like the trumpet itself. Then Louis was allowed to march in a band.

Sometimes he got jobs playing at picnics and made a little money. As he became a bigger boy, he played in small bands on the old paddle-wheel riverboats steaming up and down the Mississippi. As a young man Louis Armstrong headed a jazz band of his own in Chicago. Then he made records. Now people all over the world buy his records, and Louis Armstrong's style of playing, with its warmth and humor, has influenced a whole generation of jazz men who love golden trumpets.

Old Satch

Terry has a schoolmate named David. Because Terry and David are such good friends, Terry's father invited David to attend a baseball game with Terry. They saw the St. Louis Browns play the Yankees at the Stadium.

Satchel Paige was pitching that day. He was long, tall, and dark. When he wound up to pitch the ball, he lifted his leg like an ostrich, swung way back, and let the ball go. It seemed to hang in the air. Then, just as the batter struck at it, the ball curved slowly into the catcher's mitt. It curved just enough for the batter to miss it.

"That," said Terry's father, "is Satchel Paige's famous 'blooper' ball. That's what fans the best of them out. Nobody can hit it. They say Ole Satch is almost fifty years old now and still a great pitcher. He was forty before he got into the big leagues."

Driving David back home in the car, Terry's father told the two boys that there had never been any Negro players in the big league baseball clubs until the Brooklyn Dodgers signed Jackie Robinson in 1947. Before that time Negro ballplayers could play only on all-Negro teams.

It took many years of demanding on the part of fans and many articles by the leading sports writers to break the color line in America's most popular sport. Finally the Dodgers started by signing Robinson. Jackie became Rookie-of-the-Year his very first season. He was so popular with the fans, made so many home runs, and had such a high batting average that other teams soon hired colored players too. Finally Ole Satch, who had been a famous pitcher with Negro teams for a long time, was signed on a major league team, the Cleveland Indians. From there he went to the St. Louis Browns. And people crowded the ball parks to see him play at an age when most ballplayers, too old to pitch any more, are ready to retire.

"Ole Satch, with his slow relaxed funny kind of windups and that deceiving curve ball of his! He will always be a part of baseball history," Terry's father said. "Satch is a great example of what a man can do who keeps on trying."

Then he added, "Or what *people* can do, too, for now that everybody can play in the big leagues, baseball is really 'the Great American Sport.'"

Famous Negro Athletes

Jackie Robinson was the first Negro to play in big-league baseball. As first baseman for the Brooklyn Dodgers, he was chosen Rookie-of-the-Year and closed a pennant-winning season by playing in the world series.

Isaac Murphy was a famous jockey in the late 1800's, when he was known as the "King of the Turf."

Levi Jackson was the first Negro student at Yale University to become a captain of the Yale football team.

Althea Gibson was the first colored woman to compete in the national singles tennis championships at Forest Hills in 1950.

Jesse Owens, as a sprinter on the Ohio State University track team, was called "the world's fastest human." In 1936 he won three first places for the American Olympic Team at Berlin.

Joe Louis was heavyweight champion of the world for twelve years, the longest period in which a single boxer has held this title. As a sergeant during World War II, he boxed for the armed forces all over the world.

The Harlem Globe Trotters are expert professional basketball players who have met and defeated teams around the world and have appeared in motion pictures.

Sight-Seeing

Once when Terry's cousin, Charlene, came to visit him from Alabama, Terry's mother took them on a sight-seeing tour. Charlene, who was twelve years old, had never been in New York City. Indeed, Charlene had never been in any large city before, for she lived on a farm. She had never walked through a revolving door. So, when they went to Radio City, Charlene stepped all over Terry's heels. Charlene did not know that two people should not go through the same section of a revolving door together. This tickled Terry so much that Charlene was embarrassed. She was afraid Terry might call her his "country cousin." But Terry's mother had taught him better manners than that. Then, too, Terry realized that his cousin knew a great many things he did not know. She could tell him how to milk a cow. She could ride a horse, and Charlene even said that she knew how to clip a sheep. "You just give them a haircut all over," she declared.

Charlene's father was a cotton grower. Cotton grew right up to their porch, she said. At picking time, when the bolls were big and bursting white, school was often dismissed so the children could help pick cotton before the winter rains set in. Charlene knew how to churn butter and make fudge, and even make apple cider. Terry's mother let her make a pan of walnut fudge one night. It was very good. Then Charlene asked if sometime she could pop corn to make molasses popcorn balls, but that was before she realized that her aunt's New York apartment did not have a fireplace or a coal stove. Terry had never seen popcorn before it is popped.

Terry was interested in all the things Charlene told him about farm life. Charlene, in turn, was interested in city life. At Radio City they got on the escalator to go up to the main floor. These moving stairs were very wonderful to Charlene, for she had never imagined them before. She rode up one and down the other three times before she was ready to go any further. Then Mrs. Lane bought tickets for the Observation Roof. They got into an elevator that took them speeding up sixty-five floors in less time than it takes to climb one flight of stairs on foot. At the top of Radio City they could see twenty miles away, all the great city of Manhattan below them, and the harbor where the big boats go out to sea, Long Island, and New Jersey, and the country beyond. It was almost like being in an airplane, the two children thought, as they looked far away.

"Geeminetty!" Charlene said.

To cap the climax of wonders for the day, Mrs. Lane took her son and his cousin to luncheon at a most amazing restaurant called the Automat where people put nickels and dimes into slots in the wall, and little glass cases fly open, and there is the food inside: baked beans, or a sandwich, or hot macaroni, or almost anything you wish! Another coin in another slot, and milk, or hot chocolate, or coffee pours from a spout into your cup. Even more wonderful to Charlene was the fact that colored people and white people were all welcome there, and they sat at any tables they wished. This was the first time Charlene had ever eaten in a restaurant with white people—because in Alabama that is against the law. Terry's mother said she did not believe such laws made sense in this modern day and age, and that New York is a really democratic city because it does not have such old-fashioned ideas or customs.

"We are all Americans," she said. "Every American should be able to go into any public place anywhere."

"Do you think my home will ever be like New York?" Charlene asked.

"Of course it will," Mrs. Lane replied. "Yet no place is perfect, Charlene. In New York colored people find it hard to rent a house except in streets where Negroes live. And there are some fashionable restaurants that do not like to serve us. But most of them do, and, you see, no one minds that we are eating here. So now, if you've finished your ice cream, we'll take the subway to the Battery and see New York Harbor."

Six or eight cars long, with a great roar, the subway train raced into the underground station at Times Square, and Charlene noticed that its motorman was a Negro. Some of its guards were colored and some were white, all working together on the same train. Faster than many railroad trains, the subway tore through the tunnel and in a very short time they had gone almost five miles from the heart of Manhattan Island to its very end. When they came up into the sunlight they could smell the sea and hear the great horns of ocean-going steamers. They took a small ferry boat across the harbor to Staten Island. On the way they passed the Statue of Liberty.

"At night," Terry explained, "you can see the torch in her hand all lighted up. Look at the star on Liberty's head!"

"That has much too many points to be a star," Charlene objected. "It's a crown."

"It is not," said Terry. "Miss Liberty does not wear a crown."

Visiting the United Nations

When they came back uptown, they went to see Terry's father who works at the United Nations headquarters, an enormously beautiful skyscraper overlooking the river. Terry's father has a translator's desk there. His job is to translate speeches and documents from French, Spanish, and Italian into English.

Inside the building everything is shining and modern, and the walls of the main lobby are all glass so you can see the boats in the river outside. But Charlene and Terry were more impressed with the people there than with the building itself. They had never seen so many different nationalities before, colored and white, working together—people from far-off India, Africa, Russia, Australia, South America, and the West Indies.

Terry's father introduced them to some of the Negroes at the United Nations: Kalibala from the Sudan and Chapman of Nigeria; and James Bough of the Virgin Islands who was Chief of the Caribbean Section of the Trustee Division; and a charming French African woman, Jeanne Vialle, a member of the French Senate in Paris, who had come to New York to serve on a special committee on slavery. From Jeanne Vialle they learned that there are some parts of the world—Arabia, for example—where people are still slaves.

In one room Charlene and Terry met a young Negro officer of the United Nations, Ben Carruthers, who gave them a special children's copy of "The Universal Declaration of Human Rights." In simple language it tells how many nationalities can work together to make our world a happy place for everyone. Terry took the Declaration to school and his teacher read this part of it to the class:

> There are many who care little about the rights of others to live their own lives. Both children and adults can be unreasonable and be a nuisance to each other. It can happen that people attack each other and are cruel to each other, and time after time mankind has suffered dreadful wars. But most of us would rather live in a world where we could say and believe what we wanted, and where no one would be afraid or in need. We would like there to be justice and peace all over the world. The members of the United Nations have, therefore, promised to do everything they can so that we may enjoy such a life, whether we be children or adults.

Negro History Week

Terry's teacher was interested in the background of each pupil in her class. When Saint Patrick's Day came she told the children about Ireland. As Yom Kippur drew near, she told them about the new country of Israel. In February, at the time of Lincoln's birthday, the colored people of the United States celebrate Negro History Week. Then all the Negro papers and magazines publish pictures and stories about the contributions of the Negro to America. The teacher clipped some of these for the bulletin board, and on the blackboard she listed a few facts for the children to learn about Negro life.

John Henry, Mighty Railroad Builder

One day the teacher told her class about the John Henry legend. According to the story, she said, John Henry was a mighty Negro with muscles of steel who helped build the first railroad through the mountains of West Virginia. The tracks were laid in rock and tunnels had to be dug through solid rock, and the men had to drill out the rock. One of these tunnels was the Big Bend Tunnel. With his iron hammer and steel drill, John Henry became the best driller of all the men, white or colored. You could hear his hammer ringing all over the mountain. Folks said he made the mountains tremble each time his hammer struck. But one day the overseer bought a steam drill that could drill through rock faster than any man. John Henry didn't like this. It made him angry. So he made a bet that he could beat the steam drill. Everybody gathered around to see this race between a man and a machine.

John Henry won—because he drilled faster and deeper into the rock with his hammer and spike than the steam drill did. They say the ringing of his hammer could be heard for a thousand miles as he drove his steel drill into the rock. Sweat poured from his body. But when he finished he fell dead. Now people remember John Henry in a song which has a chorus like this:

> He died with his hammer in his hand!
> Yes, he died with his hammer in his hand!

And the last verse about his funeral says:

> They carried him down by the river
> And they buried him in the sand,
> And everybody that passed along
> Said John Henry was a steel driving man!
> John Henry was a steel driving man!

More Famous American Negroes

Gwendolyn Brooks was awarded the Pulitzer Prize for Poetry in 1950. She lives in Chicago and writes mostly about Negro life in a big city.

Phillis Wheatley, born in Africa and sold as a slave in Boston, became so famous as a poet that General George Washington praised her books.

Mary McLeod Bethune founded Bethune-Cookman College and was its president for many years. She was an adviser to President Roosevelt during World War II.

Edith Sampson is a noted lawyer in Chicago. She went around the world with Town Hall of the Air Radio Forum. She has been a delegate to the United Nations Assembly.

Lena Horne is a talented singer and entertainer.

Skating among Skyscrapers

Because Terry brought home a good report card, his father suggested that he invite his friend David to go skating with him on the beautiful outdoor ice-skating rink below the sidewalk level at Rockefeller Plaza where spectators may stand and look down upon the skaters. In the shadows of Radio City's skyscrapers, David and Terry darted around and around the gleaming rink, skimming the white ice like birds to the sound of soft music. It was snowing. With many other children and grownups Terry and David skated until dusk in the softly falling snow. Above them waved the flags of all the nations of the world with which the rim of the skating rink is decorated.

As it grew dark in the early evening a million lights gleamed in the windows of the tall office buildings above them. It was like fairyland. Terry thought to himself, "This is the prettiest city in the most wonderful country in the world, and I'd rather live here than anywhere else on earth!" And that is what he told his father as they rode home together.

His father said, "I agree, it is good to live in America, Terry. Our country has many problems still to solve, but America is young, big, strong, and beautiful. And we are trying very hard to be, as the flag says, 'one nation, indivisible, with liberty and justice for all.' Here people are free to vote and work out their problems. In some countries people are governed by rulers, and ordinary folks can't do a thing about it. But here all of us are a part of democracy. By taking an interest in our government, and by treating our neighbors as we would like to be treated, *each one of us* can help make our country the most wonderful country in the world."

The First Book of Rhythms

(1954)

Contents

Let's Make a Rhythm

It is fun to start something.

Take a crayon or pencil and a sheet of paper and start a line upward. Let it go up into a curve, and you will have rhythm.

Then try a wavy line, and you will see how the line itself seems to move.

Rhythm comes from movement. The motion of your pencil makes *your* line. When you lift your pencil as you finish, the rhythm of your line on the paper will be the rhythm of your hand in motion. Try this:

There is no rhythm in the world without movement first.

Make a point of a triangle, then a smaller one, then a smaller one than that, then a still smaller one, so that they keep on across a sheet of paper, all joined together.

Again you have made a rhythm. Your hand, your eye, and your pencil all moving together have made on the paper a rhythm that you can see with your eyes.

You can make a rhythm of sound by clapping your hands or tapping your foot. You can make a body rhythm by swaying your body from side to side or by making circles in the air with your arms.

Now make a large circle on a paper. Inside your circle make another circle. Inside that one make another one. See how these circles almost seem to move, for you have left something of your own movement there, and your own feeling of place and of roundness. Your circles are not quite like the circles of anyone else in the world, because you are not like anyone else. Your handwriting has a rhythm that is entirely your own. No one writes like anyone else.

How do you write?
Make a rhythm of peaks, starting from the bottom of one peak.

Make another rhythm like it, but start from the top.

Then do the same thing again, but put one rhythm over the other, and you have a pattern.

Fill in with your crayon and you have a pattern of diamond shapes. Rhythm makes patterns.

Draw a line. From the line make straight lines that slant up, each line growing a little longer. Or make another line and let the slanting lines cross it.

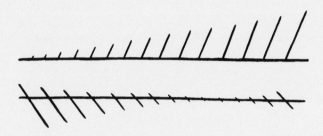

See how many rhythms you can make with straight lines, with curving lines, with circles overlapping circles, and with circles around circles, starting with a dot.

If a friend is drawing with you, see how different your friend's circles are from your circles. It is fun to make something yourself with your *own* rhythm because it will always be different from what anyone else will make. Your circles and rhythms are yours alone.

The Beginnings of Rhythm

Your rhythm on this earth began first with the beat of your heart. The heart makes the blood flow. Feel your heart. Then feel your wrist where your pulse is. That is where you can best feel the rhythm of your blood moving through your body from the heart. Doctors measure the force of the blood with an instrument which pictures this rhythm in terms of the speed of its movement. The speed varies from person to person, but when a line is used to picture this movement, it looks in general like this.

Such a diagram-drawing is called a graph. This particular line, you see, has a definite, repeating rhythm as the pulse throbs to the flow of blood pumped by the heart. The rhythm of life is the beat of the heart. The beat of the heart makes a pattern seen on paper when it is recorded by what doctors call an electrocardiograph machine. Sometimes the pattern looks like this graph.

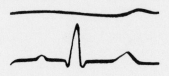

Listen to your heart. In most adults the heart beats about 72 times a minute, pumping blood through the heart into the canals of the body. When you run or when you are frightened, excited, or crying, your heart beats faster. Movement of the body, or the flow of thoughts or emotions through the mind, can change the rhythm of the heart for a while. Bad thoughts upset the heart. Happy thoughts do not disturb it unless they are sudden surprises. Usually, however, the heart pumps the same number of beats a minute, steadily, once a person becomes an adult, until he leaves our world. The rhythm of the heart is the first and most important rhythm of human life.

Thousands of years ago men transferred the rhythm of the heartbeat into a drumbeat, and the rhythm of music began. They made a slow steady drumbeat to walk to or march to, a faster beat to sing to, and a changing beat to dance to.

Try beating a slow steady rhythm with your fingers softly on the table, or on the edge of this book.

Try beating a changing rhythm that you can dance to.

Try beating the rhythm of a song you know, like "The Star-Spangled Banner."

Try clapping your hands in rhythm as people do for square dancing, the Charleston, or for games.

The rhythms of music start folks to feeling those rhythms in their minds and in their bodies. That is why music sometimes starts the heart beating faster. One rhythm may start another. The rhythm of the wind in the sky will change the movements of a kite floating in the air. The rhythm of water in the sea will make a boat rock faster or slower as the water moves. Rhythm begins in movement.

A little stream starts to flow down a mountainside from a new spring. It makes a path across the land as the water moves. Gradually the path is washed out deeper and deeper, following the course of the water's movement. If the stream keeps on flowing for a long time it will make a gully. Over the years it may even create a canyon by the rhythmical flowing of the water. Out of a wilderness of rock the steady flow of the Colorado River carved America's beautiful Grand Canyon in Arizona, until it became an immense rhythmical cleft across the land. Its rhythm began with the steady movement of the water of the river. Even, steady motion is rhythm.

Varying Rhythms

The Mississippi River flows in a slow rhythm to the sea. Niagara Falls tumbles in a swift roaring curve of rhythm over a shelf of rock from one lake to another—Lake Erie to Lake Ontario. Water from an old-fashioned hose makes a single rhythmical arch as it falls onto the grass. But a garden spray produces a hundred lines of graceful curving water.

Steady, even rhythms are the easiest to make, or to look at, or listen to, or rest by. The tick of a clock, always the same, will put you to sleep. If you bounce a ball in an even rhythm, it is easier to keep it going. To skip rope and not miss, partners must turn the rope with an even speed. A swing swoops up and down evenly as you pump it. Grandma rocks steadily, not jerkily, in her rocking chair.

But steady, even rhythms are not always the most exciting, or the most interesting. An even rhythm is restful.

But an uneven rhythm is more interesting because it seems to be changing, to be going somewhere, to be doing something.

This rhythm does not change.

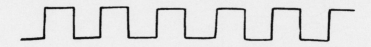

But this one does.

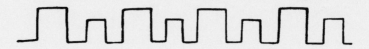

Varying rhythms are more exciting. This is perhaps why your heart beats faster when you start to school for the first time or take a trip or move to a new house and the rhythms of daily life change. Or why, when the rhythms of music vary or grow more rapid as in Ravel's "Bolero," or when the sea waves pound faster and louder, or the wind blows more swiftly and the trees sway violently, your heart beats faster, too.

One rhythm affects another rhythm. If one partner turns the end of a rope faster, the other partner must turn faster, too, to keep up. Otherwise there will be no rhythm in the turning. When two people dance together, they must dance together in the same rhythm, or it is no fun for either.

But different rhythms may sometimes be combined with interest. Straight lines make a rhythm of their own.

But with them a flowing line may be coupled to make an interesting combination of rhythms, one crossing the other,

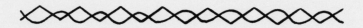

or one on top of the other,

or below the other.

There are many combinations of varying rhythms and actions. A merry-go-round goes round and round while the animals on it go up and down. If you have ever watched a sea gull flying you have noticed that it flaps its wings awhile, then glides awhile, then flaps awhile, then glides again. Flap, flap—glide—flap, flap—glide. See what other kinds of varying rhythms you can think of yourself.

Sources of Rhythm

Artists have used animals, trees, men, waves, flowers, and many other objects in nature for rhythms.

In France 25,000 years ago the cave men made animal drawings on the walls of their caves.

Later the flag lily, *fleur-de-lis*, became a rhythmical design that is the national symbol of France.

African artists a thousand years ago made beautiful masks with rhythmical lines.

Each artist makes his own rhythms out of the things he sees around him and sees in his dreams and mind.

The most beautiful rhythms seem always to be moving upward. That must be because the sun is above, and the growing things that start in the earth grow upward toward it.

A blade of grass moves upward as it grows. So does a flower, first only a little sprout, then a stem giving off other stems that turn into branches that bud as the plant grows taller. The buds turn into flowers as high above the earth and as near the sun as each plant can reach. Small plants like violets do not reach very high. Tall plants like sunflowers or hollyhocks sometimes grow taller than a man. Trees like magnolias bloom away up in the air. From the roots in the earth to the tallest flower, lines of rhythm flow upward. And in each leaf, each flower petal, there is rhythm. Nature is rhythm.

The lines of an oak leaf move outward and upward to its tip.

A locust leaf has rhythm, and a violet in bloom.

There is rhythm in a lily, and the bud of a rose before it opens much, and a many-petaled rose in full bloom.

Many vines curl upward. But some plants, like Spanish moss which lives on air, hang gracefully downward from the branches of trees. The leaves of water lilies float calmly on the surface of the water, but their blooms open toward the sun.

In growing things there is an endless variety of rhythm from the shaggy, pyramiding pine to the tall bare curve of a towering palm, from the trailing weeping willow to the organ cactus of the desert, from the straight loveliness of bamboo trees in the tropics to the wind-shaped cypress of the California coast, clinging to a rocky cliff near the sea where the waves shower their salty spray.

This is one of the many rhythms of moving water in the sea.

These are some of the many thousands of rhythms that moisture makes when it forms a tiny snowflake, or when it becomes a ball of hail, or an icicle, or when it is just, as many poets have said, "the harp-strings of the rain."

Perhaps falling rain first gave men the idea of painting stripes as decoration on their walls or on their war shields, or of weaving stripes into their garments, or making a rhythm of slanting stripes that lean as rain sometimes does, or stripes flowing as rain in the wind may seem to flow and curve.

Perhaps the curve of a waterfall or the arching stripes of the rainbow suggested the rhythms for the arches of the houses and temples and tombs and bridges of men long ago—the arch of Tamerlane's tomb at

Samarkand, the arch of a bridge in ancient China, or the Moorish arches at Granada.

When the Egyptians built their tombs and temples over a thousand years before Christ, they knew how to combine the rhythms of nature with the possibilities of stone and sun-dried brick in the structure of their buildings. And the more harmoniously they did this, the more beautiful were their buildings. In splendid palaces the pharaohs lived.

The Greeks, hundreds of years before Christ, knew the rhythmical beauty of the soaring line in a column. The rising lines of its many columns made the Parthenon one of the most beautiful buildings ever created.

The columns of Greek temples go upward.

The pyramids of the Egyptians point upward.

The skyscrapers of American cities rise into the skies.

Like the blades of grass and the stems of flowers and the trunks of trees, the houses and temples and other buildings of man rise toward the sky where the sun is. Almost nobody builds a house, church, or any kind of building underground.

The Rhythms of Nature

From the motion of the planets around the sun—Old Sol—the rhythms of the sky are charted. The sun and the planets which move around it, with the moons, the comets, the meteors, and all the smaller asteroids too far away to be seen, are called the solar system.

You with your own eyes can watch the daily rhythm of night, day, night, day, night, day, and the rhythm of the four seasons that are spring, summer, fall, and winter, regularly repeating themselves over and over again. The rhythms of the moon becoming full, then waning, then becoming full again, you can see, too, as it revolves around the earth. The magnetic pull of these rhythms is recorded in the tides of the sea.

In nature many rhythms are related, one to another, and men and animals live according to these rhythms. Fields are planted in the spring, cultivated in summer, harvested in the fall, and the grain is stored for winter when the fields lie fallow. Some birds follow the seasons, flying south to keep up with the sun. All the planets move around the sun. All the rhythms of the part of the universe we know best are attuned to the sun. The rhythms of growing things almost always move upward toward the sun. Waves begin low in a trough of the sea and rise to a crest of foam.

The rhythms of the joyful spirit are rising ones. Animals in happiness leap upward. Ballet dancers rise as high as they can on their toes when dancing. Church steeples point toward the sky. When men pray their thoughts go up, and their souls are uplifted. When people are happy they generally walk with their heads up. When they are sad and days are dark and sunless, their heads are often down.

The sun influences the moon. The sun and moon influence the sea. The tides of the sea influence the shell life of the sea, and each shell is molded into a rhythmic shape of its own by all the rhythms and pressures that bear upon it from the sea. These are a few of the many shell shapes.

On the surface of each shell the lines of some additional rhythms are etched in graceful beauty.

No one shell in the world is exactly like any other shell. There are millions of different shells. Even each shell of each family is different and the lines on each single shell are different, too.

You, like the shells, are like no one else. Even the rhythm of each line in your hands is like that in no one else's hands.

The rhythm of your walk is like no one else's walk. Some people walk with long easy steps, some trip along, some wobble. Soldiers learn to march in step together, with their walking rhythms at the same tempo, so that they all cover the same amount of ground in the same time at the same speed. They look better marching in rhythm. If one man gets out of step, he makes the whole company look bad. That is why all must follow the same marching rhythm. Forward, march! . . . One-two-three-four! . . . One-two-three-four!

At the Radio City Music Hall in New York there is a famous chorus of girl dancers called the Rockettes. Each girl's foot strikes the stage at the same time in rhythm when they are dancing. They are called precision dancers. When people are dancing together, the nearer their rhythms are alike, the better they look.

Rhythms of Music

Music sets the rhythm for dancing. The body follows the beat of the music. There are the fast whirl of the Viennese waltz, the skip and hop of the square dance, the glide of the fox trot, the step-step of the two-step, the fling of the Charleston with its flying legs, the prance of the old-fashioned cakewalk—each having its own style and rhythm. The first dances were done to the rhythms of the drums, long before other instruments were invented. And the tone of the drums and the volume of their sounds were molded by the rhythm of their shapes.

In America some of the happiest music for dancing is made by our jazz bands whose rhythms were born from the drums of Africa, and changed over to the piano, the trumpet, the bass viol, the saxophones, and all the other instruments that make up a band.

There is rhythm for dancing in words, too, like "Waltz me around again, Willie," the title of a song popular fifty years ago, which has a dancing sound.

The rhythms of music and of words cause people to want to move, or be moved, in time to them. Babies like to be bounced to

> Bye, Baby Bunting,
> Papa's gone a-hunting
> To get a little rabbit skin
> To wrap the Baby Bunting in.

Children dance to

> Ring-around-the-rosy,
> Pocket full of posy!

or play a game to

> London Bridge is failing down,
> Falling down, falling down!
> London Bridge is falling down,
> My fair lady!

In music there are simple rhythms and complicated rhythms. A popular song may follow the same rhythmical beat all the way through. In a symphony there may be many varied rhythms. The conductor of a large orchestra sets the tempo and controls the rhythms with the movement of his baton. If the men do not follow him the music is badly played and not pleasing. In the barnyard when animals are frightened and all the chickens start cackling, the dogs barking, ducks quacking, and cows mooing, each in different rhythms, the best way to describe the noise is by the word "pandemonium," which means a disorderly, inharmonious uproar. No one is moved by such noises.

But men are often moved by rhythmical music to work together better. Sailors on the old sailing ships sang sea chanteys as they hauled in the sails or lifted the anchor:

> Heave-ho! Blow the man down!
> Oh, give me some time to
> Blow the man down!

Men plowing or sawing or breaking rock like to work to music, with the rhythm of the song matching the rhythm of their bodies as they work. In this song from the deep South the "Huh!" is where the men's breath comes out as their hammers hit the rock or their picks strike the earth:

> I got a rainbow . . . Huh!
> Round my shoulder . . . Huh!
> Ain't gonna rain! . . . Huh!
> Ain't gonna rain! . . . Huh!
> This old hammer . . . Huh!
> Killed John Henry . . . Huh!
> Won't kill me, Lord! . . . Huh!
> Won't kill me!

Rhythm makes it easier to use energy. Even sweeping a rug or raking a lawn is done better if the broom or rake is handled with a steady rhythmical motion. In countries where a farmer still harvests the grain by hand, he advances across the field with the rhythmical sweep of his scythe, and the grain falls before him. Often he sings as he mows. And at the end of the harvest all the farmers sing for fun.

Rhythm and Words

Even without music there is rhythm in verses like these:

> Sing a song of sixpence
> Pocket full of rye!
> Four-and-twenty blackbirds
> Baked into a pie.
> When the pie was opened
> The birds began to sing.
> Wasn't that a dainty dish
> To set before a king?

Rhythm is very much a part of poetry. Maybe that is because the first poems were songs. In ancient Greece poets made up words and tunes at the same time. In the Middle Ages bards and troubadours sang their poems. Nowadays poets usually make up only words. But behind the words of good poems there is always rhythm. These lines by William Blake have a fine rhythm:

> Tiger! Tiger! Burning bright
> In the forest of the night!

Even when poems do not rhyme there is rhythm, as in the beautiful poetry of the Bible:

> Whither thou goest, I will go,
> And where thou lodgest, I will lodge.
> Thy people shall be my people,
> And thy God my God.

Or listen to the rolling lines of Walt Whitman:

> In the dooryard fronting an old farmhouse near the white-
>   washed palings,
> Stands the lilac-bush tall-growing with heart-shaped leaves of
>   rich green,
> With many a pointed blossom rising delicate, with the perfume
>   strong I love,
> With every leaf a miracle . . . .

Stories and sermons and speeches and prayers have their rhythms, too. How beautiful is the rhythm of Lincoln's *Gettysburg Address:*

> Fourscore and seven years ago our fathers brought forth on this conti-
> nent a new nation, conceived in liberty, and dedicated to the proposition
> that all men are created equal.

Just as the feet of soldiers marching in rhythm carry men forward, so the rhythms of sermons or speeches or poems carry words marching into your mind in a way that helps you to remember them. That is why I think

> To make words sing
> Is a wonderful thing—
> Because in a song
> Words last so long.

Most of the rhythms men put into music and poetry may be found in nature: the drumming of the rain, the rap-rap-rapping of a wood-pecker on a tree, the steady beat of the waves on the beach—breaking, retreating, breaking, retreating over and over again. The call of the whip-poorwill, the bobolink, the oriole, the sparrow, the trilling song of the canary—all these helped men to form their own rhythms and make their first music.

Some Mysteries of Rhythm

Deep inside of men and animals there are other rhythms that we cannot explain, but that are a part of life. Nobody knows why, for example, different kinds of birds always build their own particular kind of nests, each with its own peculiar rhythmical shape.

A South American ovenbird's nest is always oven-shaped.

A Baltimore oriole's nest hangs down like a hammock.

Every worker honeybee that lives knows how to help build a honey-comb, and the cells of each comb are always the same shape and of the same two sizes.

White-faced hornets' nests are always like this.

How each new brood of birds or bees or hornets knows how to create the same patterns and the same rhythmical shapes we do not know, but we call it instinct. This is nature, handing down certain ways of living and rhythms of life from one generation to another. Old swallows and young swallows all swoop through the skies in the same arcs of motion, and wild geese always fly in the same V-formations. For some reason wild geese find it easier to fly in formation this way.

Men and women create rhythms that make things easier to do, too. In fact, some things could not get done at all without rhythm. If you live in the country, watch a farmer churning butter. If he does not churn with an even up-and-down rhythm there will be no butter. Watch your mother beating cake batter. If she beats this way, that way, then slow, then stopping, then fast, the cake will not come out a good one. But if she beats her batter with a steady rhythm everything is mixed well and it is a good cake.

Athletics

When you go to the circus and see a man or a woman in spangled tights swinging on a trapeze high at the top of the tent, you remember for a long time the thrill as the trapeze artist swoops gracefully into space. The rhythm of a swimmer leaping from a diving board, cutting through the air in the swift curve of a high dive, is a beautiful picture to remember, too. In the water, the swimmer with the smoothest and most harmonious rhythm to his strokes is the one who moves the fastest and most beautifully through the water.

The word "harmonious" is a part of the definitions of rhythm in most dictionaries. Rhythm is "an harmonious flow," says one. Another dictionary says that rhythm is the measure of time or movement by regular beats coming over and over again in harmonious relationship. A good athlete must have that harmony of movement or rhythm, which is called "form."

Notice the form of a championship baseball player. Pitchers like Allie Reynolds or Satchel Paige or Ewell Blackwell wind up for the pitch and let go with a rhythm that begins in the tips of their toes and ends at the tips of their fingers as it is transferred to the ball that speeds through the air.

Watch Johnny Mize or Ted Williams, Ralph Kiner—or yourself—for when you bat a ball, your whole body turns with the bat. A rhythm is set in motion that, in its turn, carries the ball, if you hit it well, in a curve through space. The ball makes its own rhythm in the air as it moves into the outfield. The outfielder leaps into the air like a bird as his hands go up to catch the ball. From pitch, to swing, to ball, a whole series of rhythms are set off, one rhythm, or one motion, starting another. So it is in life—from sun, to moon, to earth, to night, to day, to *you* getting up in the morning and going out to play a game of ball. *All* the rhythms of life in some way are related, one to another. You, your baseball, and the universe are brothers through rhythms.

Broken Rhythms

When rhythms between people are jerky and broken—for example, when friends quarrel—life is not happy. When you row a boat you cannot make much headway with short choppy strokes. But when your body bends to the strokes of the oars with a slow easy rhythm you can feel the transfer of your rhythm to the oars. Then the boat, too, takes on a rhythm and moves forward swiftly and smoothly through the water. People and races and nations get along better when they "row together."

When a sail is unfurled properly on a sailing ship and billows out as it catches the wind you can sense its rhythm and almost hear the music of its motion. You can almost see the wind in the canvas. When a kite flies you can feel at the string's end the way it is pulled by the wind. When you spin a top you can feel in your throwing of the top the way your rhythmical unfurling of the string changes into a hum and a whirl. When ballet dancers spin on their toes they spin in rhythm. If they do not, the results are ugly. Broken rhythms usually are not beautiful.

In 1910, the lines of automobiles were not as beautiful as the smoothly flowing lines of today's models, but were broken and full of angles. And even if they had had better motors these older automobiles with their clumsy, angular, broken rhythms could not have moved as fast as the new cars with their flowing lines, for the rhythms of shape are related to the rhythms of movement.

Machines

But new things are not always better than old things. The lines of a Grecian water jar made three thousand years ago are more beautiful than some modern water jugs. One reason is that in the old days more things were made by hand. Therefore many things were different each from the other because each man, when making something, put into it his own individual rhythms.

Nowadays many things are made by machines that turn out thousands of copies, all just alike. When some of the long-ago Indians wove cloth by hand, each cloth was different and usually beautiful. Machines turn out beautiful cloth, too, and more of it, faster, by making over and over the same copies. They may be beautiful copies *if the first designs are beautiful*. But a man or a woman must *first* design the cloth. Machines cannot create beauty. They can only copy it.

Machines move in rhythm. You can hear the rhythm of a printing press. You can see the rhythms of a generator in motion making energy to start, in turn, the motion of the machine it serves. You can see the rhythms of a piston, of a ramrod, of a shuttle, of a washing machine, of an egg beater, of a propeller.

An airplane propeller thrusts forward into currents of air and on the rhythms of the wind a plane rises into the sky. A diesel engine turns its rhythms into power that carries a streamlined train rocking across the rails from city to distant city. The rhythm of a clock's balance wheel can be heard in its steady tick-tock, tick-tock, tick-tock. The rhythm of a steam shovel can be seen as it scoops up tons of earth.

Rhythms May Be Felt—and Smelled

The rhythms of the wind can be felt and certain sounds can be both felt and heard. An explosion at a distance can knock you down. Certain tones on the piano or violin hurt a dog's ears and will set him to howling. Some electronic vibrations, like those from short-wave radio transmitters, men cannot hear, but a dog can hear them, or feel them in his ears, and they hurt his eardrums. The vibrations from the sharp tone of a flute in a room have been known to break a pane of glass in a window. The flute player does not feel this tone from his flute, but it hits the pane of glass as hard as a stone, and the glass feels it. You cannot see electricity, but a shock can knock you down. Such an unseen rhythm may take on the force of a moving body. Perhaps tomorrow men may learn how to use such rhythms to shoot space ships to the moon.

In chemistry there are tiny bits of matter called molecules, too small for the eye to see. They move in a definite rhythm in liquids or gases, but we cannot see each tiny particle that makes up the gas. The air itself is gas, but we cannot see it. Instead we see *through* it.

Odors, or scents like those of perfumes, are really tiny particles, gases, or vapors in rhythmic motion. We smell them when they touch our noses although we cannot see them. In both chemistry and physics there are rhythms so complicated that it takes years of study to understand them. The rhythms of the patterns of light may be seen in colors called the spectrum. But there are many rhythms we cannot see, but which we can chart or measure.

Unseen Rhythms

Music may be heard, but not seen. It is true that the notes of music may be seen as written down on paper. But notes serve only as a guide to sound. They mean very little until they are set in motion by the human voice or by instruments, to travel in rhythmical pulsations—like the beat of the pulse—to the ears of listeners. Sir Isaac Newton, who was a great pioneer in the science of modern physics, called sound "pulses of air." Sound cannot travel far alone, but from a radio tower, through the power of electronics, sound waves are transformed into electrical pulsations which go out on invisible electro-magnetic waves in every direction. Then people thousands of miles away can hear the sound by means of electronics. Our President can make a speech in Washington and folks across the ocean in London can hear him because of this marvelous modern science.

Electronics is the science of the movement of electro-magnetic waves. In broadcasting, these waves move outward and upward and around the earth through the air. They silently carry with them sound waves in electric pulsations which become audible words or music by means of our radio sets. They carry sights, too—unseen as they travel through space—which become pictures for our television screens. They create invisible radar guides which may direct an airplane through a fog to land, or keep a ship away from a reef.

There is an instrument called a phonodeik (FO-no-dike) for picturing the vibrations of sound waves as they travel.

This is the rhythm of a single tone in a soprano voice as it moves through the air.

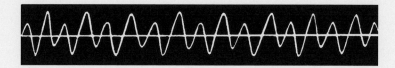

This is a graph of the tone of a violin.

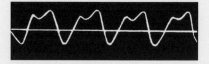

This is a bell tone.

And in the field of electronics, if the radar waves moving through space *could* be seen, they would look like this.

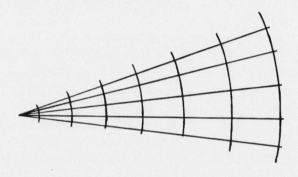

The rhythms of electronics were a mystery to men a hundred years ago. But now we know that light and sound and the force of the atom, too, each travels in its own series of rhythms. So, in this wonderful universe of ours there are rhythms that men can see, like those of sea waves. And there are unseen rhythms that we cannot see, but which we can chart and measure by scientific instruments and by mathematics. There remain to be solved tomorrow many fascinating mysteries about these unseen forces.

Rhythms in Daily Life

What is exciting about tomorrow is that it is always different from today. Back in the early 1900s the first airplane looked like a crate. But modern airplanes are streamlined.

To streamline something means to make the lines more rhythmical, more like a stream flowing. It is much more pleasing to look at a rhythmical, harmoniously shaped object than at an awkward thing. That is one reason industrial designers who create many of the things we use in daily life are paying more attention to rhythm and beauty.

The old ice box was shaped just like a box. But today's refrigerators are more graceful. And they are chilled by electricity from a dynamo whose power-rhythms are generated many miles away from your kitchen.

In grandma's day in the country, butter was put into a well to keep fresh. And cool water was drawn from the well in an "old oaken bucket." Thousands of years ago, before men learned to dig wells, they drank from springs or streams.

The first bowl to hold water was a man's cupped hand, or a pair of cupped hands.

Then the hands took clay and made a ball. A bowl is half of a ball, hollowed out. And a cup is just a bowl with a handle on it. A plate is just a bowl flattened out.

The first bowls and cups and plates were made only to be useful. Now we make them to be beautiful as well. Today fine designers like Russel Wright make beautiful dishes that are reproduced by machine methods so that people may buy them cheap. The rhythms of the hands of many makers of bowls, cups, glasses, and plates have given us the thousands of beautiful and useful shapes from which we eat and drink.

Furniture

It is interesting to observe the rhythms of furniture. The first chair was probably just a rock or a fallen log. Then a part of a log was set upright with a piece of the trunk left on it for a back. Then some planks were put together in angular fashion, very straight up and down.

Now chairs are made in many charming and graceful rhythms. Harmony or rhythm is very much a part of modern furniture-making.

And in our wallpaper and cloth, our towels and our curtains, our scarfs and neckties, the rhythms of lines and design are many. From the rhythms of nature—the pistil of a flower, the shape of an acorn, the tips of wheat stems—may come the designs on a man's tie, the patterns on living-room drapes, the border around your bedroom. At home, look and see what inspired the shapes and designs in your mother's wallpaper or the drapes at the windows.

How Rhythms Take Shape

Rhythms always follow certain conditions. Knitting creates its own rhythmical patterns by the very way the needles work in wool. So does chain stitching, cross-stitching, or featherstitching in sewing. Threads in weaving follow a rhythmical pattern according to the kind of weave being made. Pleats in dressmaking—knife pleats, accordion pleats—have a rhythm growing out of the way they are folded. When mothers curl little girls' hair they simply put the hair into the rhythm of spirals. But curls do not look well on all girls. Each person should arrange her hair to suit the shape of her face, just as a well-dressed woman chooses her hats to suit the lines of her profile, or her gowns to go well with the lines of her body.

Fashions in clothes and styles of decoration and design are everywhere influenced by other people and places around the world. That design on your father's tie may be from Persia. Your uncle's jacket is a Scotch plaid. The lines of your mother's dress are French. Her shawl is Spanish in design.

The music on your radio now is Cuban, its drums are the bongos of Africa, but the orchestra playing it is American. Rhythms go around the world, adopted and molded by other countries, mixing with other rhythms, and creating new rhythms as they travel.

In the Arctic the igloos make a curved rhythm against the sky. In America skyscrapers rear geometric towers above us. In Bechuanaland there are beehive huts, in Japan slant-roofed pagodas. Each building has its rhythms, loved by the people who made them, and often borrowed by others elsewhere. The Quonset hut of the American army is in shape not unlike an Eskimo igloo. And the East Indians are building skyscrapers in Bombay. We love Irish folk songs. The Irish love American jazz. Sometimes American jazz and Irish melodies combine to make a single song.

This Wonderful World

How wonderful are the rhythms of the world! Poets everywhere write about the drowsy hum of a bee. Farmers everywhere wake up to the cascade of a rooster's crow. In nature the rhythms we hear range from the trill of a bird to the chirp of a cricket, the lonely howl of a coyote to the thunderous roar of a lion, the gurgle of a brook to the boom of the sea, the purr of a cat to the beating of your own heart.

Look at the upward sweep of the horns of the antelope! See the outward curves of the Texas long-horned steer, the antlers of the elk, the stripes of the zebra or the tiger, the graceful neck of the giraffe, the delicate hoofs of a goat on a ledge, the curve of a sea lion on a rock, the scoop of a cat on a pillow, the flicker of a fish, the leap of a monkey, the wiggle of a puppy, the dive of a heron, the balance of hummingbirds, and butterflies, and ballet dancers, the drift of clouds across the sky in moving masses of vapor, the ever-spreading rhythm of the circles when you throw a stone into a pool of still water, the unseen rhythms of electronics that come right into your house bringing your favorite programs onto your TV screen! When a radio tower projects its electronic waves into the air, someone in Paris can hear a voice in New York saying, "Good morning"! Yet you cannot see or hear that voice on its way across the ocean. Such are the seen and the unseen, the heard and unheard rhythms of our world.

The earth which is our home moves in its own rhythm around the sun, as do all the planets. Animals, and boys and girls, and men and women, get up in the morning by the sun. Plants live by the sun. The moon moves around the earth as well as the sun. The rhythms of the sun and the moon influence the sea, the seasons, and us, and affect the rhythms of our universe, so immense in time and space that men do not yet understand most of it.

But your hand controls the rhythms of the lines *you* make with your pencil on a paper. And your hand is related to the rhythms of the earth as it moves around the sun, and to the moon as the moon moves around the earth, and to the stars as they move in the great sky—just as all men's lives, and every living thing, are related to those vaster rhythms of time and space and wonder beyond the reach of eye or mind.

Rhythm is something we share in common, you and I, with all the plants and animals and people in the world, and with the stars and moon and sun, and all the whole vast wonderful universe beyond this wonderful earth which is our home.

The First Book of Jazz

(1955)

Acknowledgments

For invaluable guidance concerning the history, development, artists, and materials of jazz music, the author is most grateful to the books, magazine articles, comments, or record notes on jazz by George Avakian, Rudi Blesh, Arna Bontemps, Sterling Brown, E. Simms Campbell, Leonard Feather, Sidney Finkelstein, Robert Goffin, John Hammond, W. C. Handy, W. E. Harper, Rex Harris, S. I. Hayakawa, Wilder Hobson, John Tasker Howard, Max Jones, Orrin Keepnews, Alan Lomax, Albert McCarthy, Mezz Mezzrow, Nestor R. Ortiz Oderigo, Frederick Ramsey, Jr., Winthrop Sargeant, Charles Edward Smith, Ezra Staples, Marshall W. Stearns, Jack Walker, and especially Louis Armstrong.

Contents

Just for Fun

When little Louis Armstrong, who was born on the Fourth of July, 1900, started singing for pennies on street corners in New Orleans, he was about ten years old. Before he was twelve, with Happy, Little Mack, and Georgie, he formed a quartet. Louis sang bass and sometimes whistled through his fingers like a clarinet. The four boys would move up and down Perdido Street harmonizing beneath people's windows in the evening. But sometimes, instead of having coins showered down upon them, they would be angrily chased away. Louis thought maybe a guitar would help their music, and be more fun, too. So he made himself a sort of ukulele from a cigar box, nailing a flat piece of wood to it for a neck, then stringing some wire from the neck tightly across the open side of his box.

The other boys probably put together homemade instruments for themselves, too, so that for fun they all could have a band. Maybe the only thing they bought was a ten-cent-store mouth organ for Little Mack. As many boys in the South have done, Happy found an old tin washtub somewhere and, at its side pointing upward, he placed a tall strip of plasterboard. From a nail hole in the center of the tub to the tip end of the board, he ran a stout brown cord and pulled it taut. That is the way Happy made himself a bass viol. Georgie borrowed his mother's washboard to stroke, putting on the ends of his fingers as many thimbles as she would let him have. When Georgie stroked the washboard it made rhythm. Maybe Mack played on his harmonica a lively little blues tune he had learned by ear. So we can imagine the four boys together in the back yard under a chinaberry tree, playing at music, with Louis picking the strings of his cigar box and singing, Happy plunking his washtub bass, Little Mack blowing his harmonica, and Georgie stroking gaily on his washboard. After a while they made such a happy beat that the other children in the neighborhood came running to sing and dance to their playing. Their band was fun.

Many young people have made such washboard bands, putting together their own instruments out of anything at hand. Some of these bands have even been recorded by the big record companies. In New Orleans before Louis was born there was a band that is still written about in books today. A blind newsboy whose nickname was Stale Bread started a little street-corner band with homemade instruments. Perhaps one of his players had a washboard. Maybe another shook two spoons together like minstrel bones. Maybe one newsie used a box for a drum, and perhaps another had a mouth organ. At any rate, they made such lively music that sometimes all of them would start jigging as they played, shaking their shoulders and bobbing their heads as if they had St. Vitus's dance, and at the same time letting their feet fly so frantically that folks started calling them the Spasm Band. From that time on throughout the South such washboard bands were called spasm bands.

Young folks—like the newsboy Stale Bread of long ago—still put together such bands, particularly in small towns and country places. In the Tennessee mountains sometimes their leader blows into a jug and the band is called a jug band. Sometimes, instead of a mouth organ, maybe a tin whistle or a kazoo is used, or tunes are played on a comb with a thin piece of paper over it. Sometimes a dishpan or a lard can is used for a drum. There is never any written music. The tunes are remembered or made up as the players play. And, to the players, it is *play*—just for fun. That is how the music called jazz began—with people playing for fun.

African Drums

Something to beat on, or thump on, or stroke on has always been a part of play-music—often the only part—for a beat or a rhythm is as important as a tune, sometimes more important. Maybe that is because hundreds of years ago music began with rhythm—with men beating on a hollow log, then singing; or beating on a goatskin drum and dancing. Men of all the ancient peoples everywhere, in Europe and Asia and Africa, beat on things to make a rhythm, just as the Indians in America long ago beat on drums as they danced. Some people in some parts of the world—in the South Seas, the West Indies, and Africa—still make music just by beating on drums alone. In parts of Africa there are whole orchestras made up of nothing but drums—big drums and little drums, tall drums and short drums, dull drums and deep drums. Each drummer may play a different rhythm, but all the rhythms are so woven together that people can sing or dance to them.

For centuries, folks in West Africa have worked to rhythm, rowed boats to rhythm, pounded their meal to rhythm, built their houses to rhythm. Then, when they were tired of working, they have danced to the rhythms of their drums, shaking little rattles made of gourds, ringing little bells, or clapping their hands to add to the rhythm. Often Africans have many different rhythms going all at once, of a kind that people nowhere else in the world can play. But all of them are woven together into a happy sound that makes folks want to get up and move in time to the rhythms. When the Africans first came to the New World almost four hundred years ago, they brought with them their wonderful rhythms. One of the chief things that makes American jazz different from the music of other countries is that it is so full of a variety of rhythms. In part, jazz grew out of the beating of African drums. The drum is man's basic rhythm instrument.

Old New Orleans

A hundred and fifty years ago in old New Orleans there was a public square called Congo Square. It was a big wide open dusty place where on Sundays, when they did not have to work, the African slaves came with their drums to sing and dance what they called the bamboula. Crowds used to gather around the square to watch the dancing slaves and listen to the music that they made on their drums. This was mostly rhythm music, unless sometimes the dancers began to sing or to chant remembered African songs against the drums, or to make up words of their own. Long after the time of the Civil War these Sunday dances continued. Little Louis Armstrong's great-grandmother remembered them well and told him about the drums.

Most people who write about the history of American jazz believe that jazz began in New Orleans, where the bands and orchestras borrowed some of the rhythms of the drums in Congo Square. The rhythms that the drummers there beat out in the dusty sunlight made the people standing around want to move their heads in time, pat their feet, and dance, too. That is one of the things about jazz: it always makes people want to *move*. Jazz music is music to move to, to dance to—not just to listen to.

The African drummers in New Orleans did not have any written music. They played from memory or made up rhythms as they went along, since they were playing just for fun. Today the best jazz is often played without music, from a tune remembered, and played as one feels like playing it for fun at that particular moment.

New Orleans had been a French city and a Spanish city before it was an American city, so, in addition to the slave drums, it knew many different kinds of music, both popular and classical. There was a great opera house in New Orleans long before the Civil War. And there were very fine orchestras and bands in the Louisiana city. But many people could not afford to go to the opera house, or listen to the symphony orchestras, or learn to play music by note as trained musicians did. So the poor people, without teachers, made their own music, playing mostly by ear for fun the melodies of old Spanish songs and French dance quadrilles and putting behind them the beat of the Congo Square drums—which made this freshly made up early music of New Orleans a very lively music indeed.

Old New Orleans had many marching bands that played a louder, livelier, more steadily rhythmical music than orchestras in opera houses or concert halls, and folks almost danced when they marched along behind such bands. On the sidewalks children did dance. When Louis Armstrong's parents were young, these brass bands often played in the streets or in parks where everybody could hear them for nothing. The sidewheel steamers that paddled up and down the Mississippi River from New Orleans to Memphis and St. Louis carried little bands on them. So the lively drum-time marching music of New Orleans, many years ago, began to spread all over the heart of America. And it turned into dancing music. Its syncopated 1-2-3-4 beat, a particular kind of 1-2-3-4 beat played with the accent shifted to the weak beat and stepped up a bit by memories of Congo Square, became a part of jazz.

Of course, people were making music in other parts of our country in early times, too—not just in New Orleans. In New England, settlers were singing their hymns. In Virginia and Kentucky the newcomers were singing their ballads. In the Far West the Indians were playing on their drums. African slaves in Georgia, the Carolinas, and other parts of the South, who did not always have drums on which to play, were making up songs to chop cotton to, load the river boats, or build the levees. They made up field hollers with long, sad, wailing blue notes in their voices that said how tired a man can be. The Negroes were also making up religious songs, called spirituals, with the rhythms of the drums in their voices. All of this—the singing, the tunes, and the rhythms—from New England to New Orleans has made American music. A part of American music is jazz, born in the South. Woven into it in the Deep South were the rhythms of African drums that today make jazz music different from any other music in the world. Nobody else ever made jazz before we did. Jazz is American music.

Work Songs

At the turpentine plant where he worked, little Louis Armstrong's father sometimes sang at his job. The stevedores on the New Orleans docks sang as they lifted their heavy loads. Today, in some parts of the Gold Coast in Africa, women pound corn for meal by putting the corn on a flat stone on the ground and beating it with another stone. As the American Indians used to do, these African women carry their babies tied on their backs. As they mash the corn they sing, and the stone in each woman's hand strikes the other stone in rhythm. As a mother's back bends and rises, the baby on her back feels the steady rhythm of this pounding of the corn. So, as the child grows older, it is no trouble at all for him to make for himself a rhythm to work by, or a song for grinding corn, rowing a boat, or cutting down a tree.

Work songs all around the world are full of rhythm—like the "Song of the Volga Boatmen," sung when men pulled barges up rivers in old Russia. Woodsmen everywhere sing tree-chopping songs, the ax striking the tree to the beat of the music. Harvest songs for the cutting of grain are thousands of years old. On sailing boats seamen sang sea chanteys when they raised the sails. On the Mississippi River slaves sang to load the cotton bales. Some of the rhythms of Afro-American work songs went into the making of jazz. "John Henry" is an American railroad-building song, sung as the picks or rock-crushing hammers struck the rock to clear the way for a roadbed or a tunnel:

> *Ain't no hammer—huh!*
> *In this mountain—huh!*
> *Rings like mine, boys!—huh!*
> *Rings like mine—huh!*

Many people who were not railroad builders liked this song and took it just to sing or play *for fun,* and not to work by. So the "huh" of the hammer's falling was dropped out. Many different people learned this song in different ways. Many singers added verses that they made up. So "John Henry" became a folk song with hundreds of different verses, sung in a great many different ways in different parts of the country. Some of the lines from English ballads got into it, like:

> *Who's gonna glove your*
> *Pretty little hand?*
> *And who's gonna shoe*
> *Your feet?*

But it always kept its work-song rhythm. A part of that rhythm, like the rhythms of many other Southern work songs, became a part of American jazz.

Jubilees

When Louis Armstrong was a boy, his relatives often sang religious tunes, and sometimes they made up their own words to go with the old melodies. Everywhere, all over the world, people have always made up songs about their God, and about the wonders and mysteries of life. The early settlers brought their own hymns from England to the New World and the slaves listened to them. But the African slaves in the American South had to learn a new language: English. So, in their new language, they made up new songs with English words, a mingling of melodies and harmonies, and African rhythms. These were called spirituals. But most spirituals had in them a more definite and lively rhythm than English hymns:

> *I got a harp!*
> *You got a harp!*
> *All God's children got a harp!*
> *When I get to heaven*
> *Gonna play on my golden harp—*
> *Play all over God's heaven!*
> *Heaven! Heaven!*
> *Everybody talk about*
> *Heaven ain't going there!*
> *Play all over God's heaven!*

Some of this rhythm from the spirituals went into the making of jazz.

The spirituals were sometimes called sorrow songs because many of them were about the sadness of life for men and women who were not free:

> *Nobody knows the trouble I've seen,*
> *Nobody knows but Jesus. . . .*

But many spirituals were very lively, too, although they were religious songs, and these were often called jubilees. Some jubilees were about the time when freedom would come:

> *This is the day of jubilee!*
> *God's gonna build up Zion's walls!*

The Lord done set His people free!
God's gonna build up Zion's walls!

On a cold autumn day in 1871 nine students, seven of whom had been slaves, started out from Fisk University in Tennessee to raise some money for their college. Singing their songs of jubilee, four ragged boys and five girls headed northward on a tour. They did not dream then that people would like their songs so well that it would be seven years before they got back to school. These young Fisk Jubilee Singers carried the spirituals over almost all America and Europe. They sang in little churches and great halls. They sang before Queen Victoria. They sent back one hundred and fifty thousand dollars to their university, and the rhythms of their jubilee songs became more than ever a part of the music of America, later influencing jazz. Jazz has in it some of the qualities of the spirituals.

Golden Slippers

While the Fisk Jubilee Singers were touring, a Negro named James A. Bland wrote a song in the rhythm of the spirituals called "Golden Slippers":

> *Oh, dem golden slippers!*
> *Oh, dem golden slippers!*
> *Golden slippers I'm gwinter wear*
> *Because dey look so neat.*
> *Oh, dem golden slippers!*
> *Oh, dem golden slippers!*
> *Golden slippers I'm gwinter wear*
> *To walk de golden streets.*

It was not a spiritual. It was a minstrel song, for James Bland was a minstrel man. He toured America and Europe singing his own songs with minstrel shows. Later on, in England, King Edward VII often came to hear him.

From about 1840 and for more than sixty years, the minstrel shows, made up entirely of men, were America's most popular entertainment. For these, such famous songs as "Dixie," "Turkey in the Straw," "Oh, Susannah," and "Swanee River" were written. Most of the minstrel songs were based on Negro rhythms and melodies borrowed from the work songs and the spirituals. The greatest of the minstrel writers, Stephen

Foster, who was white, at first called his songs "Ethiopian"—meaning Negro—songs. The minstrel shows also made popular the sand dances, the cakewalk, and the buck-and-wing, as well as the plantation jigs that later merged into tap-dancing. Minstrel music featured tambourines of Europe—similar to the African finger drums—along with the banjos and bones of the colored plantation bands. The bones were at first the ribs of a sheep or some other small animal, polished, and held between the fingers and shaken to make a dancing rhythm. Minstrel music borrowed heavily from the Negro music of the Deep South, and a great deal of the minstrel spirit carried over into jazz.

The Blues

I hate to see de evenin' sun go down—

This is the opening of W. C. Handy's famous "St. Louis Blues." Handy, who is called the "Father of the Blues," was the leader of Mahara's Minstrel Band in the 1890's. He also played a cornet. And he could read and write music, for he was a trained musician. Nobody really knows just when or where or how the kind of songs called blues began. But in 1909 W. C. Handy put down on paper and in 1912 published the "Memphis Blues" (originally called "Mr. Crump"). This was the first of many of his blues to become famous, based on the melodies and memories of the South where he was born. In 1914, W. C. Handy wrote the "St. Louis Blues," which has become one of America's best-known popular songs all over the world.

A hundred years ago there were croons, work songs, and field hollers—a kind of musical cry—whose melodies had a blues sound. To such tunes road workers or cotton pickers put whatever words came into their minds, singing out their own personal thoughts or sorrows. Maybe somebody somewhere in the Deep South long ago started to make up a song that began with a kind of field holler. Perhaps the man was working in a rice field on a hot day when a song came into his head, then out of his mouth, like this:

Oh, the sun is so hot and the day is so doggone long. . . .

Then when he couldn't think of anything else right away to go with it, he repeated the same lines:

Yes, the sun is so hot and the day is so doggone long.

But by that time he had a new thought:

And that is the reason I'm singing this doggone song.

Something like that must have happened the day the first blues was born, for that is the pattern of the blues: a twelve-bar musical pattern—one long line of four bars which is repeated, then a third line of four bars to rhyme with the first two lines that are always the same. Their melody and beat are like those of a field holler. Perhaps thousands of blues were made up in this way in the fields or on the levees, to relieve the monotony of working, to express some thought passing through a singer's mind, or just for fun. Then one day in Memphis W. C. Handy wrote down his first blues, and he and others began to use the blues as a basis for written music. Later a great singer, Bessie Smith, sang blues all over the country and made many records, some of them with Louis Armstrong. Now the blues are a part of American jazz.

Jazz took several things from the blues. It often uses the twelve-bar pattern of the blues. And it uses the "blue notes." These blue notes are "off notes," just a little bit flat and in between the usual notes. They most often are a somewhat flatted third or seventh note of the scale. They are impossible to show in written music, although they are sometimes indicated as flatted notes. But good blues players and singers always sound the blue notes, sliding in with the wailing slurring tones of a real blues song.

Blues also introduced melodies written around five notes only. Using blue notes and various note combinations, whole blues songs were written around five notes. Often instrumental blues used "riffs," also—single rhythmic phrases repeated over and over, as a background to the melody, or as the melody itself. Jazz today uses riffs. It also uses "breaks," which came from the blues. At the end of a phrase of melody or words, there is a little pause, during which one or more instruments break away from the melody and make up some fill-in music. Breaks are a part of today's jazz, but W. C. Handy's "Memphis Blues" introduced to published music the first printed jazz break of all.

The blues are almost always sad songs, songs about being out of work, broke, hungry, far away from home, wanting to get on a train but having no ticket, or being lonely when someone you love has gone. Their music says:

When you see me laughing,
I'm laughing to keep from crying.

But often there is something about the blues that makes people laugh:

I'm going down to the railroad
And lay my head on the track,
Down to the railroad
And lay my head on the track—
But if I see the train a-coming,
I'm gonna jerk it back.

In the blues, behind the sadness, there is almost always laughter and strength. Perhaps it is these qualities, carried over from the blues into jazz, that make people all around the world love this American music.

Ragtime

The first piano made in America was built in the late 1770's. But for a long time pianos were very expensive. It was not until almost a hundred years later, when several piano-making companies had been formed, that many American homes had pianos. They became almost as common as radios are today. In the evenings then, whole families played and sang for fun.

Poor Negroes, newly freed from slavery, often did not have the money to study music, but many learned to play by ear. Such Negro players transferred to the piano the rhythms of their drums, their work songs, their cakewalks, and their spirituals. By the late 1800's they had created a music which came to be called "ragtime." This meant playing a piece on the piano in a very lively syncopated manner—literally "tearing a tune to tatters." In syncopation the rhythmical accent falls on a beat that would customarily be weak, rather than on a usually strong beat. In ragtime such syncopation ran *all* the way through each piece. This syncopated ragtime piano style, along with the earlier syncopation of the marching bands, was carried over into jazz. In Sedalia, Missouri, a colored musician named Scott Joplin wrote a piece in this lively style called the "Maple Leaf Rag," published in St. Louis 1899. This happy rag became very popular, and hundreds of other such pieces were written and published. In those days, before the wide use of record players, piano music was recorded on paper rolls and played mechanically on player pianos. Many thousands of ragtime rolls were sold, as well as sheet music.

One of the great ragtime and blues pianists was a Creole from New Orleans named Jelly Roll Morton. Little Louis Armstrong, as he passed the cafés along Rampart Street or Basin Street, sometimes listened outside their doors, fascinated by the playing of Mr. Jelly Roll. Jelly Roll sometimes played on the Mississippi river boats, and at other times he traveled all over the South engaging in piano battles with other players and usually winning the prizes. In the early 1900's he was known from the Mississippi delta to St. Louis, and later all over the country. He played a thousand pianos in as many different towns. In 1938 Jelly Roll Morton spent almost two months in Washington recording his ragtime and blues for the Folk Archives of the Library of Congress. Younger Negro piano players like Fats Waller, Willie "The Lion" Smith, and James P. Johnson in New York learned a great deal from Morton. Sometimes these men would all get together and try to outplay each other. In New York's Harlem such battles of music were called "cutting contests." Other piano players, from New York's Broadway, listened to those in Harlem, and learned from them. Thus this style of piano playing spread and greatly influenced American jazz music.

Boogie-woogie

"Trilling the treble and rolling the bass" is the way some players describe "boogie-woogie." Boogie-woogie is a kind of blues-ragtime played on the piano with a strong deep powerful rolling bass added. The left hand pounds out this steady marching bass while the right hand plays a lacework of blues over the bass, often in another rhythm. One hand makes the piano a talking drum. The other hand makes it a singing voice.

The rhythms of boogie-woogie may be traced back to the plantation banjo and the minstrel shouts. But it was not until about 1930 that a long, tall tap dancer, whose name was Pine Top Smith, first made boogie-woogie on the piano popular in the Middle West with his own "Pine Top's Boogie Woogie." A little later another colored pianist in Chicago, Jimmy Yancey, made up a piece on his piano called "Five O'Clock Blues." This became so well known that some people started calling all boogie-woogie music the "fives." Others call it "eight-to-the-bar," because the rolling bass consists of eight eighth-notes in each bar. Chicago and Kansas City were boogie-woogie centers, and some of the best players—Meade Lux Lewis, Albert Ammons, Dan Burley, Count Basie, and Pete Johnson—were well known in those cities before they traveled widely over the country and their music became part of jazz.

Singing Trumpets

> *The trumpet sounds within-a my soul!*
> *I ain't got long to stay here. . . .*

says the old spiritual "Swing Low, Sweet Chariot."
   Another spiritual says:

> *When the lamb-ram-sheep horns begin to blow,*
> *Trumpets begin to sound,*
> *Joshua commanded the children to shout*
> *And the walls come tumbling down!*

Pianos were not a part of early New Orleans jazz bands. Horns were their main instruments—particularly the short cornet or the slightly longer trumpet. Perhaps there were no pianos used because the earliest jazz bands developed from brass bands. These marching bands could be heard playing for blocks. Loud and clear and strong the trumpets sounded sixty years ago, or more, in New Orleans. In those days, when he wanted to let people know a dance was taking place in Lincoln Park, one of the great horn-blowers, Buddy Bolden, would get up on the bandstand and turn loose with a raggy blues on his gleaming trumpet. Folks could hear him for many, many blocks and they would begin heading for the dance. To this day New Orleans jazz is usually loud, and the horns top all other instruments.
   Long before the days of radio or television, promoters of boxing matches, excursions, or dances often hired bands to go about in horse-drawn wagons through the streets of New Orleans to advertise these events. Sometimes one band wagon would meet another. Then each would try to see which could outplay the other. They often tied up traffic at the street corners with their wagons. They called these contests "cutting contests"—a name borrowed later by the jazz piano players in New York City's Harlem.
   In order that the slide trombone might not hit the other players in the head as its slide was pulled in and out, these wagon players let the

trombonist sit on the floor at the end of the wagon with his feet hanging over the tailgate. From this custom comes the name "tailgate" for a style of jazz trombone playing that originated in New Orleans.

Sometimes a rich young man would hire one of these wagons full of musicians to serenade his sweetheart. Then folks called them "serenade wagons." Of course, the band played softly and sweetly for a serenade. But most of the time, in a wagon or not, for dances, picnics, parades, commercials, or even for funerals, the sounding brasses of these old bands could be heard for blocks.

The Diamond Stone Brass Band, the Allen Brass Band, the Olympia, Bolden's Band, and other good ones were often parading, their golden trumpets playing gay, syncopated rhythms as the trombones bassed for people to swing along by. Always following these marching bands on the streets would be a horde of children, dancing along, some playing on their own homemade instruments, keeping time with the music. These youngsters were called the "second line." As a "second liner" young Louis Armstrong, following such bands through the streets, fell in love with their wonderful horns, and, as he grew up, he began to dream of playing a singing trumpet himself.

Louis Armstrong

The story of Louis Armstrong is almost the whole story of orchestral jazz in America. His life stretches from the very beginnings of such jazz in New Orleans until now, when jazz is played by bands everywhere from Boston to Bombay, Paducah to Paris, Memphis to Melbourne. Louis Armstrong himself has taken jazz almost everywhere on earth. He is very famous. But when he was a little boy in New Orleans plunking his music-cigar-box, he was sometimes so ragged that if anybody gave him a penny he had to put it in his mouth because he had no pockets. Since he had such a big mouth, his playmates called him "Dippermouth," and later, "Satchelmouth." That is still his nickname now, shortened to "Satchmo'."

Even as a small boy Louis always had a strong, deep, gravelly voice. Maybe that is why, when he was seven years old, he was able to get a job as a newsboy on one of the busiest corners in New Orleans. Louis could be heard for a long way yelling, *"Times-Picayune! Times-Picayune!"* And later he got a job on a coal wagon crying, "Coal! Coal! A bucket of coal!" But he always wanted to play a horn, like Buddy Bolden. He was too poor to buy a horn, so he never got his wish—never, that is, until he was sent to a reform school for firing a pistol in the street on New Year's Eve, just as 1913 was being born.

At first little Louis played a tambourine in the Colored Waifs' Band. Later he beat a mighty roll on a small drum in their favorite concert piece, "At the Animals' Ball." Then he became the school bugler. But Louis was in the Home almost a year before he was at last entrusted with a trumpet. When the bandmaster finally gave him a trumpet, Louis was so happy that he kissed it. Then he took it to the tool shop and filed notches in its mouthpiece, so that it would fit his lips better. Louis became such a good boy trumpet player that when the Waifs' Band was permitted to march in parades outside the school everybody along the streets listened to him.

After two years at the Waifs' Home, Louis was sent back to his parents. He had made up his mind to be a musician although he had to leave the trumpet at the Home. He went to work on a coal wagon again, but on Sundays he spent the whole day in Lincoln Park or Johnson Park listening to Buddy Bolden's or Freddie Keppard's bands. From the old marching bands, little dance bands had now been formed. Louis often begged for a chance to pass out handbills announcing their dances, so that he might get free passes into the halls. One night his mother pulled Louis out of a dance hall by the scruff of his neck and thrashed him good for being away from home so late. But even at home in bed sometimes Louis could hear through the summer nights Bunk Johnson's cornet blowing the "Twelfth Street Rag," or the trumpet king, Joe Oliver, holding the last high notes of the "Tiger Rag." He dreamed of the day when he, too, would play so beautifully. But Louis did not have a horn.

Then one night when he was about sixteen years old, the cornet player in a little café band near Louis' home fell ill. The Italian owner of the café sent for Louis. When he found out that the boy did not have a horn, he bought him a battered old pawnshop cornet for fifteen dollars. Louis started playing with the band that very night. He had not blown a horn in so long a time that his lips became very sore, and his notes were weak and off key. So, instead of playing much that week, Louis sang along with the band, in that deep funny rough voice of his. The people liked his singing, so the Italian owner said, "Your playing is no good but, anyhow, I'll keep you." He paid him fifty cents a night. At last Louis was a musician! Soon his lips became used to the horn again, and he was playing so loud, strong, and clear that shortly other musicians came from all over New Orleans just to hear him. Even the great King Oliver came.

Many dance band musicians in New Orleans then did not know how to read music. They learned by listening to each other's ways of playing. Many white musicians, including Tom Brown and Jack Teagarden, liked the happy rhythms that colored musicians put into their playing. So they tried to learn them by listening to piano players like Jelly Roll Morton, or trumpet players like Buddy Bolden, King Oliver, and Bunk Johnson. In 1915, Tom Brown took a white band from New Orleans to Chicago, and for the first time the word "jazz"—then spelled jass—appeared in connection with the kind of music these men played. This band was called Brown's Dixieland Jass Band. It became very popular in Chicago. A little while later King Oliver took his Negro band there, too.

Meanwhile, young Louis Armstrong began to play with a very good trombonist, Kid Ory. In the New Orleans Country Club and at the Tulane University dances folks applauded loudly when Louis played his horn or sang his sad-funny blues. Soon a very good pianist named Fate Marable asked Louis to be a part of his group, which played on the *S.S. Sidney* running between New Orleans and St. Louis. This was the first time young Louis had ever been far away from home. But he enjoyed being a part of a band taking New Orleans music up and down the river. Later Louis played on the *S.S. St. Paul* in Marable's Jaz-E-Saz Band. It had a wonderful drummer named Baby Dodds; a fine banjoist, Johnny St. Cyr; and a bass player who was the best in New Orleans, Pops Foster, also a fine tuba player. Louis became a better and better musician. When he left the river boats in 1921, he became a part of Papa Celestin's Tuxedo Band, which played at all the best balls in New Orleans. A few months later the great King Oliver, whom Louis had admired so much when he was a little boy, sent for him to be a part of his orchestra at the Lincoln Garden in Chicago.

The Birth of Jazz

By this time the word jazz was known all across America. People everywhere wanted to hear the kind of music that Louis Armstrong had been listening to in New Orleans all his life—except that Louis had not called it jazz. Nobody knows just how that name for Dixieland music got started. Some say it came from a Spasm Band player whose name was Jasper—Jas, for short. Certainly some of the first bands to use the word spelled it with an *s* or a double *s*—*jas* or *jass*. Some say the boy's name was Charles, but that he wrote it abbreviated to Chas. People who could not read very well pronounced Chas. as *chaz* or *jaz*. Others say that in New Orleans in about 1900, there was a band called Razz's Band, and that somehow this got changed to Jazz Band. Others say the word jazz had an African origin. Anyhow, by the time Louis Armstrong got to Chicago folks were calling all Dixieland bands jazz bands, and their new music was called jazz.

To Louis, of course, it was not *new* music. It was just his old famil-iar music with a new name—the music that as a child he had heard Buddy Bolden play in the marching bands, the music he had plunked out on his little cigar-box, Jelly Roll's ragtime, the blues his mother hummed, the spirituals his grandmother crooned, the drumbeats his great-grandmother told him she heard in Congo Square—all of this, too, woven into the way he and Fate Marable, Baby Dodds, and Pops Foster played on the river boats. When Louis stood up in front of a great crowd of people in Chicago and played his trumpet, his music came out of these memories. And it was different from any other music anyone had ever heard. It was fun. And it was jazz.

Improvising

Most of the old New Orleans jazz musicians played directly from mem-ory of long-familiar melodies and rhythms that all of them had heard all their lives—melodies and rhythms which were African, French, Span-ish, and Creole. They could play them together, weaving one rhythm against another, without any trouble. Once they had heard a tune by ear, they did not need any written music. It was fun to improvise—to play a piece differently almost each time they played, partly composing as they went along. It was fun to make new little breaks between the musical phrases, and to make up new riffs, runs, and the sliding notes called glissandos to suit the way a person felt at each different playing. It was no fun playing exactly the same thing over and over, each time just the same way. When you felt very happy, you might play "hot." When you felt sad, you might play "deep" blues, repeating the sad old weary wailing *tune* over and over and over, but making each chorus vary, em-broidering each phrase a little differently, and maybe "riding out" with a brand new exciting ending on the whole thing that had never been there before.

Jazz first began, not with orchestras, but with many people—thou-sands and thousands of people whose names nobody remembers any more—the drummers in Congo Square, the rivermen along the Mississippi, the musicians in the marching bands of New Orleans, the singers of spirituals in country churches, the minstrel men, the children beating out rhythms on washboards and tin tubs, the man or woman all alone on a plantation making up a field holler or a blues, the piano player who could not read music playing a tune—teasing it, "ragging" it, having a "rag time"—the untrained musicians bringing their instruments together on street corners or in lodge halls in the evening to pass the time away. That is how jazz was born. And it was not just playing *music*. It was *playing*—like a game—playing *with* music, for fun.

That is what made jazz new and different. Most trained musicians play the notes of each piece each time the same, as nearly as they can, just as it is written down on paper. But an old-time jazz musician might play each piece each time a *little differently*, improvising according to the way he felt, as long as the beat was there and the rhythm. Jazz came to be known as a playfully happy music. Even the sad old blues had, beneath the blue melodies, a steady rolling beat that seemed to be marching somewhere to something better, something happy. So, when Louis Armstrong lifted his trumpet to his mouth in Chicago, people there were happy. When he sang the blues, they were sad and happy at the same time. And when Louis sang "scat" style—"skee-daddle-de-dee-daddle," meaning nothing—folks laughed until they almost split their sides. Jazz is happy!

Syncopation

One of the things that makes jazz a happy music is its continuous syncopation—its use of surprising offbeats—and its interweaving of rhythms, one over the other. Jazz rhythms are not always simple. A march is a straight 4/4 beat such as a regular brass band plays. But when jazz began to creep in, the New Orleans bands started playing one rhythm against another, or sometimes several rhythms against one another. In jazz there are usually at least two rhythms going at once, one part of the music keeping a steady beat while the other part dodges the accent, plays around with the time, creates syncopated counter-rhythms against a 4/4 beat, jumping ahead or holding back, anticipating or retarding—skipping—hitting and missing—weaving together many rhythms, called polyrhythms. But all of it forms a teasing happy combination that comes out driving ahead, rolling smoothly and merrily on.

It is this gay going ahead, this rippling, dancing drive, in and out and around the beat, that makes jazz.

Melodies in jazz do the same things. While a cornet plays the tune, the clarinet may play a countermelody—that is one melody against the other. But off notes and blue notes, glides and slurs and slides—like an old-time Negro minister preaching a sermon—are common in jazz. The five-tone scale, frequent seventh and ninth chords, and the melody patterns of the twelve-bar blues are often used. The early jazz bands used chord combinations that no one had ever heard in European music. This "close" harmony, sometimes above the melody, like the "barbershop chords" of singing, is common in jazz—for the brasses and reeds of jazz are singing instruments, often used as if they were voices.

Chicago and New York

A teen-age schoolboy named Bix Beiderbecke used to come to the Lincoln Garden in Chicago to hear Louis. Bix later became a great hornblower himself. Art Hodes and Mezz Mezzrow, and other young musicians like Paul Whiteman and Jimmy McPartland came to hear Louis, too. Just as in New Orleans, so in Chicago, musicians learned from each other. To the Chicago boys this new Dixieland music was a wonderful and exciting thing. They began to try to play like the men from the Deep South. When the Original Dixieland Band moved on to New York, Broadway musicians began to try to play the same way. In 1921 King Oliver and his Creole Jazz Band had toured the West Coast and so, from California to New York, jazz began to go everywhere.

In 1924 Paul Whiteman and his orchestra gave a famous jazz concert at Aeolian Hall in New York. He introduced for the first time the "Rhapsody in Blue" by the young composer, George Gershwin. There were no Negro players in Paul Whiteman's Orchestra, but George Gershwin's "Rhapsody in Blue"—one of the earliest attempts at putting jazz into concert form—opened with the upward wail of a clarinet glissando and went into an echo of the sad old Negro blues of the Deep South. Jazz had begun to influence serious music. Stravinsky, Ravel, Carpenter, Bernstein, and Copland all have recognized its power. The famous American conductor Walter Damrosch once said, "Lady Jazz, adorned with her intriguing rhythms, has danced her way around the world, even to the northern Eskimos and the South Sea Polynesians."

Now jazz concerts are often held in Carnegie Hall where formerly only symphonies were heard. So from the Congo to Carnegie went the rhythms of the African drums, from New Orleans to New York, and from New York to the whole world.

What Is Jazz?

Before 1900 many of our American musicians, conductors, and composers had been born in Europe, and had come to our country as immigrants. Naturally much of our music, both popular and classical, was then greatly influenced by European music and followed its styles and forms. Strangely enough in those days, too, many Americans thought that if singers or musicians did not come from Europe they could not be very good. If songs did not sound like German *lieder,* or dance pieces were not Viennese waltzes or mid-European mazurkas or polkas, many Americans thought they did not amount to very much. Many of our most famous composers of theater music had also been born abroad. Victor Herbert was from Ireland, Sigmund Romberg from Hungary, Rudolph Friml from Czechoslovakia, and Irving Berlin, who wrote "Alexander's Ragtime Band," was from Russia. These composers writing *for* America, were nevertheless influenced by the musical styles of Europe. People enjoyed their music, but much of it was not especially American. It did not grow out of American soil. It was not until ragtime, the blues, and *particularly* jazz came along that America had a music we could call *our very own* to play and sing.

The ragtime players, blues singers, and brass band marchers whose music combined to produce jazz were all born in America. The *continuous* mounting syncopations of jazz were born here. Europeans used syncopation in their music, but not very much. The Africans used a very complex syncopation in their music, but they did not combine it with melody and harmony in the way that Americans did. And they never had the many different instruments that we use. They had no cornets, no slide trombones, no pianos, no clarinets. The way Americans began to syncopate those instruments as they played them became very much a part of jazz.

Jazz is a *way of playing* music even more than it is a composed music. Almost any music can become jazz if it is played with jazz treatment. In New Orleans there were syncopated marches and ragtime waltzes. Paul Whiteman jazzed Rimski-Korsakov's "Song of India." Ted Lewis was expelled from his home-town band when he was a child for playing a ragtime break in the "Poet and Peasant." Maxine Sullivan became famous by singing "Loch Lomond," not as it came from Scotland, but by singing it as she felt it, jazz style.

Jelly Roll Morton's "Tiger Rag" was first an old French Creole dance quadrille that he heard in New Orleans. He turned it into ragtime for the piano. Today it is played as a jazz band piece. Nobody knows on what levee the first blues song was sung. Today blues have become jazz songs. The off-beat rhythms of ragtime and blues are jazz.

Ten Basic Elements of Jazz

Syncopation. This is a shifting of the normal rhythmic stress from the strong beat to the weak beat, accenting the offbeat, and playing one rhythm against another in such a way that listeners want to move, nod heads, clap hands, or dance. Syncopation is basic and continuous in jazz, and upon it are built very complex rhythms.

Improvisation. This is composing as one plays, or making up variations on old themes directly on the instrument being played rather than from written notes. The interest and beauty of improvisation depends on the talent and ability of the individual performer.

Percussion. The drums provide jazz with its basic beat, but the banjo or guitar, the string bass or tuba, and the piano also provide percussion. Any or all of these instruments may make up the rhythm section of a jazz band. Chords may be used as a beat to create harmonized percussion.

Rhythm. In jazz this is not limited to percussion beats alone. The variations of volume, tone, and pitch may also be used in such a way as to give to a jazz performance additional accents of sound-rhythm, played against a variety of counter-rhythms supplied by the percussion.

Blue notes. These are glissando or slurred notes, somewhere between flat and natural, derived from the blues as sung, and sliding into intervals between major and minor. Blue notes are impossible to notate exactly, but when written down on paper they are frequently indicated by the flatted third or seventh notes of the scale.

Tone color. Jazz instruments may take on the varied tones of the singing or speaking voice, even of laughter or of groans, in a variety of tonal colorations. At one time different instruments may be playing different melodies.

Harmony. In jazz, harmony makes frequent use of the blue note, the blue scale, the seventh and ninth chords, and the "close" harmony of the old barbershop style of chromatic singing, which is carried over into instrumentation.

Break. This is a very brief syncopated interlude, usually of two to four bars, between musical phrases—often improvised in unwritten jazz. Armstrong is famous for his breaks.

Riff. This is a single rhythmic phrase repeated over and over, usually as a background to the lead melody. A riff may be used also as a melodic theme in itself.

Joy of playing. This is the element that gives jazz its zest and verve, its happy, dancing quality, that brings musicians of all races together in impromptu jam sessions. Here new musical ideas are born as the musicians play together for hours without written music—just for fun.

Jazz Instruments

Folks in New Orleans paid so much attention to players like old Buddy Bolden, King Oliver, and young Louis Armstrong because they were trumpeters and the trumpet was the leading instrument in their bands. The other brass instrument was a slide trombone. The reed instrument was a clarinet. Drums, banjo or guitar, tuba, or maybe a string bass were the percussion that provided the basic rhythm. Pops Foster threw away his bow and plucked the bass with his fingers. This is the way most bass viols are played in jazz today. There was no piano in the early Dixieland bands. But when King Oliver moved northward, in Chicago he added a piano. Lil Hardin, who later became Louis Armstrong's wife, played it. It was fashionable in the North for all the jazz bands to have a piano. Besides, printed music was beginning to be used for jazz, and often it was *only* the pianist who could read printed music. Lil Hardin was a college graduate. But most early jazz musicians never went to school very much.

As jazz bands grew larger—from four or five players to twelve or fifteen—the brass, reed, and rhythm sections were increased. Today, in the large bands, the brass instruments are usually trumpets and trombones; the reeds are alto and tenor saxophones and a clarinet; and the percussion is the piano, guitar, string bass, and drums.

In the old New Orleans jazz bands there were no saxophones. This instrument, invented in 1846 by a Belgian, Adolphe Sax, was used mostly in military bands until Chicago and New York jazz bands took it up, at first for comic effects. But with some of the Northern bands it grew to be almost as important a serious solo instrument as the trumpet. For fun, some bands now have a great variety of percussion-makers besides drums—rattles, bells, blocks, coconut shells, and brushes.

Rumbas and other Caribbean dances introduced into our orchestras little double drums, the bongos; the claves, two sticks that are knocked together; the guiro, a calabash that is scraped; and the maracas, seed-filled gourds that are shaken. Caribbean music is very old music from Cuba, Haiti, and other islands of the Caribbean Sea. Its rhythms also go back to Africa, but have now become a part of American jazz.

Swing Music

When Louis Armstrong came to New York in 1924, he played with Fletcher Henderson's Orchestra at the Roseland Ballroom on Broadway. This orchestra used written music, and most of its players had been trained in good music schools. So it was not easy for Louis to play with them. He had been used to not just *playing* a piece, but playing *with* it at the same time, improvising—making up the music as he went along—and letting his fancy take flight. But by 1924 there were many reasons why the younger band leaders felt that jazz had to be written down on paper. For one thing, when records were made they always had to be the same length, to play about three minutes. And, when radio programs were arranged a few years later, they had to be timed to the split second. The bands had to play things the same way and the same length all the time when they played for shows in theaters, also. So "arrangers" were employed to arrange music exactly to suit these various needs. This written and arranged jazz—less wild, less hot and strange and exciting than the old New Orleans Dixieland jazz—gradually came to be called "swing" music. When it used a great many sentimental songs for its melodies, it was called "sweet" jazz.

Louis Armstrong's wife Lil helped him learn to read music better, and to understand written arrangements quickly. In a little while, just as he had been a star of the old Dixieland groups, Louis became a star of the new swing bands. No matter what kind of band Louis played in, his trumpet sang out. Broadway liked Louis. Ted Lewis, Paul Whiteman, Muggsy Spanier, and the former schoolboy who had listened often to him in Chicago, Bix Beiderbecke, all were at the Roseland to hear him and to study his style. On the West Coast many other young musicians heard Louis at the Cotton Club in Hollywood. Louis made hundreds of records and often played on the radio. In the years that followed, Armstrong's once improvised riffs, breaks, and solos became a part of modern American jazz.

Many good swing orchestras developed before World War II, some playing "sweet" and some playing "hot." Duke Ellington, Glenn Cray, Benny Goodman, Red Nichols, Glenn Miller, Vincent Lopez, Cab Calloway, Bunny Berigan, Charlie Barnet, Jimmy Lunceford, Artie Shaw, Woody Herman, Bennie Moten, Tommy Dorsey, and Count Basie all had bands that millions of people enjoyed. Louis Armstrong, too, had his own band. And, in the past twenty years, he has traveled almost all over the world playing jazz from the Palladium in London to the great halls of Tokyo. When big bands were no longer so popular, and many smaller jazz band combinations were formed, Louis had one of the best, with white and Negro musicians playing together: Earl Hines, piano; Jack Teagarden, trombone; Barney Bigard, clarinet; Cozy Cole, drums; and Arvell Shaw, bass. From Chicago to Copenhagen they played jazz.

But by this time Copenhagen had its own jazz bands, as did Tokyo, London, Paris, and every other big city in the world. By 1940, the music of America had gone everywhere and people everywhere were trying to play it. In Paris there was a society called *Le Jazz Hot*. Brussels had a jazz magazine called *Music,* and London had another named *Jazz Forum. Downbeat* and *The Record Changer* came out in our country. Critics and commentators began to give lectures on American jazz and to write books about it in many languages: Robert Goffin in Belgium, Baron Timme Rosenkrantz in Denmark, Hughes Panassié in France, Ortiz Oderigo in Argentina, and Albert McCarthy in England. By 1950, Marshall Stearns, John Hammond, and George Avakian were giving a course in the history and appreciation of jazz at New York University, while Rudi Blesh had already given a series of lectures at the San Francisco Museum of Art, introducing Bunk Johnson there. An Institute of Jazz Studies has been formed in New York. And every summer now near Tanglewood, a famous music center in the Berkshire Hills, a round table on jazz is held.

About 1945 a young trumpet player named Dizzy Gillespie began to blow on his trumpet a saucy, more offbeat than ever kind of jazz called "bebop." At jam sessions for several years before this, a few musicians had been playing bebop, or bop—Thelonious Monk and Bud Powell on the piano, Max Roach improvising on the drums, Lester Young and Charlie Parker on the saxophone. Small bands soon took up the new bebop riffs and chords and bongo drumbeats. For a while this ultra-modern music was much talked about. When the bebop wave passed, it left its influences behind on what is called "cool" or "progressive" jazz, which often is played for listening rather than dancing, and which does not always have the steady rhythms of Dixieland jazz or swing. Clashing chords and dissonances may be more prominent than in older forms of jazz. Stan Kenton's and Dizzy Gillespie's bands feature this style of music.

Sometimes for fun, singers sing "oo-ya-koo" syllables to boppish backgrounds today, as Cab Calloway in the 1930's sang "hi-de-hi-de-ho-de-hey," meaning nothing, or as Lionel Hampton sang "hey-baba-re-bop" in 1940, or as Louis Armstrong used to sing "scat" syllables to his music in Chicago in the 1920's, or as Jelly Roll Morton shouted meaningless words to ragtime music in the early 1900's, or as the Mother Goose rhyme said, "Hey-diddle-diddle, the cat and the fiddle," even before that—for fun. Nonsense syllables are not new in poetry or music, but they are fun.

Musicians today are still having fun with jazz—as the boys in the old Spasm Bands did—and people all over the world are enjoying it. Jazz, America's music, *is* fun.

Famous Jazz Musicians

Trumpet

Louis Armstrong
Bix Beiderbecke
Bunny Berigan
Buddy Bolden
Buck Clayton
Wild Bill Davison
Sidney De Paris
Harry Edison
Roy Eldridge
Dizzy Gillespie
Erskine Hawkins
Harry James
Bunk Johnson
Max Kaminsky
Freddie Keppard
Tommy Ladnier
Howard McGhee
Jimmy McPartland
Bubber Miley
Frank Newton
Red Nichols
King Oliver
Hot Lips Page
Louis Prima
Henry Rena
Joe Smith
Muggsy Spanier
Rex Stewart
Lu Watters
Cootie Williams

Clarinet

Buster Bailey
Sidney Bechet
Barney Bigard
Buddy De Franco
Johnny Dodds
Irving Fazola
Benny Goodman
Edmond Hall
Woody Herman
Mezz Mezzrow
Jimmie Noone
Leon Rappolo
Pee Wee Russell
Artie Shaw
Larry Shields
Omer Simeon
Frank Teschemacher

Drums

Ray Bauduc
Louis Bellson
Denzil Best
Manzy Campbell
Sidney Catlett
Cozy Cole
Jimmy Crawford
Baby Dodds
Buddy Gilmore
Sonny Greer
Lionel Hampton
J. C. Heard
Joe Jones
Gene Krupa
Kaiser Marshall
Chano Pozo
Max Roach
Zutty Singleton
Dave Tough
Chick Webb
George Wettling
Shadow Wilson
Herbert Wright
Steve Wright

Trombone

Lawrence Brown
George Brunies
Wilbur De Paris
Tommy Dorsey
Amos Gilyard
Tyree Glenn
Charlie Green
Jimmy Harris
J. C. Higginbotham
Lou McGarity
Glenn Miller
Miff Mole
Benny Morton
Kid Ory
Jack Teagarden
Dickie Wells
Trummy Young

Saxophones

Georgie Auld
Charlie Barnet
Sidney Bechet
Tex Beneke
Chu Berry
Don Byas
Harry Carney
Benny Carter
Bud Freeman
Stan Getz
Wardell Gray
Coleman Hawkins
Johnny Hodges
Illinois Jacquet
Lee Konitz
Jimmy Lunceford
Dave Matthews
Eddie Miller
James Moody
Gerry Mulligan
Charlie Parker
Flip Phillips
Ike Quebec
Paul Quinichette
Don Redman
Willie Smith
Joe Thomas
Frankie Trumbauer
Ben Webster
Lester Young

Piano

Albert Ammons
Count Basie
Dave Brubeck
Dan Burley
Herman Chittison
Nat King Cole
Duke Ellington
Erroll Garner
Johnny Guarnieri
Lil Hardin
Fletcher Henderson
Earl Hines
Art Hodes
Tony Jackson
James P. Johnson
Pete Johnson
Scott Joplin
Porter King
Billy Kyle
Meade Lux Lewis
Cripple Clarence
    Lofton
Marian McPartland
Dodo Marmarosa
David Martin
Thelonious Monk
Jelly Roll Morton
Bennie Moten
Benny Payne
Oscar Peterson
Bud Powell
Luckeyth Roberts
Hazel Scott
George Shearing
Pine Top Smith
Willie the Lion Smith
Jess Stacy
Joe Sullivan
Art Tatum
Billy Taylor
Lennie Tristano
Fats Waller
Teddy Weatherford
Mary Lou Williams
Teddy Wilson
Jimmy Yancey
Bob Zurke

Violin

Ray Nance
Stuff Smith
Eddie South
Joe Venuti

Banjo

Eddie Condon
Johnny St. Cyr
Elmer Snowden
Dave Wilborn

Guitar

Bernard Addison
Irving Ashby
Teddy Bunn
Charlie Christian
Eddie Condon
Freddie Green
Lonnie Johnson
Barney Kessel
Eddie Lang
Carl Lynch
Brownie McGhee
Oscar Moore
Les Paul
Tampa Red
Django Reinhardt
Johnny St. Cyr

Harmonica

Larry Adler
Sonny Terry
Les Thompson
Toots Tilman

Bass

Artie Bernstein
Jimmy Blanton
Wellman Braud
Ray Brown
Red Callender
Israel Crosby
Pops Foster
John Kirby
Oscar Pettiford
Junior Ragland
Slam Steward
Billy Taylor

Vibraphones

Terry Gibbs
Tyree Glenn
Lionel Hampton
Margie Hyams
Milt Jackson
Red Norvo

Records

Illustrating the historical stages of jazz and the influence of jazz on contemporary popular music, currently available on long playing reissues, speed 33 1/3 RPM, unless otherwise indicated.

Primitive Sources

African Coast Rhythms
Native musicians
Riverside 4001

African Tribal Music
Native musicians
Esoteric 513

African and Afro-American Drums
Including Brazil, Caribbean, U.S.A.
Folkways P 502

Negro Folk Music of Africa and America
Drummers, folk musicians, singers
Folkways EFL-P 500

American Negro Folk Sources

Sonny Terry
"Lonesome Train"
Asch 550–3A (78 RPM)
(Collector's item)

The Jug Bands
Dixieland and Memphis jug bands
"X" Vault Originals 3009

Leadbelly (Huddie Ledbetter)
Vocals with guitar and zither
Capitol EAP 1–369 (45 RPM)

Leadbelly Memorial Album—Volume 1
"John Henry" and other songs
Stinson SLP 17

Ragtime

Jelly Roll Morton
"Maple Leaf Rag" played in both St. Louis and New Orleans styles
Jazz Man 21/22
also included in the Morton Album—Volume 3
Circle L 14003

Ragtime Piano Roll
Early rags played by Scott Joplin and others
Riverside RLP 1025

Blues *(78 RPM, old issues)*

Bessie Smith with James P. Johnson
"Back Water Blues"
Columbia 14195-D

Bertha Chippie Hill with Louis Armstrong
"Trouble in Mind"
Okeh 8312-A

Leroy Carr with piano and guitar
"How Long, How Long Blues"
Vocalion 1191

Woody Herman and his orchestra
"Dupree Blues"
Decca 1288-A

Count Basie with Jimmy Rushing
"Good Morning Blues"
Decca 1446-A

Charles Brown
"Black Night"
Aladdin 3076-A

Louis Armstrong
"The St. Louis Blues"
Decca

New Orleans Jazz

King Oliver's Creole Jazz Band
With Louis Armstrong
Riverside RLP 1029

Louis Armstrong and His Hot Five
Twelve selections recorded 1925–1927
Columbia ML 4383

Johnny Dodds Washboard Band
"X" Vault Originals LX 3006

Original Dixieland Jass Band
Earliest recorded jazz by whites
"X" Vault Originals LX 3007

Jelly Roll Morton's Red Hot Peppers
With Kid Ory, Barney Bigard, Omer Simeon
"X" Vault Originals LX 3008

New Orleans—Jazz Volume 3
Jug bands, brass bands, Oliver, Armstrong, Morton, and others
Folkways FP 57

Chicago Jazz

Bix Beiderbecke and the Wolverines
Bix's earliest recordings
Riverside RLP 1023

Eddie Condon's Hot Shots
With Miller, Hawkins, Teagarden
"X" Vault Originals 3005

Chicago Jazz Album
Representative white bands
Decca DL 8029

Kansas City Jazz

Bennie Moten's Kansas City Jazz
"X" Vault Originals LX 3004

Count Basie's Kansas City Seven
Mercury 25015

Kansas City Jazz
Famous Negro Bands
Decca 8044

Boogie-woogie

Pine Top Smith
Also Jelly Roll Morton
Brunswick 58003

Jimmy Yancey
Blues and boogie
"X" Vault Originals LX 3000

Meade Lux Lewis
"Boogie Woogie"
Blue Note 7018

Pete Johnson and Albert Ammons
"8 To The Bar"
Victor LPT 9

Pioneers of Boogie Woogie—Vol. I-II
Cow Cow Davenport and others
Riverside 1009/1034

Harlem Piano

James P. Johnson
"Early Harlem Piano"
Riverside 1011

Fats Waller
"Jivin' with Fats"
Riverside 1022

Swing

Fletcher Henderson's Orchestra
With Rex Stewart and Coleman Hawkins
"X" Vault Originals 3013

Duke Ellington and Orchestra
"Ellington's Greatest"
Victor LPT 1004

Duke Ellington and Orchestra
"Masterpieces"
Columbia ML 4418

Woody Herman's Band
"Classics in Jazz"
Capitol H 324

Jimmie Lunceford and Orchestra
Decca DL 8050

Benny Goodman Quartet
Early white and Negro combo
Victor LPT 3004

Benny Goodman Band
Carnegie Hall jazz concert
Columbia SL 160 (4358/9)

Erskine Hawkins
"After Hours"
Coral 56061

Wingy Manone
Small band swing
"X" Vault Originals LVA 3014

Goodman, Dorsey, Shaw, Miller
"Up Swing" by famous bands
Victor LPT 12

Afro-Cuban

Tambores Afro-Cubanos
Cuban drums
Spanish 535

Machito's Afro-Cubans
Caribbean rhythms
Decca 5157

Bebop

Dizzy Gillespie
With Charley Christian
Esoteric 4

Dizzy Gillespie Band
Volume I and II
Atlantic ALR 138/142

Thelonious Monk
"Genius of Modern Music"
Blue Note 5002

Stan Getz and Lee Konitz
"New Sounds"
Prestige 108

Tadd Dameron
With Clifford Brown
Prestige 159

James Moody
With Chano Pozo
Blue Note 5006

Thelonious Monk Trio
Prestige 142

Cool Caribbean

Tito Puente
Mambo rhythms
Secco 23

Joe Loco Trio
Volumes I and II
Tico 109/III

Tito Rodriguez
Caribbean jazz
Spanish 504

Piano Stylists

Earl Hines
Piano solos
Atlantic 120

Art Tatum
Piano solos
Decca 5086

Barbara Carroll
"Piano Panorama"
Atlantic LP 132

Progressive Piano
Previn, Booker, and others
Victor LJM 3001

Hazel Scott
"Great Scott"
Columbia CL 6090

Marian McPartland
"Moods"
Savoy 15022

Jess Stacy
Piano solos
Brunswick BL 58029

Eddie Heywood
Eight selections
Commodore 20007

Teddy Wilson and his piano
Columbia CL 6098

Mary Lou Williams
"Piano '53"
Contemporary 2507

Progressive Sounds

Woody Herman
"Third Herd"
MGM E-192

Stan Kenton
"Progressive Jazz"
Capitol H 172

Sauter-Finegan
"New Directions in Music"
Victor LPM 3115

Duke Ellington
"Ellington Uptown"
Columbia ML 4639

Cool Combos

Chet Baker Quartet
With Russ Freeman
Pacific 6

Dave Brubeck Octet
Fantasy 3-3

Lennie Tristano
With Lee Konitz
Prestige 101

Erroll Garner
Trio and solos
Dial 205

George Shearing Quartet
MGM E-518

Billy Taylor
With guitar, bass, drums
Atlantic 113

Oscar Peterson Quartet
"Willow Weep For Me"
Clef 8999 (78 and 45 RPM)

Gerry Mulligan Quartet
With Lee Konitz, Chet Baker
Pacific 2

Bud Powell Trio
Roost 401

Classics in Jazz
"Cool and Quiet"
Capitol H 371

Documentaries

The Jazz Scene
Numerous famous instrumentalists with photographs, 2 LP records
Clef Special Edition Album Series

From Barrelhouse to Bop
"A History of Jazz Piano"
Narrated and played by John Mehegar
Perspective Records PR 1

Jam Session No. 4
With Count Basie, Stan Getz, Buddy Rich, Wardell Gray, Benny
Carter, Willie Smith, Buddy De Franco, Harry Edison and others
Clef MG C-4004

Hot vs. Cool
"A Battle of Jazz"
New Orleans style: Jimmy McPartland and Dixieland Stars
Modern jazz style: Dizzy Gillespie and Birdland Stars
MGM E-194

Jazz at the Philharmonic
Willie Smith, Wardell Gray, Krupa and others
Stinson 23

Great Trumpet Artists
Bunk Johnson, Beiderbecke, Berigan and others
Victor LPT 26

100 of My Favorite Recordings of Jazz, Blues, Folk Songs, and Jazz-Influenced Performances

After Hours, Erskine Hawkins, Bluebird
After You've Gone, Benny Goodman Trio, Victor
Any Old Time, Artie Shaw (with Billie Holiday), Bluebird
A-Tisket A-Tasket, Chick Webb (with Ella Fitzgerald), Decca
At the Jazz Band Ball, Bix Beiderbecke, Columbia
Aunt Hager's Blues, Paul Whiteman (with Jack Teagarden), Decca
Back Water Blues, Bessie Smith, Columbia
Begin the Beguine, Tiny Grimes, Atlantic
Begin the Beguine, Eddie Heywood, Commodore
Big Noise from Winnetka, Bob Crosby, Decca
Blue Skies, Benny Goodman, Victor
Body and Soul, Coleman Hawkins, Bluebird
Boogie Woogie Prayer, Lewis, Johnson, and Ammons, Columbia
Bugle Call Rag, Jimmy Yancey, Riverside
But Officer, Sonny Knight, Aladdin
Call of the Freaks, Luis Russell, Okeh
Careless Love, Josh White, Asch
Carson City Stage, Gerry Mulligan Quartet, Pacific
Casbah, Tadd Dameron, Capitol
Chattanooga Choo Choo, Glenn Miller, Victor
Cherokee, Charlie Barnet, Bluebird
Chica Boo, Lloyd Glenn, Swing Time
Christopher Columbus, Fletcher Henderson, Decca
Danny Boy, Glenn Miller, Bluebird
Dear Old Southland, Duke Ellington, Victor
Dippermouth Blues, King Oliver's Creole Jazz Band, Brunswick
Drifting Blues, Johnny Moore's Three Blazers, Exclusive
Flat Feet Floogee, Slim Gaillard and Slam Stewart, Vocalion
Flying Home, Lionel Hampton, Decca
For You, Tommy Dorsey, Victor
Fox Chase, Sonny Terry (with Red on Washboard), Columbia

Good Morning Blues, Count Basie (with Jimmie Rushing), Decca
Hambone, Red Saunders (with the Hambone Kids), Okeh
He's a Real Gone Guy, Nellie Lutcher, Capitol
He's the Best Little Yankee to Me, Una Mae Carlisle (with Ray Nance),
    Joe Davis
Hey Baba Rebop, Lionel Hampton, Decca
Honky Tonk Train, Meade Lux Lewis, Victor, Decca
How Long Blues, Count Basie, Decca
How Long Blues, Jimmy and Mama Yancey, Atlantic
I Cried For You, Benny Goodman Quintet (with Teddy Wilson),
    Bluebird
I'm Going to Sit Right Down and Write Myself a Letter, Fats Waller,
    Victor
It's Only a Paper Moon, King Cole Trio, Capitol
Jingle Bells, Joe Loco, Tico
Lemon Drop, Woody Herman, Capitol
Lonesome Road, Tommy Dorsey, Victor
Lonesome Train, Sonny Terry, Asch
Lover Man, Charlie Parker, Dial
Mamie's Blues, Jelly Roll Morton, Commodore
Mardi Gras in New Orleans, Professor Longhair, Atlantic
Marie, Tommy Dorsey, Victor
Me and My Chauffeur, Memphis Minnie, Okeh
Memphis Blues and Others, W. C. Handy (with narration), Audio
    Archives
Minnie the Moocher, Cab Calloway, Brunswick
Miss Brown to You, Teddy Wilson (with Billie Holiday), Columbia
Mobile Bay, Rex Stewart, "X" Vault Originals
Night Life, Mary Lou Williams, Brunswick
Old Man Mose Is Dead, Louis Jordan, Decca
One O'Clock Jump, Count Basie, Decca
Pine Top's Boogie, Pine Top Smith, Brunswick
Rag Mop, Doc Sausage and His Mad Lads, Regal
Rhapsody in Blue, Paul Whiteman (with George Gershwin), Victor
Round about Midnight, Thelonious Monk, Musicraft
St. James Infirmary, Artie Shaw (with Hot Lips Page), Victor
St. Louis Blues, Larry Adler (with John Kirby's Orch.), Decca
St. Louis Blues, Louis Armstrong, Okeh
St. Louis Blues, Earl Hines (Boogie Woogie), V-Disc
St. Louis Blues, Hall Johnson Choir, Victor

St. Louis Blues, Johnny Moore's Three Blazers, Exclusive
St. Louis Blues, Bessie Smith, Columbia
Salted Peanuts, Dizzy Gillespie, Manor
See See Rider, Ma Rainey (with Louis Armstrong), Paramount
September Song, Morris Lane's Combo, Continental
Shadow of the Blues, Wilton Crawley, Okeh
Sit Down, Sister Rosetta Tharpe, Decca
Skin Deep, Duke Ellington (with Louis Bellson), Columbia
Skylark, Harry James, Columbia
Snowy Morning Blues, James P. Johnson, Folkways
Solid Rock, Rex Stewart (with Django Reinhardt), H. R. S.
So Long, Marl Young's Orchestra, Sunbeam
Sparrow's Flight, Johnny Sparrow, Melford
Star Dust, Artie Shaw, Victor
Stormy Weather, Buddy Johnson (with Ella Johnson), Decca
Straighten Up and Fly Right, King Cole Trio, Capitol
Suite in Four Comfortable Quarters, Leonard Feather and Dan Burley,
    Continental
Tea for Two, Johnny Hodges, Clef
Tea for Two, Willie Smith, Mercury
Texas and Pacific Blues, Frenchy's String Band, Columbia
The Mooche, Duke Ellington, Victor
Tiger Rag, Original Dixieland Jazz Band, Columbia
Traveling Blues, Ma Rainey (with Jug Washboard Band), Paramount
Trouble in Mind, Bertha Chippie Hill (with Armstrong), Okeh
Tuxedo Junction, Erskine Hawkins, Bluebird
Well, All Right Then, Jimmie Lunceford, Vocalion
West End Blues, Louis Armstrong, Columbia
What's Your Story, Morning Glory, Andy Kirk, Decca
When the Saints Go Marching In, Bunk Johnson's Brass Band, Victor
Willow Weep For Me, Oscar Peterson, Clef
Winter Wonderland, Bonnemere, Roost
Yazoo Blues, Bennie Moten's Kansas City Orchestra, Victor
Yellow Dog Blues, Bessie Smith, Columbia

The First Book of the West Indies

(1956)

Contents

The West Indies

Lands of palm trees and blue-green water, dancing waves and sandy beaches, fishermen and fishing ships, bright birds and butterflies, sugar cane and spices, bananas, coconuts, sunshine and blue skies—these are the islands of the West Indies.

Beginning near the tip of Florida, they curve out from the Gulf of Mexico in a long tropical arch all the way down to the northern coast of South America. Cuba, Hispaniola, Puerto Rico, the Virgin Islands, the Leeward and Windward Islands, Tobago, and Trinidad form a border on the eastern side of the Caribbean Sea. Out in the Atlantic Ocean, off the tip of Florida, stand the Bahama Islands, and much farther south is Barbados, most eastward of the islands. Off the northern coast of Venezuela are Aruba and Curaçao. And surrounded by the Caribbean itself is Jamaica, south of Cuba. The coasts of Mexico and Central America and the northern shoulder of South America border the Caribbean Sea to the west and south.

For more than four hundred years thousands of ships have been sailing to the Caribbean Sea. The golden galleons of the explorers, Spanish caravels, Yankee clippers, four-masted schooners, cruisers and battleships, merchant vessels and oil tankers, pleasure yachts, and beautiful white ships carrying tourists on happy winter cruises—all these have come to the West Indies. Before the Europeans arrived, the native Carib and Arawak Indians put to sea in long canoes. Today, in addition to sturdy cargo ships, thousands and thousands of little fishing boats with colored sails carry food to the people who live on the islands of the Caribbean.

So far as we know, the tiny caravels of Columbus were the first European ships to reach Caribbean waters. In August, 1492, Columbus left Spain on the *Santa Maria,* with two other ships, the *Niña* and the *Pinta.* He sailed into the unknown distances of the Atlantic Ocean, seeking a new route to India. For two months he did not see land. Some of his crewmen became frightened and wanted to turn back, but Columbus would not do so. Each night he noted from the deck the position of the stars—the ever-faithful stars that were familiar to him. So long as the stars did not disappear, Columbus felt that he was safe under heaven. Each night by flickering candlelight he made entries in his journal. And each morning he said to his helmsman, "Sail on! Sail on!"

At last one morning the crewmen saw signs of land life—floating twigs on the water, and land birds in the sky. Then they saw land! It was a small island southeast of what is now Florida, among the many islands we have since named the Bahamas. The people Columbus found there called the island Guanahani (gwahn-a-HAH-nee). He renamed it San Salvador. Just which small island this was is not certain, but historians think it is the one now called Watlings Island.

Sailing on, Columbus found other islands, among them Cuba and Hispaniola. Finally, after leaving some men behind to form a colony on Hispaniola, Columbus sailed back to Spain to tell the King and Queen he had found India. When he returned on a second voyage he discovered more islands, among them Puerto Rico and Jamaica. On a third voyage in 1498 he touched the coast of South America.

Columbus never knew he had found a brand-new world, the Americas. He thought he had simply discovered the eastern coast of India. To this day the islands where he first landed, and all the others in the area, are called the West Indies. Since most of the West Indian islands border the Caribbean Sea, they are also called the Caribbean islands. Another name for them is the Antilles (an-TIL-eez), as the Italians once called all uncharted land west of the Azores.

Through its support of Columbus, Spain opened up a new world to explorers. Not long after the exciting news of his discoveries spread over Europe, the English, the French, and the Dutch were sailing across the Atlantic too, in search of the warm and sunny lands of the west. In the names of their various kings these early explorers laid claim to the places where they landed. Then colonists came, some speaking English, some Spanish, French, Dutch, or Danish. So, even today, the languages spoken in the West Indies are not the same from island to island.

The gentle Arawak and the fiercer Carib Indians whom the Europeans found on these warm islands were not used to hard labor. Many of them soon died when the colonists forced them to work from dawn to dusk. Before long, slave ships began to bring captured Africans whom the settlers drove by whip and gun to clear the forests and cultivate the rice, sugar cane, and spices that grew so richly. When slavery ended in the islands—in some places long before it did in others—there were more people of African blood than of any other race. That is why most of the folks in the West Indies today are colored—black people or brown— mixed Indians, Africans, Europeans.

Pirates and Parrots

Among the bright birds on some of the Caribbean islands and in the tropical jungles of the bordering mainland are thousands of parrots. The explorers and adventurers of far-off sailing-ship days loved parrots, the strange, gay-colored, sharp-beaked birds that could learn to talk, or squawk, in any language. On every galleon sailing into a European port from the Caribbean there were seamen with parrots perched on their shoulders—brilliant, screeching, green and red and orange-mixed-with-blue birds, sometimes spitting out a word or two to the astonishment of docksiders.

The sailing vessels of those days, with their rich cargoes, were tempting to dishonest sea captains. Many of them became pirates, attacking ships on the high seas and robbing them of spices and gold. These pirates had golden earrings in their ears, curly locks dangling in front of fierce eyes, a cutlass in hand, and often a parrot on one shoulder. Parrots have rather mean-looking faces. So had pirates. The two went well together.

One pirate named Blackbeard prided himself on looking fierce and frightful. He let his sooty beard grow so long he could plait it into two enormous braids which he hung about his ears. Under the brim of his hat he stuck lighted torches so that he resembled the very devil himself. And no devil was more cruel. Once, to amuse himself on a dull night at sea, he proposed to some of the crew that they make believe he was the devil and follow him down into a dark hold of the ship. There Blackbeard locked the hatch and lighted sulphur candles that gave off horrible fumes and sputtered with a ghostly yellow light. All the men except Blackbeard began to cough and wheeze and gasp for breath. Their eyes ran water. Some of them fainted. They begged to be allowed out. But Blackbeard did not even cough. He laughed and finally freed the men, panting for air. He was a tough and terrible fellow.

Blackbeard's real name was Edward Teach. He was an English sailor who in 1717 gave up honest sailing in Jamaica to become a pirate. Perhaps because there were then so many pirates in the Caribbean, Blackbeard finally sailed northward with three ships and began to attack boats off the coasts of the Carolinas and Virginia, then still colonies of England. But at last he was killed in hand-to-hand fighting with Lieutenant Maynard of Virginia, who was sent from Jamestown to capture him with two small sloops of the colonial navy.

Before he fell, Blackbeard had received twenty-five wounds—twenty from pistol shots and five from Maynard's sword. He died still trying to fire an empty pistol. Lieutenant Maynard sailed back to the James River in Virginia with Blackbeard's hairy head hanging from the bowsprit of his sloop. Nobody knew where Blackbeard had buried his treasure. He once said that only he and the devil could find his gold, and if the devil lived the longest he could have it.

The pirates of the West Indies were also called buccaneers, a name which comes from the French word *boucanier*—person who dried beef in the sun, then smoked it over a fire. In the early days of the Spanish Main, as the Caribbean area is often called, there were many wild beeves and boars on the island of Hispaniola. Englishmen and Frenchmen sold the wild meat, smoked or dried or salted, as provisions for ships bound to and from Europe in the West Indian trade. But the Spanish objected to this business and attacked the *boucaniers,* who fought back. The Spanish also attacked the Dutch and other newcomers trading anywhere in the Caribbees. To protect themselves, men of various nationalities banded together with the *boucaniers* on the Isle of Tortuga-de-Mar—Sea Turtle Island—off Hispaniola. As buccaneers, they began to raid Spanish ships, taking jewels and gold and casks of money.

At first only Spaniards were attacked, but as piracy grew any settlements and any ships from New England to Panama were in danger. It was in the Spanish Main, however, that the black flag of the pirates with its skull and crossbones was most often seen.

Port Royal in Jamaica was a great pirate center, wild and wealthy, gay with music and dancing, the clink of gold, and the squawking of parrots. There Bloody Henry Morgan, a pirate with hundreds of men and a large fleet of ships, brought his loot. Morgan stripped cities in Cuba and Panama and on the northern coast of South America of their treasure. He robbed rich monasteries and cathedrals, held monks and nuns as prisoners, and sometimes even made them march in front of his rascals as shields against Spanish gunfire.

In later years Morgan gained the king's favor and became Lieutenant-Governor of Jamaica. But before he retired from piracy his name had become so fearful that at the very sight of his fleet offshore soldiers fled, forts were left unguarded, and towns were left undefended, to be robbed and burned by his ocean bandits. However, because of earlier pirate attacks, one large city had become too well protected for Morgan, greatest of the buccaneers, even to attempt to raid. That was Havana, the Queen City of Cuba.

Cuba

Cuba once belonged to Spain and its language is still Spanish. The pirates and their attacks three hundred years ago were the beginning of Spain's battles in the West Indies. In Europe wars with the British and French took place. Spain sent against England her famous Armada, a fleet of beautiful sailing ships armed with great cannons. When Sir Francis Drake defeated the Armada off the English coast, England ended Spain's command of the seas.

The French and Dutch also fought Spain in the West Indies. When the Dutch established a colony on St. Croix in the Virgin Islands, a Dutch admiral lashed a broom to the topmast of his galleon as a sign that he would sweep the seas clean of Spanish ships from that day on.

Spain was weakened by fighting the galleons of war, the pirate ships, the Indians, and the Negro slave revolts. Her power in the West Indies began to go down. One by one she lost her colonies. Finally in 1895 the people of Cuba revolted against Spanish rule. The United States sent gunboats to protect its citizens in Cuba. One of these American ships, the *Maine,* was sunk in Havana harbor—no one will ever know how. But Spain was blamed, and our country went to war. Spain was defeated. As a result of the Spanish-American War, Cuba, the largest island in the West Indies, became a free republic in 1902.

Today Cuba is a busy island—the world's greatest producer of cane sugar. Many Cubans work the year round in the cane fields or in the sugar mills. There is a great deal of cattle raising on the island. Cuba is famous for its tobacco, too; the finest cigars in the world come from Havana. Cuba also exports tropical fruits, coffee, cocoa, dyewoods, mahogany, and cedar. And the music of its rumba bands has gone around the world.

>From a ship approaching Havana, Cuba's capital looks like an all-white city in the brilliant sunshine. But it is really a city of many soft colors: mossy stone-grays, pale pinks, rose, orange, and delicate greens. In the tropics people paint houses all sorts of colors. But no matter how bright the walls may be when freshly painted, the sun soon fades them to gentle shades. That is why, a long way off in the sun, Havana seems entirely white. The great stony old forts which formerly guarded either side of the entrance to the harbor are really brownish-gray. These forts were no doubt the reason Morgan and his pirates did not attack Havana, for their ancient cannons were once very powerful.

Havana today is an attractive modern city with flashing neon signs and traffic-filled streets. A section called Vedado has handsome homes and gardens; and along the ocean there is a wide avenue, El Malecón, where blue waves break in white spray on the sea wall. But many of the streets are still narrow, lined with handsome old colonial buildings which have arched doorways, decorated iron gates, and wide courtyards like those of ancient Spain.

The University of Havana was founded more than two hundred years ago, but today its buildings are almost all newly built. At the center of the city stands the modern, air-cooled, white marble capitol with its gleaming golden dome. Old buildings and new often stand side by side in Havana, and both add to the beauty of the city.

Ships from all over the world now come into Havana's harbor. As they dock, dozens of brown boys in little boats call to the passengers to throw down coins. Passengers can see their shining coins going away down, down, down into the clear water while dark bodies dive after them, swimming like fish under the sea's surface. Shortly the swimmers come up, each holding a coin high above the water to show he has recovered it. Since they live surrounded by the ocean, the people of the West Indies are almost all good swimmers. They are also great fishermen.

Fish is very much a part of Cuban meals—tiny little fishes fried very crisp; pink shrimp; baby oysters; or red lobsters served with fried bananas and yellow rice. Often people drink large glasses of cool fruit juice with their meals—pineapple, tangerine, coconut, or even watermelon juice. On the main streets of Havana shining modern fruit-juice stands hold great ice-cold containers of delicious juices—lime, orange, lemon, and such strange tropical fruits as papaw, mammee, tamarind, and mango.

Winter in Cuba does not bring snow and ice, zero weather, and gray skies. Every month is warm and sunny. There are fine beaches bordering emerald-green seas. No wonder that when Columbus first saw Cuba he said, "It is the loveliest land human eyes have ever seen!"

Haiti

Across the Windward Passage from the eastern end of Cuba lies the island of Hispaniola. Today that island is divided into two countries: the Dominican Republic on the east and Haiti on the west.

Haiti is a mountainous country; its name was an Indian word meaning "high ground." Even today Haiti keeps many of the customs brought from Africa by slaves. Some of the people still practice an ancient African religion of many gods called *vodun*. And some believe in ghosts called "zombies," who come back from their graves to walk about like sleepy men and women. In the hills many of the people still play Congo drums with their bare fingers and worship their many gods. But other Haitians do not believe in *vodun* at all, for they have been educated in the universities of Europe or America.

Haiti occupies one third of the area of Hispaniola, and has a population of about four million, whose language is French. The capital is Port-au-Prince, a seacoast city with a backdrop of mountains. On the lower slopes of the mountains coffee, the country's chief crop, grows wild. Cocoa, sugar, bananas, tobacco, and sisal—a kind of hemp from which rope is made—are other valuable products. There are hardwood forests of mahogany, ebony, and rosewood, too. And, like all the other Caribbean islands, Haiti is rich in fruits and flowers, and its waters swarm with fish.

When Columbus's flagship, the *Santa Maria,* was wrecked off Haiti's coast on Christmas Day, he left there a colony of forty men under the flag of Spain. Later the French took Haiti from the Spaniards. In 1791 the descendants of African slaves rebelled and took the country from the French. They became free, and in 1804 set up their own government. Haiti was the first Negro Republic in the world, and the second country in the Western Hemisphere to gain its independence. The United States was the first.

The stories of the three Negroes who led Haiti to freedom are thrilling ones. These men were slaves, but they became rulers and national heroes. In the late 1700s one of them, Toussaint, was only a coachman driving a carriage for his French master. But he had learned to read and write, and some think he must have studied books on military science; in his old age he became a great general who defeated the trained armies that Napoleon sent to conquer him. The French finally got rid of Toussaint by tricking him onto a gunboat and carrying him away to Europe, where he died in a dungeon. But by that year Haiti was free, so the people named their leader Toussaint l'Ouverture—"Toussaint, the Opener of the Way to Freedom."

After Toussaint was kidnapped, his fellow-leaders, Dessalines and Christophe, carried on the protection of the country. Dessalines was killed and Christophe became king. Ever since his rule ended in 1820, Haiti has been a republic with a president.

When Christophe was king, he completed the Citadel, a mighty fortress on a mountaintop overlooking the harbor of Cap Haitien. Its walls, six feet thick, still stand like the giant prow of a ship, high above the mountain forests. The underground caverns of the Citadel could house fifteen thousand troops and hold enough supplies for a year. Men had to drag its great cannons inch by inch up the steep mountainside. Each stone in its walls had to be cut by hand and hauled up the soaring slopes. Thousands of men worked for years to build this strong and beautiful fortress. Of course, today its guns are rusty and the Citadel is no longer useful as a fort. Men hope for protection now through treaties and good will rather than cannons. Today the ancient Citadel is open to tourists who ride up the mountainside on donkeys to visit this surprising building.

>From the top of the mountain the Cap's lovely harbor may be seen, dotted with the white sails of fishing boats, and, here and there, the smokestack of a great steamship or a visiting freighter. Sometimes in the valley distant drumbeats sound. Just as their ancestors did in Africa, the Haitians still use drums played with bare fingers to send messages, or to announce a dance or a *vodun* meeting. Haiti is a land of drums— wonderful, living, heart-throbbing drums.

For dancing, the country people often make only drum music, and play no other instruments. They dance out of doors on the bare ground. Haitians are very good dancers. Some of them are also very good paint- ers. Lately their painting has been helped greatly by the interest of DeWitt Peters, an American artist who in 1944 started the Haitian Art Center at Port-au-Prince. Here artists or even people without training may come for paint, paper, canvas, brushes, and help. Then they go their way, painting what they wish as they choose. Some of the artists in the mountains formerly painted on wrapping paper with a chicken feather for a brush. But now, with more materials to use, some of them have become interesting painters; their pictures are shown in New York and Paris, and many people have bought them.

Today everyone who visits Port-au-Prince goes to see the wall paint- ings that the artists of the Haitian Art Center have done inside the old Episcopal Cathedral. They have painted the Bible stories of Adam and Eve, the Birth of Christ, the Last Supper, and other Gospel scenes in terms of life in Haiti, with Negro angels and black disciples. Looking at the bright colors of the paintings, one American visitor described this church as "the happiest I ever saw."

The Dominican Republic

The boundary between Haiti and the Dominican Republic is 193 miles long and stretches across the width of the island of Hispaniola. Although the Dominican Republic is about twice as large as Haiti in area, its population is about one-half million less. Its language is Spanish.

The land is rich and fertile. Farming and cattle-raising are the main occupations; rice, coffee, sugar, cocoa, tobacco, and corn are the chief products. And there are rich deposits of silver, copper, iron, and petroleum which have not yet been used. In the Dominican mountains logs from the thick forests of mahogany, pine, and cedar are cut and floated downstream to the sea. On the coastal plains there are thousands and thousands of acres of sugar cane, and rich orchards of banana and cacao, or cocoa, trees. Ships from all over the world put into Dominican ports, for there is a great deal of trade with other countries.

The Dominican Republic was formed through revolution in 1844, after the country had been ruled by the Spanish for centuries, then by the French, and for a short time by the Haitians. A constitution modeled after that of the United States was adopted.

Santo Domingo, as the capital was formerly called, is the oldest city in the Western Hemisphere. There the first permanent European settlement was made a few years after Columbus discovered the island. Now Santo Domingo is called Ciudad Trujillo (sy-oo-THATH troo-HEE-yo), Spanish for Trujillo City, after the president who has now ruled the republic for many years.

The first university in the New World, the University of St. Thomas Aquinas, was started in Santo Domingo in 1535. And during the years of Spanish rule many beautiful colonial mansions and churches were built. Beneath the stone floor of the Cathedral of Santo Domingo Columbus was buried.

The Dominicans are very proud of the past history of their country. From there Cortes, Balboa, and other explorers sailed to discover new lands in the two Americas, North and South.

Puerto Rico

When the Spaniards were defeated in Cuba, they also lost the island of Puerto Rico, which became a possession of the United States. Puerto

Rico means "rich port." At one time it was Spain's most important American colony, since it guarded the entrance by sea from Europe into the Caribbean. San Juan, Puerto Rico's capital, became the second most strongly fortified city in the West Indies. It was made a free port—allowed to trade without customs regulations with all countries. For years it was very rich and busy. The citizens of Puerto Rico loved their mother country and were faithful to Spain. The King of Spain gave them a motto for their coat of arms: *Most Noble and Most Loyal.* The Puerto Ricans were somewhat surprised then when they suddenly became Americans in 1898.

Today San Juan is part Spanish, part American, in language and in appearance. It has big autobuses and flashing electric signs, old-world buildings and modern apartment houses, rich avenues and poor slums. The University of Puerto Rico in San Juan has about eight thousand students. In the center of the city there are fine shops and excellent restaurants that serve spicy fish soup, oysters with slices of lime, fried plantains (a kind of coarse banana), yellow rice, giant shrimp, rock lobsters, and delicious ice cream flavored with ginger root.

Puerto Rico is a mountainous island, but almost every foot of its soil is cultivated. Even high up into the hills sugar cane is planted. Sugar, tobacco, and coffee are the chief crops. Oranges, mangoes, and bananas grow wild, for Puerto Rico, like the other islands of the Caribbean, is warm and sunny. But it is crowded with too many people—almost seven hundred inhabitants for each square mile. Most of its clothing and food have to be imported. This makes living difficult and very expensive. Although Puerto Rico is fourteen hundred miles from New York, many of the islanders come that far looking for work in the United States. By a Congressional resolution passed in 1952 their land is classed as a "free commonwealth associated with the United States," but electing its own president and legislature. The Puerto Ricans are citizens of the United States.

The Virgin Islands

The Virgin Islands, just east of Puerto Rico, are the farthest eastward of the United States possessions. They are a cluster of about fifty small islands, the largest of which are St. Thomas, St. Croix, and St. John. These islands were purchased from Denmark in 1917 for 25 million dollars. Their whole population is only about twenty-six thousand people, hardly as many folks as work in a single skyscraper block in New York City. The islanders are mostly tradesmen, truck gardeners, dairy farmers, and fishermen. Their language is English.

The Virgin Islands are quiet and peaceful and sunny, washed by clear blue seas and cooled by the trade winds. The capital, on the isle of St. Thomas, is Charlotte Amalie (SHAR-lot a-MAHL-ye), a quiet, pretty little town named for a former queen of Denmark. It lies nestled about a beautiful harbor whose West Indian Docks fuel ships from all over the world. Its houses run back up into the hills where there stands an old pirates' tower built in 1666. Some of the steep, sloping streets are stone stairsteps, not sidewalks or pavements. Near the center of Charlotte Amalie there is the iron-roofed Bungalow Market to which islanders bring their produce, balancing it on their heads or carrying it on donkeyback. Here housewives bargain with market women over many-colored piles of red peppers, oranges, limes, beets, celery, squash, pigeon peas, and yams. Stacked in the market stalls are prickly cucumbers, juicy mangoes, dried conchs from the shells of the sea, and bright straw baskets, along with wide handwoven straw sun hats.

The people who live in Cha Cha Town, the French village at the edge of the capital, are especially good at weaving straw hats. When early French settlers were driven off the tiny island of St. Barthélemy more than two centuries ago, they came to St. Thomas. Their descendants have remained there, speaking French and living to themselves. They are great fishermen; some of them put far out to sea in small boats, and others sink huge nets near the shore. The women make and mend nets, weave hats and baskets, and cook for the men in small out-of-door ovens in the yards of their pink and yellow and blue houses. The French have a beautiful church on Gallows Hill, and their white-robed Catholic nuns have organized a choir of boy singers—one of the finest choirs in the West Indies.

On the island of St. Croix, forty miles from St. Thomas, there are two small cities, Frederiksted (FRED-rik-sted) and Christiansted (KRIS-chan-sted). At the time of the American Revolution there came from Christiansted to New York a young man who enrolled for studies at King's College, now Columbia University. This young student had been born on the West Indian island of Nevis, but had been brought to the Virgin Islands as a child. In his teens he worked as a clerk in a waterfront store. In keeping track of the cargoes that went in and out of St. Croix he learned accounting and bookkeeping. When his employer went away on trips, young Hamilton was left in charge of the business. He was such a bright boy that his father decided to send him to the mainland for an education. The rest is history. Alexander Hamilton joined George Washington in the fight for freedom, became his aide-de-camp on the battlefields, and later was appointed the first Secretary of the Treasury of the United States.

In the Virgin Islands the countryside is always green, although water is scarce and people must catch rain in containers on their rooftops and save it carefully. The roads are lined with coconut palms, silk-cotton trees, mahogany and mammee trees. Almost everywhere there are many-colored flowers, flame trees, hibiscus, orchids, and Chinese roses. People driving into the country pass farmers on little donkeys, dozens of goats jumping playfully about, and herds of cows sometimes so friendly that one of them may look right into a car window.

In the forests doves coo gently or flocks of wild geese may streak across the sky. The ruins of old windmills and the tall stacks of ancient sugar factories dot the land. There are plantations centuries old with such names as Wheel of Fortune Plantation, Upper Love, Orange Grove, and Peter's Rest.

Near Sugar Bay, where Columbus filled his water casks in 1493, is the Little Princess, one of the most beautiful plantations that tourists may visit today. Here waving palm groves border the white sands of the beach. Ancient mahogany trees spot the hillsides, and coconut groves are heavy with hard sweet nuts that may be tapped for their cool white milk. In the woods of the Little Princess Plantation there is the grave of an old settler who was buried with his horse. He sometimes comes back at night and rides about the plantation to see how things are, so they say, and to haunt the place. But he is a pleasant ghost who never bothers anybody.

The Lesser Antilles

Two groups of many islands, mostly British and French, curve southward from the Virgin Islands for more than six hundred miles, almost to the coast of Venezuela. They are the Leeward Islands and the Windward Islands, together called the Lesser Antilles. The Leeward Islands include the British Virgin Islands, Antigua, Sombrero, Montserrat, Nevis where Alexander Hamilton was born, St. Kitts, Redonda, and Guadeloupe. The southernmost group, the Windward Islands, includes Martinique, St. Lucia, St. Vincent, Grenada, and the twenty little islets of the Grenadines.

Great Britain has transferred Dominica from the Leeward to the Windward Islands. Columbus himself named Dominica from the Spanish word *domingo,* meaning Sunday, because he discovered it on that day. It is a lovely little island of bamboo and orchids, valleys of lime trees and parrots, and 365 rivers, one for each day of the year. Dominica also has a boiling sulphur lake, and many hot springs in the dead craters of its old volcanoes. Its capital city has the charming name of Roseau (ro-zo).

Another volcanic island of striking mountains and valleys is Montserrat—only eleven miles long and seven miles wide. It was once the home of numerous Irish settlers, and the Irish brogue is still a part of the native speech. Only one third of the 32 square miles of British Montserrat is cultivated. The rest of the island is taken up by rugged volcanoes. One of them is still active and gives off steam and the smell of sulphur. But the hillsides and valleys of Montserrat are beautifully green, with fields of waving cane and groves of sweetly scented lime trees.

The strange Dutch island of Saba, in the Lesser Antilles, is less than five square miles in size. It is almost nothing but the cone of a dead volcano rising steep and rocky from the surf of the sea. The chief village, away up almost one thousand feet, is on the crater floor of the volcano; it is sensibly called the Bottom.

To land on Saba from the big ships that anchor far offshore, passengers must climb into tiny rowboats. When the boats approach shore they wait for a big wave so that they may ride like surfboats to the narrow beach. Then the passengers must climb up, up, up on foot to the volcano's rim. >From there they see below them in the crater the red tile roofs and Dutch gables of the little town of the Bottom. It is reached by a series of steps in the rock, called the "Ladder." The Bottom's inhabitants are mostly fishermen, seamen, or boatbuilders. Their boats are built in the Bottom at the bottom and are lowered by ropes from the peak of the volcano down the steep cliffs to the sea.

The largest of the French islands in the Lesser Antilles are Martinique, and the two main islands of Guadeloupe known as Grande Terre and Basse Terre. Associated with Guadeloupe are a number of much smaller islands with such charming names as Marie-Galante, St. Barthélemy, Désirade, and Les Saintes. Martinique and Guadeloupe have belonged to France since 1635. Each sends two senators and three deputies to the French Parliament at Paris, in addition to having its local government.

The soil of these islands is rich and grows many crops. Most of the coffee and sugar used in Paris now come from Martinique. On that island was born the beautiful Empress Josephine, who married Napoleon and became a great lady of the court in France. A white marble statue of her now stands in the public square of Fort-de-France, the capital of Martinique.

Many of the women of the French West Indies are very beautiful. They dress in the colors of bright birds, with golden earrings and many necklaces and bracelets. High on their heads they wear many-colored bandanna handkerchiefs with the ends rising in butterfly-like points above their foreheads. Some wear turbans fastened with golden pins. Their complexions are of all shades from rich, deep, dark chocolate or cinnamon-brown to coffee-and-cream or peach or white. But most of the people in Martinique are a handsome brown.

One of the prettiest of the smaller West Indian islands is Grenada, a British island at the southern end of the Windward Islands. Grenada has only 133 square miles of land, and a small population; it has no large sugar cane plantations, bustling industries, or busy cities. But its largest town, St. George's, is the capital of all the British Windward Islands.

Behind the city the mountains rise. High in the hills, more than two thousand feet above the sea, there is a lovely lake called the Grand Etang, in the crater of an old volcano. On its shores wild monkeys play. Flame trees, nutmeg trees, and cocoa trees dot the mountainsides below. In the valleys orchids and tree ferns grow, and all around the island sandy-white beaches shine in the sun.

Almost everyone in Grenada owns a little plot of land where fruit and vegetables grow. Pomegranates, mangoes, and tamarinds are plentiful. So are star apples, a delicious, very sweet fruit so named because when it is cut in half its seeds can be seen forming a dark star in the apple's white flesh. The chief crops of the island are bananas, cotton, nutmeg and other spices, and cocoa beans.

Plantains, rice, and fish are the favorite foods of the people of Grenada. St. George's fish market is a colorful spot; its stalls are piled high with all sorts of fish fresh and glittering from the sea, and even with ancient sea turtles whose steaks are delicious. Coconut oil is used for cooking. Ginger beer, lime- and orange-ades, and a cool red liquid called "sorel" are favorite soft drinks. Grenadan children love shaved ice sweetened with anise or ginger syrup.

Almost all the boys and men of Grenada swim, and cricket is a favorite sport with young men. There are only a few motion picture theaters on the island. Mostly the people make their own amusements. Since there are no factories, they make most of their own furniture and clothing, too. Many of the folks who live on Grenada have never been anywhere else at all. They are happy on their quiet, sunny little island at the outer edge of the Caribbean, far from the hustle and bustle of industry.

Children in the West Indies

Busy machines that turn out thousands of objects, one just like another, are not very common anywhere in the West Indies. And factories are not found at all on the smaller islands. People make things by hand, and children soon learn to use their hands well and to work along with their parents. In fact, most of the children of the Caribbean work as much as they play, if not more. Youngsters in the country districts help their parents cultivate the fields, pick coffee beans, and even cut sugar cane. They learn to load little donkeys with produce and drive them to market. If boys live near the sea they go on fishing trips with the men. There they learn to lower and bring up the nets, and to throw back into the sea the kinds of fish that are not good to eat. They learn how to spread fishing nets on the sand to dry, and how to tie the cords in mending them. Some of the boys learn to build and repair boats.

Little girls soon learn how to cook on open fires of brush or charcoal in the yards around the tiny thatched huts. They learn how to clean fish or fowl, how to fry plantains, roast breadfruit, and boil rice. They learn, too, how to weave straw mats and hats, or saddlebags to hang from the backs of the little donkeys. And girls are always taught how to buy and bargain in the marketplace. When they are still quite young, some of them learn how to sell, too, sitting in the market beside their mother's stock of peppers, lemons, limes, or whatever else the family grows on its plot of land. Children of the West Indies are seldom idle, for there is a great deal of work to be done.

In Haiti young Jacques and his sister, Marie, get up with the sunrise and go to the nearest spring for water. Then they get coconut fiber brooms and sweep clean the yard before their hut. Perhaps later their mother puts them to work weaving a mat of palm thatch. Or she may send them in search of wild mangoes or oranges. When they come back, they may both go with her to the brook. There she pounds clean the family laundry on a stone in the running water, making lather from a soapweed. The children may carry the clothes home in basins on their heads, balancing their loads without using their hands. Almost everyone in West Indian country districts knows how to balance things on the head in this way without any trouble at all.

Much of the furniture is made by hand, for machine-made furniture from America or Europe is very expensive. There are expert woodworkers throughout the Caribbean. While Jacques is still very young his father teaches him to cut planks from Haitian logs, and to make from them chairs and tables and cabinets. Marie learns how to make water dippers from gourds, and fans from palm thatch or even from the feathers of birds. It is fun doing these things, and when the children of the Caribbean grow up they know how to make many useful objects from the plants and trees that grow naturally around them.

Leather is rather scarce in the West Indies and shoes are expensive. On most of the islands the country children—and many city children too—usually go barefooted. Some never own a pair of shoes until they are grown.

Instead of candy the children suck a sweet stalk of sugar cane. Instead of ice cream they eat juicy oranges or tangerines or cool melons. And at night, instead of amusing themselves with radio or television, they listen to the older folks singing, or watch them dancing out of doors to the rhythms of the deep drums. Many teen-agers learn to play drums themselves. And in Aruba, Curaçao, and Trinidad boys are particularly fond of the steel drums which they make from oil cans. On these they can play melody as well as rhythm.

Trinidad

Trinidad, the farthest south of the West Indian islands, is near the South American coast—only a stone's throw from Venezuela. It is a shipping center and a very busy place. Then too, it has a great lake of pitch, a natural black tarlike substance that is shipped around the world for the making of asphalt. Pitch Lake is almost three hundred feet deep and from it millions of tons of pitch have been shipped abroad. Trinidad is also rich in petroleum.

Port of Spain, the capital, is far from quiet. It is a bustling city of trade, alive with the sound of children, steel bands, songs, and the babble of various languages. Its official language is English, but people of many races and nationalities—English, Spanish, Portuguese, Negro, East Indian, Chinese, and American—live and work there.

The rhythmical tunes called "calypsos" (kuh-LIP-sohz) come from Trinidad. Calypsos are songs about news events of the day, politics, famous people, or things the singers see around them as they perform. Like the old-time bards and wandering troubadours of Europe in the Middle Ages, calypso singers make up their songs on the spot. Night after night in carnival season the Negro calypso singers stand in dusty open-air pavilions, thinking up their funny rhymes. These singers have nicknames such as Lord Invader, Duke of Iron, Sir Lancelot, and Attila the Hun. Some songs and singers have become famous on records, but most calypsos are never recorded or written down.

At Port of Spain the best calypso singer each year is chosen Calypso King of the Carnival. Carnival starts just before Lent. Then for two days the people dance and sing indoors and out, and listen to street singers. At carnival time in Port of Spain steel bands march through the streets. Sometimes they have as many as thirty players, with each man playing on a brightly painted gasoline-can drum. Each drum is tuned differently and is of a different size. Discarded oil drums are cut, heated, and hammered in such a way that each has its own pitch and tone. Those that carry the melody are called "ping pongs." Those that supply the harmony are "tune booms." The music they make together is soft and melodious, yet ringing, like that of a xylophone or a combination of steel guitars. Steel drums, unknown until recently, are a new musical instrument created in the West Indies.

For the yearly carnival before Lent almost everybody puts on a mask and dresses up in a gorgeous costume or a comic outfit. Some people may dress as kings and queens grand in velvet and ermines, while others appear as devils, clowns, or red Indians with feathers. Some citizens turn themselves into Supermen; others into walking buildings like Buckingham Palace; and still others into clocks, vampire bats, or butterflies with silken wings. And many people who do not especially costume themselves are naturally in carnival colors, for every day on the streets of Port of Spain there are turbanned Hindus, bandannaed belles, East Indian girls in long thin saris, and country women in bright skirts. All the year round, Trinidad is an island full of color and a great variety of people. Those who live there call it the "land of hummingbirds, calypsos, and carnival." Some fun-makers even go further and claim that in Trinidad the frogs whistle, the birds speak French, and oysters grow on trees.

Quite different from busy, crowded Trinidad is the nearby island of Tobago. Tobago is very quiet and uncrowded. It has long stretches of sandy beach without a soul in sight. In its waters are coral reefs where divers with marine goggles may see bright underwater creatures swimming lazily in the sunny seas. Tobago and tiny Ingram Island to the north are sanctuaries for the rare birds of paradise that no hunters are allowed to kill.

Curaçao

Belonging to the Netherlands West Indies are Curaçao, Aruba, and Bonaire, all together near Venezuela, and the islands of St. Eustatius, Saba, and a part of St. Martin, across the Caribbean in the Leeward Islands. These islands are administered by a governor appointed by the Dutch queen. They have an executive council of Landsministers, and an elected body called the Staten.

Curaçao is the largest Dutch possession in the West Indies. Its city Willemstad (VIL-em-staht) is the capital of all the Dutch islands, which first belonged to Holland in 1634, passed to the British for a while, then back to Holland again. The official language of Curaçao is Dutch, but most of the people speak a strange mixture of Spanish, African, Dutch, Portuguese, French, and English. Very few foreigners can understand the mixture, which is called Papiamento (PAH-pya-MEN-toh).

Curaçao is a rather barren island, and Aruba is a windswept, rocky bit of land. Both Aruba and Curaçao are drenched in sun and are often very hot. Corn, beans, and lentils grow there, but little else except, on Curaçao, the bitter oranges from whose rind the liqueur called *curaçao* is made. Salt and phosphate, a natural chemical material used in fertilizers, are the main products of these two rocky islands. Their chief industry is the refining of oil from nearby Venezuela, less than forty miles away. There is a huge American Standard Oil refinery on Aruba; and the Royal Dutch Shell Oil Company controls the refineries of Curaçao. Into the ports of these islands come oil tankers from all over the world. Seamen of all nationalities throng the main streets of Willemstad.

Every day hundreds of sloops bringing food and other goods from Venezuela sail into the harbor of Willemstad. Along the sea wall everything from red peppers to bandannas, guava jelly to roasting hens, may be bought directly from the sloop decks.

The old colonial part of Willemstad is solidly built, with gabled, Dutch-style houses, white walls, and neat stone fences. But most of the town's dwellings are frame cottages and tiny shacks, many of them painted in bright colors. Some of them even have stripes on their walls, like stick-candy houses in the sun.

Jamaica

Jamaica, a beautiful British island about a hundred miles south of Cuba, is entirely surrounded by the blue-green waters of the Caribbean. It has one of the loveliest coves in the world—the palm-fringed Blue Lagoon, near the town of Port Antonio. From the roadway above, its deep smooth water looks like a rich blue jewel. Another beautiful spot on Jamaica's north shore is Ocho Rios, which means Eight Rivers. Here eight little rivers come together to bound over a rocky ledge in little waterfalls of dancing spray which drop into the Caribbean Sea.

At Doctor's Cove children may build castles in the sand all day long. Or they may hunt sea shells, or ride in a glass-bottomed boat and watch the tropical fish in the water. For those who like to hike or ride horseback there are trails winding up into the hills and on through what is called the "Cockpit Country" and the "Land-of-Look-Behind." Here splendid old mansions are still standing on ancient plantations. From this region come the famous Jamaica ginger, and cashew nuts, pimentos, many spices, and copra, the dried meat of the coconut from which oil is made. Other Jamaican products are coffee, sugar, cocoa, and bananas.

The white sands of the beaches at Montego Bay are world-famous. Luxury hotels house thousands of winter visitors. There are music, dancing, bathing, and deep-sea fishing. From Montego Bay's charming seacoast town, country trails lead through forests of ferns as tall as a man, or beneath shady bamboo groves of the most delicate yellows and greens. Brilliant butterflies flutter down the lanes, and harmless little lizards scoot along the gullies. Overhead jabbering crows may fly, or the black grackles that the Jamaicans call "kling-klings." Tiny hummingbirds on whirring wings balance above bright flowers. Parakeets cry. A hawk may wheel and dive. A flock of whitewing doves passes. Maybe a giant buzzard called a John Crow glides through the sky after food. Perhaps you might even see a nightingale in a dusky glade, or a sleepy tropical owl, blind in the daytime, yet with sightless eyes wide open in a bayam tree.

Jamaican towns and villages have such odd names as Puppy Hill, Devil's Race Course, Barbecue Bottom, Taketime Town, Bog Walk, Wag River, Happy Retreat, and Bamboo Gulch. Jamaican people often give their houses odd names, too. On the gate over a porch there may be a sign reading BUTTERFLY MANOR, WIZARD COTTAGE, HAPPY HOME, or just MY HOME. Visitors to Kingston, the capital, are impressed with such unusual street names as Minstrel Road, Puss Gully, Rumbo Lane, and many names from the Bible such as Luke Lane, Matthew Lane, and Mark Lane. There is also a Love Lane.

At Hope Botanical Gardens, one of the beautiful parks near Kingston, visitors may see most varieties of Jamaican plants. There grow the tallest and most feathery of palm trees, enormous old cottonwood trees from which canoes are made, bay trees, candle trees, and the lovely flame-of-the-forest. There is a tree, too, whose seed-filled pods, rattling in the wind, give it the name of "woman's tongue." Among the flowers are bright Christmas-red poinsettias and delicate tree orchids in almost all shades from creamy white to rich purple.

Across the harbor from Kingston is the historical old city of Port Royal, where Bloody Henry Morgan and other pirates came with their treasure to trade and spend wildly. Port Royal was once the most famous city in the West Indies. But more than two hundred years ago a great earthquake shook down most of it. Thirty years later a hurricane blew away much of the newly rebuilt town. Then a tidal wave came in from the sea and washed half of the rest of the town into the ocean. Pirates, earthquakes, hurricanes, tidal waves, and time all have attacked Port Royal. Today it is a rather sad little tropical village where breadfruit trees, lignum vitae—a tree with very hard wood—junipers, and palms grow in and about the ruined walls of the buildings that were once so grand. And some of the little Jamaican children in Port Royal now have never heard of pirate Henry Morgan.

The new University of the West Indies is located near Kingston, and to it come students from all the British islands in the Caribbean. The well-educated, of course, speak perfect English, but the uneducated people of Jamaica have strange ways of speech which North Americans find hard to understand at first.

One little Jamaican boy, watching another one boxing, may say, "Him thump him down," instead of "He knocked him down." And in the evening when people come calling or pass each other in the streets they say "Good night" as a form of greeting instead of "Hello."

Sometimes a carpenter may sing as he works on a little cottage beside the road:

Hosanna! Me build me house oh!

For him, "I build my house" becomes "Me build me house."

A well-known Jamaican folk song goes:

Me donkey want water—
Hold 'im, Joe!
Him want sugar water—
Hold 'im, Joe!
Him want coconut water—
Hold 'im, Joe!
Me jackass want water—
Hold 'im, Joe!

A very popular song for dancing starts:

Me carry me ackee to Linstead Market . . .

An ackee is a fruit that came long ago from Africa. It grows on a flowering tree and its pods of brilliant red have yellow pulp and very shiny black seeds. When cooked, the pulp of the ackee is delicious served as a breakfast dish with salt fish and rice.

Curried goat is a popular food often eaten by the poor in Jamaica. The hotly flavored combination of spices called curry was brought to Jamaica by the East Indian workers who came in the middle of the 1880s when slavery ended. At the same time many Chinese arrived. Today Jamaica has a mixture of races. Along King Street, the main street of the capital, there are English shops, Chinese shops and Indian shops. But most of the people of Jamaica have ancestors who came from Africa and they are very dark. The governor-general is English and is appointed by the English king or queen, but the Prime Minister of the island and most of the other government officials are colored men—from the treasurer of the island who handles all the taxes to the smartly uniformed police in the streets or the customs officials in their white suits who examine your bags at dockside or airport.

Islands outside the Caribbean

Barbados, the most eastern of the West Indian islands, lies outside the waters of the Caribbean in the Atlantic to the north of Trinidad. It is an island without much trade or excitement, but its shining beaches and bright flowers have made it a popular winter resort and a place where many retired British government workers live. A common but delicious food there is flying fish. And one of the sights to see in Bridgetown, the capital of Barbados, is the now rebuilt church which George Washington attended when he visited the island in 1751.

The Bahamas, too, are restful English islands that lie outside the Caribbean Sea. These islands begin just east of Palm Beach, Florida, and stretch for more than seven hundred miles down toward the northern coast of Haiti. The Bahamas are made up of almost seven hundred islands and more than two thousand little islets and low reefs. Many of the smaller isles are almost wholly uninhabited, so that they are fine living places for wild life and tropical birds. But the island of New Providence, containing half the population of the Bahamas, is a popular center of large tourist hotels and guest houses. To its capital, Nassau, come thousands of visitors in the winter season. Since Nassau is less than an hour by plane from Miami, many Americans fly over there just for a day's visit. There are many-colored reefs and undersea gardens to explore in glass-bottomed boats. And there is a racetrack where very small horses race, ridden by boy jockeys twelve or thirteen years old.

To a visitor Nassau and the whole island of New Providence seem to be one large flower garden with bright colors everywhere. Tall palms border the beaches, and inland there are giant silk-cotton trees whose great roots rise above the ground. The little thatch houses of the native people are almost all surrounded by plants and shaded by semi-tropical trees.

Winter visitors spend a great deal of money in the Bahamas, especially at Nassau, so the tourist trade is very important. The islanders also earn money from the sale of hardwoods, crawfish, salt, tomatoes, and attractive handwoven hats, purses, and straw mats.

Our Neighbors

Air travel has helped to make the West Indies ever more popular. In recent years airplanes have made it possible to reach the Caribbean from the United States within a day, whereas ships take several days. And travel between the islands now has become very easy indeed—sometimes a matter of only a few minutes. The tourist business is now a very big one in such popular West Indian sunlands as Jamaica, Cuba, Haiti, the Virgin Islands, and Barbados.

So near to the United States are the Caribbean islands that in years to come more and more of us will visit them and become better friends with their people. And each of us will bring home our own memories of the West Indies, islands that are alike because they all have a way of living which is ruled by the sea around them, yet unlike because of the little differences that make each island like no other—the clipped Spanish speech and the rumba bands of Cuba; the English customs of Jamaica or Barbados where cars drive on the left; the traces of Africa in Haiti's ancient *vodun* ceremonies; the Dutch houses of Curaçao and Aruba; the colorful streets of Trinidad, thronging with people of many nationalities; Saba's boatbuilding town in a volcanic cone; the turbanned creole women of Martinique; the birds of paradise of Tobago; and over all, sunshine, trade winds, and bright blue skies.

Some Plants of the West Indies

ackee (uh-KEE)—the podlike fruit of the ackee tree; often cooked with salt fish

amaryllis (AM-uh-RIL-is)—the belladonna lily, with large red blossoms

avocado (AV-oh-KAH-doh)—the alligator pear, a shiny green, pulpy fruit

bamboo (bam-BOO)—a reedlike plant with tough, hollow, jointed stems

bayberry (BAY-beh-ree)—a Jamaican tree whose leaves supply an oil used to perfume bay rum

bougainvillaea (BOO-gan-VIL-ee-uh)—a vine with small flowers, cultivated for ornament

cassava (kuh-SAH-va)—a rootlike vegetable used whole and for meal

frangipani (FRAN-ji-PAN-i)—a shrub whose blossoms are used in perfume-making

hibiscus (hy-BISS-kus)—a plant or small tree with large bell-shaped flowers

lignum vitae (LIG-num VY-tee)—a hardwood tree producing very durable lumber used in making pulleys and blocks

mammee (MAM-mee) or mamey—a tree which has an extremely sweet fruit

mango (MANG-goh)—a fruit with a reddish rind, a sweet yellow pulp, and a single large seed

mimosa (mih-MOH-suh)—a plant with prickly leaves and white or pink blossoms

palmetto (pal-MET-oh)—a palm tree with fan-shaped leaves

papaya (pah-PY-a) or papaw (pah-PAW)—a sweet, reddish, melonlike fruit with a juice that renders tough meat tender

pimento (pih-MEN-toh)—a Jamaican allspice berry which grows on a glossy laurel tree

plantain (PLAN-tan)—a variety of banana with a large coarse fruit that is cooked as a vegetable

pomegranate (POM-gran-it)—an acid fruit with a hard rind filled with soft reddish pulp and many seeds

sapodilla (sap-oh-DILL-a)—a hardwood tree with sweet edible fruit

silk-cotton or ceiba (SAY-e-ba)—a very large tree sometimes fifteen
   stories high with enormous fencelike roots growing partly
   aboveground
sisal (SY-sal)—a plant producing hemp fiber for rope-making
soursop (SOUR-sop)—a large, slightly acid, pulpy fruit from which a
   soft drink is made
tamarind (TAM-uh-rind)—an acid-tasting fruit with beanlike pods on a
   tall, thickly-leaved tree
tangerine (tan-juh-REEN)—a small, easy-to-peel type of orange, also
   called a mandarin orange
yam—an edible tuber similar to a sweet potato
yucca (YUK-uh)—a sub-tropical, treelike plant with clusters of white,
   bell-shaped flowers

Some Famous Men and Women of West Indian Birth

Antigua

Bert Williams, 1875–1922, *Comedian*

Barbados

Frank Collymore, 1893–1980, *Author*
George Lamming, 1927– , *Author*

Cuba

Alicia Alonso, 1921– , *Ballet dancer*
Sandy Amoros, 1932–1992, *Baseball player*
Desi Arnez, 1917–1986, *Actor*
José R. Capablanca, 1888–1942, *Chess champion*
Nicolás Guillén, 1904–1989, *Poet*
José Maria de Herédia, 1803–1839, *Poet*
Ernesto Lecuona, 1896–1963, *Composer*
Antonio Maceo, 1848–1896, *Revolutionary general*
Jorge Mañach, 1898–1961, *Author*
José Marti, 1853–1895, *Revolutionary leader*
Minnie Minoso, 1922– , *Baseball player*
Fernando Ortiz, 1881–1969, *Author*
Plácido (Gabriel de la Concepción Valdés), 1809–1844, *Poet and
    Patriot*

Guadeloupe

Chevalier de St. Georges, 1745–1799, *Violinist and composer*

Haiti

Dantès Bellegarde, 1877–1966, *Diplomat and author*
Alexandre Dumas, 1762–1806, *General of Napoleon's cavalry*
Oswald Durand, 1840–1906, *Poet*
Jacques Roumain, 1907–1944, *Author*
Toussaint L'Ouverture, Pierre Dominique, 1743–1803, *General*

Jamaica

Louise Bennett, 1919– , *Folk singer*
Claude McKay, 1891–1948, *Poet and author*
Victor S. Reid, 1913– , *Author*
Walter Adolphe Roberts, 1886– , *Author*
Louis Simpson, 1923– , *Poet*

Martinique

Aimé Césaire, 1913– , *Poet and member of French Chamber of Deputies*
Josephine de la Pagerie (Mme. Napoleon Bonaparte), 1763–1814,
    Empress of France
René Maran, 1887– , *Author*
Clement Richer, 1914– , *Author*

Nevis

Alexander Hamilton, 1757–1804, *The first Secretary of the Treasury of
    the United States*

Puerto Rico

José Ferrer, 1912– , *Actor*
Eugenio Maria de Hostos, 1839–1903, *Author and educator*
Luis Muñoz-Marín, 1898–1980, *Poet and governor*
Luis Palés Matos, 1898–1950, *Poet*
Moro Morales, 1911– , *Composer and band leader*

Vic Power, 1931– , *Baseball player*
Arthur Schomburg, 1874–1938, *Book collector*

St. Vincent

Hugh H. Mulzac, 1886– , *The first Negro Captain in U.S. Merchant Marine*

Trinidad

Beryl McBurnie, 1913–2000, *Folk dancer*
C. L. R. James, 1901–1989, *Author*
Hazel Scott, 1920–1981, *Pianist*

Virgin Islands

Bennie Benjamin, 1907– , *Song writer*
J. Antonio Jarvis, 1905–1963, *Poet and painter*
Camille Pissarro, 1831–1903, *Painter*

The West Indies[1]

	Capital	Population	Area in square miles	Products
INDEPENDENT COUNTRIES				
Cuba	Havana	5,870,000	44,206	Sugar, tobacco, dyewoods, hardwoods, coffee, bananas, citrus fruits, pineapples
Haiti (HAY-tee)	Port-au-Prince	4,000,000	10,714	Coffee, sugar, cotton, sisal, cocoa, rice, hardwoods, bananas
Dominican Republic (do-MIN-i-kan)	Ciudad Trujillo	2,291,000	19,333	Sugar, coffee, cocoa, rice, corn, tobacco, salt, cattle
UNITED STATES				
Puerto Rico (PWER-to-REE-ko)	San Juan	2,210,703	3,435	Sugar, tobacco, coffee, fruits, coconuts, vegetables, rum
Virgin Islands	Charlotte Amalie	26,655	132	Sugar, bay rum, rum, cattle, hides

1. These statistics have been retained as in the original publication of 1956.

	Capital	Population	Area in square miles	Products
NETHERLANDS				
Netherlands West Indies	Willemstad	175,631	403	Petroleum products, phosphates, salt, corn
Aruba (a-ROO-ba)			69	Petroleum products
Bonaire (boh-NAHR)			95	
Curaçao (koo-ra-SAH-oh)			210	Petroleum products
Saba (SAH-ba)			5	Boatbuilding
St. Eustatius (SAYNT YOO-STAY-she-us)			7	
St. Martin (1/2)			17	Salt
GREAT BRITAIN*				
Jamaica (ja-MAY-ka)	Kingston	1,430,000	4,411	Cocoa, sugar, bananas, citrus fruits, coffee, spices, coconuts, ginger, rum
Turks Island and Caicos (KAY-kus)		6,600	166	Salt, sponges
Cayman Islands (kay-MAN)		7,000	100	Sea turtles, boatbuilding
Bahama Islands (ba-HAH-ma)	Nassau	84,390	4,404	Hardwoods, tomatoes, salt, crawfish
Barbados (bar-BAY-doz)	Bridgetown	212,000	166	Sugar, cotton, molasses rum

* In 1955, plans were approved for the creation of the West Indies Federation, to be made out of the British islands of Jamaica, Trinidad, Barbados, and the Leeward and Windward Islands. The Bahamas are not included. The mainland colonies of British Guiana and British Honduras may join later. The West Indies Federation will have island governments in charge of local affairs, but a central administration run from a capital yet to be chosen.

	Capital	Population	Area in square miles	Products
Trinidad (TRIN-i-dad)	Port of Spain	669,650	1,864	Petroleum, pitch, sugar, cocoa, rum, citrus fruits
Tobago (to-BAY-go)			116	
British Leeward Islands	St. Johns, Antigua	120,145	422	Sugar, cotton, coconuts, tomatoes, onions, sisal, charcoal, salt, spices, fruits
British Virgin Islands Antigua (an-TEE-guh) Barbuda (bar-BOO-duh) Redonda (re-DON-duh) St. Kitts or St. Christopher Nevis (NEE-vis) Anguila (an-GWIL-luh) Montserrat (mont-seh-RAT) Sombrero (som-BRAYR-oh)				
British Windward Islands	St. George's, Grenada	283,000	810	Sugar, cotton, copra, cassava, cocoa, arrowroot, spices, citrus fruits, molasses, rum
Dominica (do-mi-NEE-kuh) Grenada (gre-NAY-duh) Grenadines (gren-a-DEENZ) St. Lucia (SAYNT LOO-shuh) St. Vincent				
FRANCE				
Guadeloupe (gwad-LOOP)	Basse-Terre	278,864	583	Sugar, cocoa, vanilla, bananas, rum, coffee
Basse-Terre (bahs-TAIR)				

	Capital	Population	Area in square miles	Products
Grande-Terre (grahn-TAIR) Désirade (DAY-ZEE-RAHD) Les Saintes (lay SANT) Marie Galante (ma-REE-ga-LANT) St. Barthélemy (SAN bar-tail-MEE) St. Martin (1/2) (SAN mar-TAN)				
Martinique (MAR-tee-NEEK)	Fort-de-France	282,600	380	Sugar, cocoa, pineapples, bananas

NOTE: Population figures are as up-to-date as possible, but in some instances may have increased within the past few years.

The First Book of Africa

(1960)

Contents

Unknown Africa

Long after other continents were quite well known by the people of the world, Africa remained almost unexplored. Until the eighteenth century little but the fringes of the continent had been touched by outsiders. A hundred years ago, or a little more, large parts of Africa were still known as "darkest Africa," and they really were dark as far as knowledge of them went in other countries.

Why?

For one thing, the terribly hot, dry Sahara Desert in the north was a barrier to outsiders trying to reach Central Africa from that direction. Then, too, much of the African land away from the coast is a high plateau from which many rivers run in rocky rapids to the ocean; the boats of earlier days were not built to journey up such rivers. In addition, there were jungle thickets, strange wild animals, a frightening swarm of insects, an unfamiliar and often uncomfortable climate, tropical diseases, and unknown tribes that might be unfriendly.

North Africa was known because it could be reached by way of the Mediterranean Sea. In many ways it was almost a part of Europe. But the Africa farther south—the Africa we are chiefly concerned with in this book—was little known until the past century. Then came a time of great exploration. Here are some of the things we know about Africa now.

Africa Today

Of the world's continents, Africa is second in size. It has an area of more than eleven millions of square miles and makes up about one-fifth of the land surface of the earth; it is bigger than the United States, India, and China put together. It has perhaps 224 millions of people; this is a guess, however, for not all its people have been counted. Not all its land has been explored, either, though its chief lakes and rivers are charted, and its mountains, deserts, and plains are properly shown on maps.

Its climate varies from temperate to tropical. The equator runs near the very middle of the continent. As a result, the heart of Africa has a tropical climate, hot, moist, and sunny except in the mountains, where some peaks have snow all the year round. In South Africa there is often snow in winter, but North Africa is temperate. If it were not for the warm waters of the Mediterranean Sea, however, winters in North Africa might be very cold.

Africa is one of the richest lands in the world. Most of the diamonds and almost half the gold on earth come from that continent. Uranium, copper, tin, iron, and other minerals of great value are found there, and so are cocoa beans, from which chocolate is made, rubber, coffee, cotton, palm oil, and ivory. Ebony, mahogany, and many other hardwoods are also products of Africa.

Because the continent is so rich in raw materials, Europeans settled there long ago, and now control most of the area. They are white people. But in all of Africa there are only about five millions of such settlers, and more than half of them live at the very top or the very bottom of the continent—either in North Africa or in South Africa, where the climate is closest to that of Europe.

Most of the native peoples of Africa are black or dark brown, though some are lighter, and in the Arab countries of North Africa they may be tan or ivory white.

The greater number of the peoples of tropical Africa have their own tribal religions. They worship many varied gods. But about sixty million Africans are Moslems (also called Mohammedans) and about twenty-one million have been converted to Christianity. Most of the Moslems live in North Africa, and most of the Christians are in the coastal regions where European and American missionaries have been most active. There are also some African Jews, like the Falasha of Ethiopia.

Africa has many countries, which are grouped to make over forty political units. They have fascinating names, such as Tanganyika, Togoland, Nigeria, Senegal, Morocco, and Ethiopia. No two of the countries are alike, and they have many different tribes and different languages. More than seven hundred languages and dialects are spoken in Africa.

Before the coming of the Europeans, most of the African peoples had their own tribal governments, usually ruled by a chief who in many cases was advised by the elders of the tribe. Now the different countries have a variety of kinds of government. Some countries are completely independent, each with its own ruler, or with officials elected by the people. Some are self-governing members of the British Commonwealth. Others are colonies of a European power; they are under the protection of a European power; or they are watched over by the United Nations. England, France, Belgium, and Portugal control large areas of the African continent. But the aim of African peoples today is to be free of foreign management and to have the right to govern themselves.

Ancient Africa

Africa has had a long and fascinating history. Prehistoric skulls have recently been found in Kenya. They seem to show that more than a million years ago man may have had his beginnings on the African continent. Rock paintings of the Bushmen in South Africa seem to date from the early part of the Stone Age. And beautiful bronze heads discovered in Benin show that in ancient times people who were fine artists lived near the river Niger.

Before the Golden Age of Greece or the rise of the Roman Empire both Ethiopia and Egypt had firmly established governments and standing armies. The people built great cities and carved enormous statues from stone. As early as 2600 B.C. the Egyptians had beautiful temples, tall pyramids, and handsome palaces. Herodotus, the "Father of History," recorded the splendor of the Pharaohs.

After a time, European peoples came into Egypt from across the Mediterranean, and others came from Asia. In the fourth century B.C. the Greeks built schools there, and a thousand years later the Romans built roads. These invaders, as well as the Arabs, mixed with the Africans and produced along the Mediterranean a people with the many shades of skin coloring seen in Egypt today. In ancient times Egypt became the "crossroads of civilization."

The Egyptian kings were rich; many of them owned slaves. Some of the slaves were from the dark heart of Africa south of the Sahara, and at one time some were Jews or members of other captive groups. About three thousand years before Christ it became fashionable for wealthy Egyptians to own Pygmies, the little men from Central Africa who almost never grow more than four and one-half feet tall. Later, Homer speaks of Pygmies in his *Iliad*, as do Aristotle and the ancient Roman writer, Pliny, in their works. Apparently some knowledge of Africa has been recorded since the beginning of written history.

About 332 B.C., Alexander the Great added Egypt to his empire. He built there the city of Alexandria, which became a great center of learning and trade. Alexandria's lighthouse on the island of Pharos was one of the Seven Wonders of the Ancient World; and the city's library, later destroyed by Julius Caesar, contained thousands of books written on rolls of papyrus. Students from many parts of Africa and Asia visited Alexandria, and ships sailed from its port to all the world then known.

Long before Alexander's time, however, Phoenician sailors had explored the North African coastline, and Phoenician pioneers had founded the city of Carthage on what is now the shore of Tunisia. The Carthaginians, braving the vast, unknown waters of the Atlantic Ocean, ventured down the west coast of Africa as far south as Sierra Leone, but they did not go inland. The heart of equatorial Africa and all the region of the south remained unknown to outsiders for centuries until, early in 1488, the Portuguese rounded the Cape of Good Hope. Ten years later, on his way to India, Vasco da Gama visited the Kenya coast. Before the end of the Middle Ages trading had developed between Africa and Europe, and European ships were bringing home gold, olive oil, tropical fruits, nuts, and slaves. By then, as European explorers realized more fully the riches to be found in Africa, they were venturing ever farther up its rivers. But, hemmed in by the rivers and by mountains and jungles, and fearful of the natives, the explorers did not dare attempt many expeditions overland.

Great Kingdoms of Black Africa

Long before Columbus discovered America, there had flourished in black Africa a number of large Negro kingdoms. The most remarkable were Ghana, Melle, and Songhay. By A.D. 300 the old state of Ghana stretched from Senegal southward to the sources of the Niger River. Its citizens worked farms, raised cattle, trapped elephants, and mined gold. Their largest city, Kumbi-Kumbi, was an important trading center. From the countries across the Sahara caravans came, laden with sugar, wheat, and cloth; they returned northward with gold, ivory, and rubber.

In 1067 a fierce fighting band of Moslems invaded Ghana and from then on its power grew less. Meanwhile, to the west, another Negro kingdom grew up, called Melle or Madingoland. It stretched from the Atlantic Ocean to Lake Chad, and within its borders were the rich gold mines of Bure. The rulers of Melle became so wealthy that in 1324, when King Gonga-Mussa, a Moslem, made a pilgrimage to Mecca, he took with him five hundred servants, each of whom carried on his head a slab of pure gold. In all, sixty thousand persons—soldiers, secretaries, camel drivers, and attendants—went with the king on his pilgrimage. Along the way he gave gifts freely to provincial governors, and ordered beautiful mosques built so that the distant towns of his realm might remember him. On his return from Mecca, King Gonga-Mussa brought with him an Arabian architect, Es Saheli, to help beautify the cities of Kangaba, Jenne, and Timbuktu.

Timbuktu was then a busy trading center, famous for its leatherwork, its white embroidered robes, its silks and pearls, perfume, ostrich plumes, dates, cloves, tea, and coffee. Timbuktu was also a center of learning, known for its libraries and bookstalls. To its University of Sankoré came students and teachers from Cairo, Baghdad, and even as far away as Europe. From Sankoré professors carried their learning to other countries. One of the sheiks of Sankoré, Ahmed Baba, was a learned man, the author of some twenty books.

In 1469 the ruler of the kingdom of Songhay, Sunni Ali, sent his river navy down the Niger to capture the cities of Timbuktu and Jenne. Sunni Ali eventually gained control of all the land of Melle. By the beginning of the sixteenth century Songhay had become the most powerful state in West Africa. Under King Askia Mohammed, who was a great traveler, Songhay became friendly with surrounding states; new systems were set up for governing, trading, and banking; new schools were started. At the University of Sankoré the departments of surgery, law, and literature attracted students from the whole Moslem world. Until the Moors conquered Songhay in 1591 it was one of the most enlightened countries of its time, and in the Middle Ages the city of Timbuktu became one of the greatest centers of learning. But today it is only a drab West African town of about seven thousand inhabitants, at the end of a caravan route across the Sahara.

White Explorers

Although Portuguese seamen had sailed a short way up the Congo River in the late 1400's and by the 1600's had penetrated farther inland, and the Dutch had built a supply station for ships on the Cape of Good Hope in 1652, no large-scale European exploration into the heart of Africa began until the end of the eighteenth century. In 1795 Mungo Park, a Scottish traveler, was sent out from England by the African Association, a society whose purpose was to learn more about Africa. Park went up the Gambia River and later explored the Niger where it flows eastward before turning toward the south and west. In 1822 three Englishmen, Denham, Clapperton, and Oudney, began a historic crossing of the Sahara Desert. In 1851 David Livingstone discovered the Zambezi River, and a few years later reached Victoria Falls. In 1877 Henry Stanley traced the flow of the

Congo. Wherever such Britishers went, others followed, claiming land for the English crown. At the same time explorers for other European powers were active.

Much of Britain's early interest in Africa came about through its part in the slave trade. To compete with the Dutch, the French, and the Portuguese in the ugly business of selling human beings, the King of England chartered the African Company in 1672. Thereafter England began to build forts and settlements along Africa's Atlantic seaboard. The other large European powers did the same thing. It was not long before almost the entire West African coast was under the power of Europeans who at the same time controlled all of North Africa and portions of the East Coast.

As early as 1575 the Portuguese took over the coast of what is now Angola. But Europeans were much longer in gaining control over the vast African interior, because of the lack of exploration, the difficulty of travel, and other drawbacks. The first white man, John Hanning Speke, did not go into Uganda until 1862. A few years before, he had discovered the source of the river Nile. In 1884 the Germans took over the Cameroons; in 1885 the Belgians began their rule of the Congo; and a little later the British South African Company began to gain control of Rhodesia and other inland territories in the queen's name. By the beginning of the twentieth century almost all of Africa belonged to Europe.

Livingstone and Stanley: Explorers

The two greatest African explorers were David Livingstone and Henry Morton Stanley, both born in Great Britain. Livingstone was a missionary, and Stanley a newspaperman. Livingstone studied medicine at the University of Glasgow, and first set out for Africa a year before Stanley was born. Thirty years later their paths were to cross on that continent in a most dramatic way.

It was in 1840 that the London Missionary Society sent David Livingstone to Bechuanaland to pick places for the setting up of missions, to help convert the tribes to Christianity, and to see what could be done about stopping the slave trade. On his first trip Livingstone remained in Africa for nine years. In his travels he discovered Lake Ngami and the Zambezi River. On a second trip he followed the course of the Zambezi to the Indian Ocean and on the way discovered, in 1855, a mighty waterfall that he named after Queen Victoria. In 1858 he was made British consul to Quelimane. At the same time he continued his explorations.

Livingstone kept records and made maps of all his discoveries, and for the first time charted routes into the dark heart of Africa. He was past fifty when he organized an expedition to map the headwaters of the Nile. On this trip he disappeared into the Lake Tanganyika region and was not heard of for many months. His silence caused great anxiety among his friends. After more than two years the New York *Herald* sent its most famous reporter, Henry Stanley, in search of the famous missionary-explorer.

In his youth Stanley, an orphan, had shipped to New Orleans as a cabin boy. There he found a foster parent and remained in the United States. He served in the Confederate Army, and later in the United States Navy. Still later he became a foreign correspondent, making his first trip to Africa in 1867 to cover a British military invasion into Abyssinia.

In the spring of 1871 Stanley organized an expedition of 192 men to find Livingstone. They set out from Zanzibar and traveled by boat up rivers and on foot through jungles for more than six months before they located the aged missionary. On November 10, 1871, Livingstone was found in the village of Ujiji on the shores of Lake Tanganyika.

The first person to sight Dr. Livingstone was a native guide; he brought word to Stanley of a very old man with a very white beard. Stanley later wrote in his journal that at this news his heart began to beat very fast. He was so excited he wanted to turn handsprings and slash trees. But dignity would not allow such behavior. Instead, when he reached the village he walked with great ceremony through a throng of natives that surrounded the old missionary. Then, taking off his hat, he bowed and said quietly, "Dr. Livingstone, I presume?"

It was indeed Dr. Livingstone. Warmly he welcomed Stanley, and together they spent some four months. But Livingstone did not wish to be rescued. He wanted only to continue his explorations and his work as a missionary. After Henry Stanley left, Livingstone went farther into the jungle world and lived with the Africans. At the age of sixty he died on the shores of Lake Bangweulu, where his heart is buried beneath a tree. The natives wrapped his body in salt and carried it to Zanzibar. From there his remains were sent to London, to be buried in Westminster Abbey with other great men of English history.

In 1874 Stanley returned to Africa as an explorer in his own right. He became the first European to circle Lake Victoria and to chart its size as the second-largest fresh-water lake in the world. He was also the first white man to see Mount Ruwenzori, the Mountains of the Moon, and to travel by boat down the entire length of the Congo River. Riding the rapids on the Congo trip, his three white companions died before reaching the coast, and he lost two-thirds of his African carriers.

Stanley became famous for his explorations of the Congo, and he tried in vain to interest the British government in the niches he had found along the river's banks. He failed. Instead, King Leopold II of Belgium commissioned him to head an expedition into the Congo country. Within five years Stanley had set up the framework for complete Belgian control over the region, which was named the Congo Free State. Later, in England, Stanley was knighted for his contributions to the knowledge of Africa. As Sir Henry Morton Stanley he became a member of the British Parliament in 1895.

Both Stanley and Livingstone left behind them many books, records, and journals of their African discoveries. Stanley, in particular, wrote and lectured a great deal. But it was the missionary David Livingstone, rather than the more colorful and pushing Stanley, who expressed a modern feeling toward Africa and the values of exploration. Livingstone said that the exploration of a new country should be "a matter for congratulation *only* in so far as it opens up a prospect for the elevation of the inhabitants." If all European explorers and settlers had followed this noble belief, there might be no trouble in Africa today.

Cecil Rhodes: Empire Builder

Explorers were not the only men fascinated by the almost unknown continent that was opening up. Pioneers like Cecil Rhodes soon learned that here they might find great wealth and power. Rhodes, the son of a minister, was born in England in 1853. As a youth he was frail, and for his health's sake doctors advised him to seek a warmer climate. At seventeen he set sail for South Africa; soon after he arrived he went into the Kimberley region to dig for diamonds. Two years later young Rhodes was a millionaire. At twenty-three he returned to England to enter the university at Oxford, but every year he went back to South Africa during his vacations, for Africa had become his home.

In addition to his diamond properties Rhodes soon had large interests in the mining of gold. Wealth gave him political power, and in 1881, the same year he received his degree from Oxford, he was elected to the Parliament of the Cape Colony. He was called an "unscrupulous land-grabber" by many, but Rhodes insisted that he had no interest in money for its own sake. His real aim was the advancement of the British Empire, he said, and his dream was that England should rule all of Africa, and in time, all the world. To this end he devoted his energies and his fortune.

In 1888 Rhodes founded De Beers Consolidated Mines, Ltd., which became one of the greatest mining combinations ever formed. At thirty-seven he was made Prime Minister of Cape Colony. He had already set up the British South Africa Company, which governed the area later named for him, the Rhodesias. He had also forced the annexation of Bechuana-land, and he bought from King Lobengula, king of the Matabele peo-ple, all the rights to search for minerals within an area of 75,000 square miles, for a payment of about $500 a month, 1,000 rifles, 100,000 rounds of ammunition, and the promise of an armed steamboat, which the king never received. Even Queen Victoria of England was shocked to hear of King Lobengula, especially when Rhodes employed a num-ber of the king's sons as his servants. This "great empire builder" had little regard for the African people as he pushed British control north-ward from Cape Town almost to the Congo. Eventually he put some 800,000 square miles of land under English control.

"In Africa, think big," was one of his mottoes. He dreamed of a Cape-to-Cairo railroad to cross the length of the whole continent, and he brought about the building of long stretches of this railroad. It still is not finished. At Victoria Falls the line crosses one of the world's highest bridges, which allows passengers a view of one of the mightiest waterfalls on earth.

Rhodes was much against the Dutch government in the Transvaal, and his policies helped to bring about the Boer War in 1899. In this war the Dutch were defeated, and their colonies became a possession of Great Britain. The same year the war ended, Rhodes died and was buried in Rhodesia, the rich area of gold, copper, cobalt, zinc, and manganese that he had taken over for the English. In Rhodesia's meadows fat cattle graze; fertile fields grow wheat, corn, cotton, and tobacco. Across the grassy plains, leopards scream and lions roam. There, on a high, lonely hill that he himself had purchased for his tomb, Rhodes is buried; only by an act of Parliament may anyone else be laid to rest near him. He willed a part of his great fortune to Oxford University for the creation of the famous Rhodes scholarships, given annually to students of many nations.

Rhodes, Livingstone, and Stanley, all British, were the great pioneers in the opening up to Great Britain of Africa south of the equator. North of the equator, too, Britain had gained control in one way or another of enormous territories stretching south from the Mediterranean. At one time it was possible to map a route entirely on British-dominated territory from Cape Town northward across South Africa, through Bechuanaland and the Rhodesias into Tanganyika, Kenya, Uganda, then over the former Anglo-Egyptian Sudan through Egypt to Cairo near the northern coast—across the whole length of Africa.

Today Britain no longer has such power, although its holdings on the Dark Continent are still enormous and Africa is one of the great sources of its wealth. A sizable part of the wealth results from the efforts of Cecil Rhodes.

Albert Schweitzer: Missionary

One group of men and women who have had a tremendous influence on Africa have been neither explorers nor money-makers. They have been missionaries, both Protestant and Roman Catholic. The missionaries have been responsible for a good part of the education, hospitals, and health agencies that Africa now has. Almost the entire school system in the Belgian Congo is in the hands of hard-working monks and nuns of the Catholic faith. The most famous hospital on the continent, that of Dr. Albert Schweitzer at Lambaréné in jungle Africa, is a Protestant mission. It lies just north of the Congo River in the republic of Gabon. Founded by Dr. Schweitzer in 1913, it has become known around the world as a great center of tropical medicine.

Dr. Schweitzer has always been a scholar, and became first a Doctor of Philosophy at the University of Strasbourg, then a Doctor of Theology and the pastor of a church in Strasbourg. He was already an excellent organist, and later took a degree in music and became an authority on the music of Bach. At the age of thirty he decided to become a physician. For six years Albert Schweitzer studied medicine, and in 1911 was graduated as a medical doctor. Two years later he and his wife sailed for Africa as representatives of the Paris Missionary Society. He was then thirty-eight years old.

Dr. Schweitzer paid for all the first equipment for his hospital from his own earnings as a minister, public speaker, and organist. For its site he chose a lonely spot just south of the equator and almost two hundred miles from the African coast, because there a hospital was badly needed. The climate of Gabon is hot and humid. Leprosy is a common disease.

Wild animals abound, and dangerous mosquitoes and the tsetse fly are widespread.

Except for brief returns to Europe, Dr. Schweitzer remained at Lambaréné for nearly fifty years. The story of his devotion to the saving of human lives in the heart of the African jungle is one of the great sagas of medical history. Albert Schweitzer himself has written a number of books. From them and from the many volumes that others have written about his work, the full story of this great man and his remarkable hospital may be learned. During his long life numerous honors have come his way, including a series of postage stamps bearing his picture and pictures of his hospital. Dr. Schweitzer received the 1952 Nobel Peace Prize for, in part, the belief he has often expressed that it is wrong "to regard the life of any living creature as worthless." His work and that of many other missionaries in both the medical and educational fields show what can be done to help Africa take her place in the modern world.

Primitive Peoples of Africa

Through the work of the explorers, the missionaries, and now the modern businessmen and representatives of foreign governments, most of Africa has been influenced by white people in one way or another.

There are still some people like the Bushmen, however, whose tribal life remains much as it has been for centuries. The untouched people were formerly called "savages," but today we use the word "primitives"; the word points out that although their civilization is not modern, they nevertheless do have a civilization of their own. Often their basic ways of living are more suited to the climate and the conditions under which they exist than European ways are. When white customs are introduced, the primitive peoples sometimes do not fare well. Tribal laws go to pieces, for certain parts of white civilization do the people more harm than good. But there is no stopping the changes that are taking place in Africa. It is a land that is rapidly passing from one stage of development to another. Before the end of the twentieth century there may no longer be any truly primitive peoples left on the continent.

Primitive government in Africa usually began with the clan, a group of blood relatives who formed a cluster of villages. As the clan grew, people were less and less directly related through family ties but still had a common language and common customs; the tribe came into being. A tribe may inhabit many hundreds of square miles and have many villages within its area. Usually the ruler is a chief. Often the chieftainship is handed down from father to son, but on the other hand a chief may simply be the strongest or wisest man in the tribe or a man chosen by a council of elders. Some tribes have a queen, but usually a male rules and the older and wiser men of the tribe help him to make decisions.

Land usually belongs to the tribe as a whole, but is parceled out to families for farming. Women do most of the planting and sowing of crops, and sell at the market the produce they do not need. Women also cook, weave, and tend the children. Primitive men usually hunt and fish, killing game for food. Men herd the cattle, clear the land, and build the houses. They protect the villages from wild animals; if there is a war, men are the fighters.

In many African tribes a man may marry more than one wife. There are practical reasons for this. The more women there are in a family, the more help there is for tending the gardens and fields. Moreover, the more sons a man has, the more protection he and his village will have in time of war. Men take pride in many wives and large families. All are members of the tribe and no one is neglected or goes hungry. Brides are usually purchased from their parents, or a dowry of cattle, grain, or money is given to the girl's family. In some tribes, women take part in making important decisions, but in others they have no word of authority except in the household.

Primitive Africans respect many gods. In some tribes like the Yoruba of Nigeria there are more than four hundred deities. Often each god represents some part of nature, such as water, thunder, lightning, or the sun. There may also be a god of war, of love, of planting, or of the harvest. In English, primitive priests are often called "witch doctors" or "medicine men" for, besides calling on the powers of various gods, they work to cure illnesses. Primitive people often think a cure is made by the casting out of the evil spirits that cause sickness.

Almost all ceremonies in tribal life are in some way related to the gods, and drums and music play a great part in the primitive religions. The gods are called on by music to bless the planting and the harvest, or to make successful a hunting expedition—or to receive thanks when a son is born. Drums are also used in trials of wrong-doers, to emphasize a chief's judgments; in warfare they excite men to a fighting pitch; on happy occasions they are used for dancing. Drums may still carry messages from one village to another in some places. Faster than a man can talk, drumbeats can tell of a missionary approaching up the river, of a lion in the vicinity, or of danger from a neighboring enemy tribe.

Even the most primitive of the Africans, as Livingstone discovered, are not savage in the animal sense, nor are they dangerous to strangers unless they are angered or harmed. Many tribes are most kindly to travelers passing through their villages. A recent American writer has said that today it is possible for a white man to travel from one end of Africa to the other without danger from the natives. Most wild animals in Africa will also leave men alone, if men have not frightened or disturbed them. Human beings had best watch out for snakes and crocodiles, however, for they attack without warning.

Home Life and Arts in Primitive Africa

Primitive men seldom live apart from one another. They usually dwell in villages, and sometimes their huts are grouped around a central clearing. The huts are often built of stout poles, roofed with palm thatch or mats of tightly woven grass. Some tribes use a mudlike brick for building, and others a kind of adobe plaster over a framework of woven twigs. There are tribes whose huts of mud and straw are shaped like beehives, and other tribes whose homes are rounded, like igloos. Usually African homes are very clean—swept often, and with little or no furniture except mats spread on dirt floors. Cooking is usually done over outdoor fire-places, and washing is carried to the nearest lake or creek, where baths are taken, too. Festivals are held outdoors.

Carved wooden pillars or statues dedicated to one's ancestors may decorate homes or shrines, but usually African art is not "art for art's sake." Rather, it is art applied to useful objects: a beautiful carved cup of wood or ivory in the shape of a head, a decorated bowl or spoon, a hand-carved chair or stool, a shield for hunting or for war, a handle for a spear, or a mask for a religious ceremony. Art like the great Benin heads of bronze and other similar ancient objects is not being created in Africa today. Yet, in areas seldom touched by European traders with their factory-made articles, handmade objects that are both useful and lovely to look at are still being produced.

African music and its rhythms came across the seas to the West Indies and the Americas three hundred years ago, and in the United States helped to make jazz. The same ancient rhythms may be heard in many parts of Africa today. Drums of varying tones are the basic instruments, but there are other percussion instruments such as gourds, rattles, sticks, and stamping-tubes of bamboo. Various kinds of reeds and flutes are

376 Works for Children and Young Adults

played, also. A small flat frame crossed by strips of metal or bamboo is in common use; it is played with the thumbs and is called a "sansa" or "thumb piano." The Watusi of Ruanda play large stringed harps. The Bapende of the Congo have long xylophones, wooden slabs mounted on a set of hollow gourds and played with sticks that have gummed heads. They make beautiful melodies. Music-making, singing, and dancing are favorite pastimes with Africans everywhere.

Africans love to tell stories, riddles, and proverbs, too. There is much wisdom in a Ewe proverb that says, "Until you have crossed the river, never tease a crocodile." Another proverb from the same people advises, "An animal with a long tail should not try to jump over a fire." And from the Kru people: "A dog says, 'I have never called a man to come to me and then beaten him.' "

Each African tribe usually has one or more official storytellers, usually old men who act as tribal historians also. Since primitive peoples have no books, all the history of a tribe must be handed down by memory from one generation to another. Early in life young men are chosen to learn from older storytellers all that has happened to their ancestors. These men are the "human books" of tribal lore and wisdom. Aside from being teachers they often tell stories around an outdoor fire at night, just for fun. Sometimes the stories try to explain *why* things are, as this tale from the Ibibio tribe in Nigeria does.

Many years ago the Sun and the Water were great friends, and both lived on the earth together. The Sun very often used to visit the Water, but the Water never returned his visits. At last the Sun asked the Water why it was that he never came to see him in his house. The Water replied that the Sun's house was not big enough, and that if ever he came with all his people they would drive the Sun out.

The Water said, "If you wish me to visit you, you must build a very large yard—but I warn you that it will have to be a tremendous place, as my people are very numerous and take up a lot of room."

The Sun promised to build a very big yard. Soon afterward he returned home to his wife, the Moon, who greeted him with a broad smile when he opened the door. The Sun told the Moon what he had promised the Water, and the next day he started building a huge yard in which to entertain his friend. When it was completed he asked the Water to come and visit him. When the Water arrived, he called out to the Sun and asked him whether it would be safe to enter.

The Sun answered, "Yes. Come in, my friend."

The Water began to flow in, accompanied by the fish and all the other water animals. Very soon the Water was knee-deep, so he asked the Sun if it was still safe.

The Sun said, "Yes."

At that, more water creatures came in.

When the Water was level with the top of a man's head, the Water said to the Sun, "Do you want more of my people to come?"

The Sun and the Moon both answered, "Yes," not knowing any better.

Water continued to flow until the Sun and the Moon had to perch on the top of the roof. Again the Water addressed the Sun. And again he received the same answer. More of his people rushed in. Very soon, the Water overflowed the top of the roof. Then the Sun and the Moon were forced to go up into the sky, where they have remained ever since.

And that is why they are so far above the earth.

Children of Africa

The children of primitive Africa are seldom separated from their elders. They listen to their stories at night, and work or play beside the older folk in the daytime. Early in life, children are given little tasks to do, and they gradually grow into the work habits of the tribe. The boys herd cattle, aid in clearing the fields, or go with the men on hunting or fishing trips. The girls help tend the huts and sweep the village yards. Usually the girls and women cultivate the village gardens in which maize, beans, cassava, and peppers are grown. Children dig for peanuts (called groundnuts in Africa) and pick papaws, mangoes, bananas, and coconuts.

But there is plenty of playtime, too, and African children have their own games, many of them somewhat like American games. The children learn to make drums and flutes, to sing and dance, and to repeat riddles and stories. In most tribes, when boys and girls approach their teens they go through ceremonies that teach them the things they will need to know as grownups. These ceremonies are different from tribe to tribe, but usually the boys spend a time apart in the forest where they are tested for their bravery and their readiness to become strong men. The girls may live in huts apart from others for weeks, too, while they are advised by older women of the tribe as to the duties of wives and mothers. Great feasts and dances are usually held when the time comes for bringing the young people into the tribe as grown-up members.

In most of the large cities of Africa, however, tribal customs are disappearing, and life for children is now much the same as it is in other lands. The old ways are being forgotten under the influence of missionary education and European ways of living. Today there are Boy Scouts in the Congo, and many students in Cape Town study Latin. In recent years young African delegates have attended international high school forums in New York City. And, although the number is not yet large, more and more young Africans are going to Europe or the United States for college education.

Changing Africa

Not only in the cities, but over most of Africa the coming of the Europeans has brought many changes. Mining and the starting of industries have made new kinds of work. Natives in remote villages are meeting Europeans, and some of the tribesmen have been educated by missionaries. Western clothes and western habits are being introduced even to some lonely settlements. American jazz is in some places beginning to have an influence on African tribal music. Roads have been built, and motor cars imported; as a result, men can now travel in an hour the same distances that once took days. Airplanes make it possible for African leaders and chiefs to attend meetings in cities like Accra or Cairo; they can come from their far-off countries within a day, whereas it would formerly have taken weeks, perhaps even months, to make so long a journey. Messages once relayed overland by the beat of drums may now be sent by telegraph or radio. The changes on their continent have been so great that now the Africans can never go back to their former ways.

Part of the changes that the Europeans have brought to some areas have been good—things such as education, better health arrangements in large cities, the possible end of slave trading, and in some places, a chance to see how a democratic government works.

Not all the changes have been good, however. At first, the white newcomers did not understand tribal customs and they tried to do away with them in many areas. Or they tried to change African ways too quickly. The new methods brought about great confusion, upset the old, time-tried ways of doing things, and caused many Africans to hate Europeans.

Then, too, when the white settlers made the mining of gold, diamonds, and uranium into great industries, Africans were lured away from their tribes into the mines. They were also offered work in the homes, shops, and factories of great cities like Johannesburg, in South Africa. In recent years some forty millions of natives have left their tribal villages and their families behind them to work in European centers and industries. But they have not been given the same rights or wages as white workers. The unfair treatment they have received and the breakdown of the old tribal customs have made serious problems for everyone.

Now the ugly situations that the coming of the Europeans created need to be settled. What happens in Africa is bound up today with the affairs not only of Europe but of the United States as well. If answers for Africa's problems are not found, the peace of the whole world may be upset.

But what are the answers? What will take the place of the old tribal customs that are disappearing? How quickly can an African tribesman become used to modern civilization, and what happens when he does? How can the Africans best take their place in the modern world, and how can they be sure of fair treatment under new conditions?

Searching for ways to solve their problems, the various African people feel the need to control their own governments. Let's look at some of Africa's modern governments.

Africa's Governments

Africa has ten completely independent countries: Cameroun, Egypt, Ethiopia (also called Abyssinia), Libya, Liberia, Morocco, the Sudan, Togoland, Tunisia, and the Republic of Guinea. Here the countries govern themselves. The oldest of the independent nations in Africa are Ethiopia and Egypt; their histories go back many centuries, and during this time they have been independent except for brief periods. Ethiopia is a kingdom, ruled by an emperor. Egypt is now a republic, although it has not always been one. Liberia, however, is the oldest republic in Africa, dating its formation from 1847. Among the new completely independent nations of Africa are the United Kingdom of Libya, formed in 1952; the Republic of the Sudan, the Republic of Tunisia, and the Kingdom of Morocco, all of which achieved independence in 1956; the Republic of Guinea, formed in 1958; and Cameroun and Togoland, independent early in 1960.

The Union of South Africa and the new state of Ghana, as free members of the British Commonwealth, have like Canada only slight ties to the British Empire.

Aside from these twelve countries all the other lands of Africa were, early in 1960, a part of the colonial world, and had ties with governments outside the African continent.

Ways of running the government, and the treatment of the native peoples, varied widely from country to country—even in different countries under the same European ruler. For example, the native peoples of Nigeria, under the British, had much more political freedom than the natives of Kenya. As a result, Nigeria went through a peaceful change toward statehood, whereas Kenya experienced a dangerous native revolt against the British government. In French Algeria there was unrest and rebellion, but in French West Africa there was peace. The formerly French Guinea, like the formerly British Ghana, was freely building its own future.

Kenya: A Trouble Spot

In contrast to Ghana and Nigeria, where the future looks hopeful, Kenya is an unhappy land where whites fear blacks and blacks hate whites. Yet Kenya, too, is a part of the British Empire. Its strip of coast is a protectorate, and the rest of Kenya is a crown colony. This country, lying on the equator between Ethiopia and Tanganyika, runs from the Indian Ocean to Lake Victoria and the borders of Uganda. Its climate ranges from temperate in the high plateaus to hot and humid in the lowlands, and its scenery is as varied as its climate. There is snow at the top of 17,040-foot Mount Kenya, yet along the coast regal palms and brilliant tropical flowers grow. Kenya's railroad, built largely by East Indian labor, runs from Lake Victoria to the sea through one of the most exciting big-game areas in the world. From the train windows a passenger may sometimes see not only untamed lions, but enormous elephants, tall giraffes, and graceful gazelles.

Kenya has a population of about six millions of people, yet only about sixty thousand, or 1 per cent of them, are white. The whites, however, rule the country and have taken possession of almost all the best land.

Most of the British live on the high plateaus where the climate is cool, much as it is in England. They have staked out large farms and cattle-grazing meadows on land taken from the Africans. This area, called the White Highlands, is so productive that there are two harvests a year. Only white men may own land here. All that is left to the native tribes are the most arid and hard-to-cultivate areas, known as reserves—and the natives may even be moved from this land without notice or without their consent. The largest tribes are the Kikuyu, the Kamba, and the Masai. Many of their members leave the overcrowded reserves to work under a sort of plantation system for British farmers whose chief products are coffee, tea, sisal, and grain.

But even so, about a million of the Kikuyus of the region have been crowded into some two thousand square miles of unfertile land, although less than four thousand whites occupy sixteen thousand square miles.

Seeking to get some of their land back, the Kikuyus took up arms against the British settlers and through their secret society the Mau Mau began a campaign of death and terror. In 1954 the Mau Mau were crushed by the military might of the whites, and were arrested in masses and confined to reserves. They are no longer openly active, but the natives still feel a smoldering hatred and the white farmers must sleep with guns beside their beds.

Some way will have to be found in the future for the natives to have a share of Kenya's good things. But most of the whites in Kenya do not wish to grant the Africans land, education, or political equality. In public places the color line is strictly drawn. In Nairobi, the capital, neither Africans nor East Indians are admitted to the hotels, cafes, or clubs of the white people. The situation is not a happy one, but in the Commonwealth of South Africa conditions are even worse for people of color.

South Africa: Land of Apartheid

South Africa has the largest white population of any country on the continent—about three million, almost evenly divided between those of Dutch and those of British descent. But people of color far outnumber the whites. The country has nearly ten million Africans, a million and one-half people of mixed blood, and a half million Indians and Malayans. Yet South Africa has stricter laws against people of color than any other country in the world. Under its system of "white supremacy," called *apartheid* (pronounced a-PART-hate), black Africans may not vote, attend schools with whites, or travel without a pass. There are separate living areas in the cities, separate buses, and separate railway cars for persons of color. Forced labor exists, and the workers in the gold and diamond mines are treated almost like slaves. Even missionaries are hindered in their work in churches and schools. Those who protest against these unfair conditions are arrested for "treason," whether they are black or white.

The Union of South Africa has a British governor general, but the country is actually run by its own parliament, a premier, and his cabinet. The administrative center is at Pretoria, while the seat of the parliament is at Cape Town. The descendants of the Dutch, called Boers or Afrikaners, have the balance of power in the government and, because for years they fought against the Bantu tribes in the old days, they now oppose any advancement for the natives or East Indians.

The climate of South Africa is temperate; there is summer and winter as in Europe; and there are fine beaches and high mountains. The largest city, Johannesburg, is more than a mile high, on the Witwatersrand, a ridge where gold was discovered in 1886. There are skyscrapers in Johannesburg, and beautiful theaters and parks—for whites only. Other fine South African cities are Cape Town, at the foot of Table Mountain; Durban, with miles of sandy beaches on the Indian Ocean; and Kimberley, where the deepest man-made hole on earth is located, created by the diamond-mining operations. In the Transvaal there are lovely old Dutch towns surrounded by orchards and vineyards. And the world's largest sanctuary for wild animals is Kruger National Park near the border of Mozambique.

South Africa has a high intellectual level compared to the rest of the continent. Famous writers like Alan Paton, white man who wrote *Cry, the Beloved Country,* and Peter Abrahams, colored man who wrote *Tell Freedom,* are South Africans. In Johannesburg the largest magazine for African readers, *Drum,* is published, with writers and editors of color on its staff. Nevertheless, as regards fair rights for all races, South Africa, like Kenya, is most backward. New and even harsher laws have lately been passed to keep the native peoples from advancing any further in education or politics. Although all of the South African mines and industries depend on native labor for their output, the natives themselves are not permitted to share in any of the benefits of their country's wealth.

And, with its diamonds, uranium, and gold, the Union of South Africa has great wealth; it is the most advanced country on the continent—for Europeans. It produces more than a million tons of steel a year. Its cities are the largest and most modern. It has excellent universities. But for the native peoples it is, with Kenya, the worst place to live—and even educated natives are seldom permitted to travel outside the country. The

South African system of white supremacy permits persons of color almost no freedom at all, therefore today they are in a state of half-rebellion which newspapermen predict is likely to burst into violence at any time.

Belgian Congo: Troubled Colonialism

Next to the Union of South Africa, the most industrialized region on the continent is the Belgian Congo. It has over 900,000 square miles of land, is nearly eighty times the size of the European country that controlled it for many years, and has a population more than a third greater than that of Belgium itself. It has the tallest people in the world, the Watusi; one of the longest rivers in the world, the Congo; and the largest uranium mine on earth, Shinkolobwe. The material to produce the first atom bomb came from this mine, and the United States is still Shinkolobwe's leading customer.

The Belgian Congo is the world's largest source of industrial diamonds. Gold, tin, copper, cobalt, used in jet engines, germanium, used in transistors, and manganese also add to its enormous mineral wealth. Palm oil and hardwoods are a part of its riches. Exports amount to more than $3,000,000,000 a year. Belgium is a great European power because of what it has taken from the Congo.

In recent years the Belgians have hoped to keep the African mine and foundry workers happy by making their living conditions as good as possible. In the cities modern housing, hospitals, and missionary schools have been built for the natives brought from their tribal areas to the mines and industrial districts. In the native quarters of the larger cities more new housing, bright movie houses, and good restaurants were to be found than in any other part of colonial Africa. To keep away mosquitoes, helicopters sprayed entire cities regularly. Belgian foremen and officials even went to the trouble of learning tribal languages, a task which few whites bothered with in other colonies. Africans themselves held many office jobs, acted as customs officers, tax collectors, and postal clerks, and worked at skilled and semi-skilled labor. But the races have been kept strictly apart. In Léopoldville, capital of the Congo, Europeans and Africans live in separate sections. Colored peoples have been made to carry passes permitting them to walk about the city, and for them there has been a nine o'clock curfew after which they could not be seen in white districts.

Nobody in the Congo, white or black, has voted in the past. Whites have occupied all the top positions, and the government has been directed from Brussels, in Belgium. Many native Africans in the Belgian Congo wanted to vote, and wished to have a say in running the affairs of their land. Like the New England colonists in the 1770's, who grew tired of British control, so the Congolese finally asked for reforms. But the Belgians then took away their right to hold meetings, banned African papers and political parties, and put native leaders in prison. In 1959 riots broke out in Léopoldville, Matadi, and other cities. Police and soldiers fired on the natives, and almost two hundred were reported killed. Many others were imprisoned.

In all the Belgian Congo there are only about 125,000 whites, as compared to 13,000,000 blacks. The National Congolese Movement, under the leadership of native Africans who up to 1960 had no part at all in their own government, has stated that it aims finally to obtain the freedoms guaranteed by the United Nations Charter, and to obtain, through discussion and after a reasonable time, the independence of the Congo. Africans feel that when they first asked for discussions of the subject they should not have been arrested, met by police with armored cars, and forbidden to hold public meetings. There is now a troubled peace between the Europeans and the Africans in the Congo. But there is a feeling of hope, too. The Belgian King Baudoin has made the first official promise of independence to the people. An early date has been set, and everyone waits to see what this promise will achieve.

Guinea: Freedom by Ballot

Just across the river from the Belgian Congo lies the vast territory of Equatorial Africa. It stretches away, northward and westward around Nigeria, to join with West Africa. This French community of nations has an enormous number of natives—about 25 millions of them. In Paris, in 1958, the French Premier Charles de Gaulle offered his African territories the right to make a choice by voting. They were to choose between being completely independent or remaining within the French Overseas Community, either as a part of France or as a country with local self-government.

Several of the colonies chose to remain in the French Overseas Community as semi-independent republics. These include Mauritania, Chad, Gabon, the Congo Republic, the Malagasy Republic (formerly Madagascar), Dahomey, and Senegal, now joined with the French Sudan into the Mali Federation. Only Guinea chose to separate itself completely from France and form an independent republic under the leadership of Sékou Touré, who became its first African premier. There were no violent uprisings or long-drawn-out conferences. Guinea took de Gaulle at his word and simply voted to be free.

Many people predicted that the country would have a difficult time in governing itself—particularly in obtaining enough money. But Sékou Touré said, "We prefer poverty in liberty to riches in slavery." He immediately set about trying to make his country's trade, industry, and banking secure. Shortly after freedom, Guinea joined with Ghana to form a union which both states hope will in time lead to a sort of "United States of Africa."

Guinea is located on the West Coast just north of Sierra Leone. It has a population of over two and a half million; its area is 105,200 square miles; and it has rich deposits of iron ore, bauxite (used in the making of aluminum), and diamonds. This buried wealth, as yet only partly mined, now produces more than $5,000,000 a year in export value. But most of Guinea's laborers work on plantations, raising coffee, bananas, oranges, peanuts, pineapples, and palm oil. Rubber plantations also bring in money. France still carries on business and banking in Guinea, and Frenchmen are still big investors there, but the people of Guinea now control their own government.

Liberia: Godchild of the U.S.A.

Liberia is a child of American freedom. In 1822 the land it occupies was purchased by the American Colonization Society as a haven for freed slaves; twenty-five years later Liberia became a republic. Its government was modeled after that of the United States. Its flag is red, white, and blue, but has only a single star. Like the United States, Liberia has a Congress of both senators and representatives, and a Cabinet selected by the President. All its citizens who own property or pay hut-taxes may vote, women as well as men. The President is head of the military forces.

Liberia lies just north of the equator on the Atlantic Ocean. Its climate is humid, with a heavy rainfall, and much of the land is covered with tropical jungles. It is one of the smallest countries in Africa, being only about the size of Pennsylvania. Its population is probably less than three millions of persons, who are either the descendants of the freed slaves who settled there, called Americo-Liberians, or members of twenty-three native tribes. The largest of the tribes are the Mandingo, Kru, Bassa, Grebo, and Vai. Long before outsiders brought the English alphabet, the Vai had a written language, one of three in all of primitive Africa. And the Krumen were an enlightened people, great fishermen and seamen, many of whom now work on foreign ships during voyages up and down the African West Coast.

Most of the people are very poor, but under President William V. S. Tubman the country has increased its income enormously, largely with the aid of such American investors as the Firestone Tire and Rubber Company and the Liberian Mining Company. Each year Liberia now exports enough rubber to make tires for almost half the cars manufactured in the United States. Besides that, it exports over a million tons of the world's richest iron ore, and much cocoa and palm oil.

Liberia was long neglected by the land that created it, but America has now begun to take a new official interest in it. Through the Point Four program, a plan for giving technical aid, the government of the United States today contributes more than $1,000,000 a year to Liberia. A number of experts trained in agriculture, public health, education, and other fields have been sent from America to help the country. The capital and port of Monrovia, named after United States President James Monroe, has been made larger and brought up to date by American engineers, who have also built a large airport and an American military base at Roberts Field and have designed a system of highways. President Tubman has paid an official visit to the White House, and numbers of Liberian students now come to the United States for higher education. Today there are many American technicians, teachers, and missionaries living in Liberia. The country remains all-Negro, however, in that persons of other races may not become citizens or purchase land, although they are welcomed as investors, technicians, teachers, and advisers.

Ghana: A Free Commonwealth

One of the most interesting African republics is Ghana, which in 1957 was made a member of the British Commonwealth. Ghana was formerly the territory of British Togoland and the Gold Coast; it took its new name from the ancient African kingdom whose center was Timbuktu. Its first premier, Kwame Nkrumah, was educated at Lincoln University in Pennsylvania, and later lived in London.

Though many of its people are poor, Ghana is a wealthy country, well able to support itself. It exports two-thirds of the world's cocoa and has the largest supply of bauxite ore on earth. There are also diamonds in Ghana, besides gold, manganese, and great forests of hardwood. Accra, its capital, is a city on the Gulf of Guinea, where once slave ships plied their trade.

The population of Ghana is about five million. In proportion to the number of its inhabitants this new republic has more children in school than any other land in Africa. For the future, the people of Ghana have great plans for improving their country. They plan to dam the Volta River, then build one of the largest hydroelectric plants in the world. They also intend to erect on the banks of the Volta a plant to make aluminum of the bauxite deposits along the river. The project will give low-cost electrical power and lighting to a large area of the country.

In Ghana all grownups can vote. The country is governed by a parliament, and the whole plan of government and courts is like that of England. Kwame Nkrumah, Ghana's first prime minister, also founded the leading political group, the Convention People's Party, in 1949. Most other political parties in the country have banded together into a single opposition force called the United Party. But there are important tribal chiefs who still have the power to act as tyrants. Nkrumah must bring these chiefs into line with the democracy he is trying to form. Yet at the same time he must try to allow those who do not agree with him the right to criticize and oppose him freely. This is a problem, for a new democracy.

Since Ghana's independence, foreign investments and advisers are welcomed. Many white English judges and civil servants have been kept in their former positions, and white people continue to live and work in Ghana without harm. Nkrumah does not hold a grudge against the British who once, he feels, ruled his country unjustly. In his public speeches he has stated that there should be "an absence of the desire for vengeance for our wrongs . . . in a world sick of injustice, revenge, fear, and want." And he has said this about independence: "Self-government is not an end in itself. It is a means to an end, to the building of the good life for the benefit of all."

Today the eyes of the world are on Ghana because in that country is a test whether native Africans can make a success of self-government. Ghana has many different tribes speaking forty-six languages within its borders, and it has believers of many different religions. The uniting of so many varied peoples into a common democracy is not easy. But

Prime Minister Nkrumah is a very able man, and other natives high in the government are capable, too.

The people have given Nkrumah the nickname of "Show Boy." This name means that they are proud of him and like to show off his abilities to the rest of the world. The black peoples of Africa and the forward-looking white residents on the continent hope Ghana will succeed in becoming a successful modern state. But some white colonizers in Kenya or South Africa hope that Ghana will fail and thus discourage further efforts at freedom on the continent. They are fearful that someone like "Show Boy" may gain popular favor with the natives in their countries. These white people aim to keep all the governing power in the hands of Europeans and to allow the Africans no political rights at all. What happens to Ghana in the near future will influence the history of all Africa.

The U.S.A., the U.N., and Africa

The United States, through its Point Four program, gives teaching and technical assistance to a number of African countries besides Liberia. With the building of demonstration houses from a new type of sun-baked brick in Egypt, the killing of swarms of crop-eating locusts in Ethiopia, and many other activities American experts have brought Africa a practical kind of assistance that was not known before. The Point Four Visual Aids program has introduced new educational methods to African teachers. And, of course, the United States contributes both money and workers to such United Nations organizations as UNESCO (United Nations Educational, Scientific and Cultural Organization) and the World Health Organization; their work is of great value in colonial countries. All the free nations of Africa are members of the United Nations. But the Union of South Africa has recently been at odds with the United Nations over the South African "apartheid" policy of extreme color discrimination, which is directly contrary to the ideas put forth in the United Nations covenant. With representatives of black Africa now taking part in United Nations councils, the problems of colonial rule and the color bar are bound to become more and more a part of United Nations discussions.

Africa Tomorrow

The eyes of the world are upon the "trouble spots" of Africa. Among the troubled areas are Algeria, where the native peoples no longer wish to be a part of France, Kenya, South Africa, and the Rhodesias, where the governments show great injustice to the colored races. Meanwhile, Nigeria's independence within the British Commonwealth of Nations will give that country a chance to develop a democracy. If Ghana successfully weathers the early years of its new self-government, more and more of the African colonial states will become impatient to have independence. Most authorities on Africa today agree that terrible violence can be avoided only by paving the way for such independence.

"For better or for worse the old Africa is gone and the white races must face the new situation which they have themselves created," said Jan Christian Smuts, the white South African leader, before his death.

"Our struggle is simple: it is for political freedom, economic opportunity, and human dignity for all Africans," says the young black chairman of the first All-African People's Conference, Tom Mboya. "We want in our countries to have the right to self-determination, to have a government elected by our people, responsible to our people, and accountable to our people."

The new leaders of black Africa like Mboya of Kenya, Touré of Guinea, Nkrumah of Ghana, and Azikiwe of Nigeria know that independence brings problems. They know that many African regions just freeing themselves from foreign government will need to be guided as they take their first steps toward independence. They realize that their people cannot get along without work, food, and money. They will need investments and practical help from other countries, to develop fully the rich natural resources of Africa. They ask the other nations of the world to be patient with them.

Africa's leaders of color today are aware of the many tribal and religious differences on their vast continent, where about one-fourth of the population is Moslem, one-tenth Christian, and the rest worship various gods, and where there is great variety in languages and ways of living. They know that four-fifths of Africa's enormous population cannot read or write, and that most are unfamiliar with modern machinery.

But Africa's leaders know that the natives can learn to read and write, as the people of Ghana are doing. In the Congo the leaders have seen that Africans can operate complicated machinery or become skillful in industrial laboratories. And they believe that Africans can govern themselves, as they have been doing for generations in those countries that did not come under colonial rule.

Although mistakes may be made at first, African leaders feel that people can learn to govern only by practicing government. For the sake of their own dignity, they must have the opportunity to try. Leaders admit that there are difficulties to be faced in independence. When Nkrumah says, however, "We prefer self-government with danger to servitude in tranquillity," he is expressing the feeling of most of the people of black Africa today.

It is a world-wide aim that people of all races should be able to live together in peace and freedom. May that aim be reached in the future of Africa, a country whose earth is rich, whose landscape is beautiful and varied, and whose native peoples eagerly seek a better life as they step forward into the modern world. For a very long time white Europeans ruled Africa, and many Europeans will wish to continue to live in the Africa of future days. Concerning them and their responsibilities toward the new Africa the great South African writer, Alan Paton, has written: "They brought a new life to this country. They changed the old life beyond recall. It goes on changing, and it is our duty to see that it changes for the good of all who live here. . . . Justice in the ideal is a powerful thing, but justice in practice is more powerful still, and can influence powerfully all the peoples of the world."

The Countries of Africa[1]

(Since in many areas no complete census has ever been taken, the population figures for some countries can only be estimated)

Country	Area [sq. mi.]	Population	Capital
INDEPENDENT			
Cameroun (Republic)	166,489	3,187,000	Yaoundé
Egypt (Republic)	386,198	24,410,000	Cairo
Ethiopia (Kingdom)	350,000	19,500,000	Addis Ababa
Guinea (Republic)	105,200	2,505,000	Conakry
Liberia (Republic)	43,000	2,750,000	Monrovia
Libya (Kingdom)	679,358	1,091,830	Tripoli and Bengazi
Morocco (Kingdom)	172,104	9,823,000	Rabat
The Sudan (Republic)	967,500	10,000,000	Khartoum
Togoland (Republic)	21,893	1,088,000	Lomé
Tunisia (Republic)	48,313	3,800,000	Tunis
INDEPENDENT MEMBERS BRITISH COMMONWEALTH			
Ghana	91,843	4,763,000	Accra
Union of South Africa	472,550	14,418,000	Pretoria and Cape Town
BRITISH COLONIES OR PROTECTORATES			
Basutoland	11,716	634,000	Maseru
Bechuanaland	294,020	327,000	Mafeking
Central African Federation			
Northern Rhodesia	290,323	2,180,000	Lusaka
Southern Rhodesia	150,333	2,480,000	Salisbury
Nyasaland	47,404	3,266,000	Zomba
Gambia	4,005	311,000	Bathurst
Kenya	224,960	6,261,000	Nairobi
Mauritius and dependencies	720	596,857	Port Louis

1. These statistics have been retained as in the original publication of 1960.

Country	Area [sq. mi.]	Population	Capital
Nigeria (Independence in 1960)	373,250	34,700,000	Lagos
St. Helena and dependencies	119	5,355	Jamestown
Seychelles	156	40,417	Victoria
Sierra Leone	27,925	2,500,000	Freetown
Somaliland	68,000	640,000	Hargeisa
South-West Africa	317,887	458,000	Windhoek
Swaziland	6,704	241,000	Mbabane
Tanganyika Territory (U.N. Trusteeship)	362,688	8,452,619	Dar es Salaam
Uganda	93,981	5,680,000	Entebbe and Kampala
Zanzibar and Pamba	1,020	285,000	Zanzibar
FRENCH COLONIES OR PROTECTORATES			
Algeria	852,600	9,530,500	Algiers
Central African Republic (Ubangi-Shari)	238,000	1,121,000	Bangui
Chad Republic	496,000	2,521,000	Fort-Lamy
Comoro Archipelago	790	180,000	Pamanzi
Congo Republic	132,000	745,000	Pointe Noire
Dahomey Republic	45,900	1,614,000	Porto-Novo
French Somaliland	9,071	65,403	Jibuti
Gabon Republic	103,000	420,000	Libreville
Ivory Coast Republic	123,200	2,481,000	Abidjan
Malagasy Republic (Madagascar and dependencies)	241,094	4,913,000	Tananarive
Mali Federation			
French Sudan	450,000	3,346,900	Bamako
Senegal	80,600	2,220,000	St. Louis
Mauritania	415,900	615,000	St. Louis (Senegal)
Niger Republic	494,500	2,334,000	Niamey
Réunion	969	274,370	St. Denis
Upper Voltiac Republic	105,900	3,324,000	Ouagadougou
BELGIAN COLONIES AND U.N. TRUST TERRITORY			
Congo (Independence promised in 1960)	904,757	12,660,000	Léopoldville
Ruanda-Urundi (Trust Territory)	20,742	4,424,573	Usumbura

Country	Area [sq. mi.]	Population	Capital
PORTUGUESE COLONIES			
Angola	481,351	4,354,000	Luanda
Cape Verde Islands	1,557	166,000	Praia
Mozambique	297,731	6,170,000	Lourenço Marques
Portuguese Guinea	13,948	554,000	Bissau
São Tomé-Principe	372	53,000	Santo Antonio
SPANISH COLONIES			
Ifni	740	38,000	Sidi Ifni
Spanish Guinea	10,852	212,000	Santa Isabel
Spanish Sahara			
Rio de Oro	73,362	23,000	Villa Cisneros
Sekia el Hamra	32,047	10,000	Smara
ITALIAN U.N. TRUST TERRITORY			
Somalia (Trusteeship ending 1960)	194,000	1,255,000	Mogadiscio